But What Will People Say?

'It bridges gaps where Western mental health drops the ball. It is accessible, truthful and healing – what we need to decolonize our therapies and address our people's historical trauma' Dr Jennifer Mullan, author of *Decolonizing Therapy*

'Sahaj writes with great insight, clarity and an uncommon grace and warmth . . . this book approaches with nuance (and love) the complex and multidimensional challenges and blessings, heartaches and joys that we go through as we grow into ourselves' Farnoosh Torabi, author of *A Healthy State of Panic*

'With radical honesty and empathy, Sahaj breaks the traditional self-care model for community care, returning us to true belonging rooted in love' Valarie Kaur, bestselling author of *See No Stranger*

'Sahaj Kaur Kohli [. . .] compassionately shares her own story, and guides readers through the nuances and pain of assimilation, individuation and mental health' Ramani Durvasula, PhD, Clinical Psychologist, author of *It's Not You: How to Identify and Heal from Narcissistic People* and Professor Emerita of Psychology, California State University, Los Angeles

'Sahaj writes with compassion and expert authority, guiding us along a path to honour where we come from, our communities and ourselves. A heartfelt, thought-provoking and deeply tender book that I will carry with me for the rest of my life' Sarafina Nance, author of *Starstruck*

'This wonderful book is a compass, a blueprint, a mirror and a friend. Kohli gives language to what many of us feel but can't yet articulate' Erika L. Sánchez, *New York Times* bestselling author of *I Am Not Your Perfect Mexican Daughter*

T0322268

About the Author

Sahaj Kaur Kohli is a licensed therapist, a columnist for the advice column 'Ask Sahaj' in the *Washington Post* and the founder of the Instagram page @browngirltherapy, the first and largest mental health and wellness community organization for children of immigrants. Sahaj also serves as an international speaker, and she has sat on panels and delivered workshops and keynotes at companies including Amazon Inc., Google, LinkedIn and UNICEF, among others. This is her first book.

But What Will People Say?

Navigating Mental Health,
Identity, Love and Family
Between Cultures

Sahaj Kaur Kohli, MAEd, LGPC

Founder of Brown Girl Therapy

PENGUIN LIFE

AN IMPRINT OF

PENGUIN BOOKS

PENGUIN LIFE

UK | USA | Canada | Ireland | Australia
India | New Zealand | South Africa

Penguin Life is part of the Penguin Random House group of companies
whose addresses can be found at global.penguinrandomhouse.com.

First published in the United States of America by Penguin Life 2024
First published in Great Britain by Penguin Life 2024
001

Printed and bound in Great Britain by Clays Ltd, Elcograf S.p.A.

The authorized representative in the EEA is Penguin Random House Ireland,
Morrison Chambers, 32 Nassau Street, Dublin D02 YH68

A CIP catalogue record for this book is available from the British Library

ISBN: 978–0–241–58489–7

www.greenpenguin.co.uk

MIX
Paper | Supporting
responsible forestry
FSC
www.fsc.org   FSC® C018179

Penguin Random House is committed to a
sustainable future for our business, our readers
and our planet. This book is made from Forest
Stewardship Council® certified paper.

*To anyone who straddles between cultures
and questions if—and where—they belong.
You're not alone. Come sit, stay awhile.*

"The first generation thinks about survival; the ones that follow tell the stories."

—HUA HSU

Contents

But What Will People Say?

Introduction

"You never talk about your assault or your depression with me," my father blurted unprompted as we were driving up Interstate 295 between Portland and Bar Harbor, Maine.

It was 2015, I was twenty-six years old, and we were on day two of our first-ever father-daughter trip. My dad, a stoic immigrant with a slight Indian accent and, almost always, a blue or purple pagri on his head, was sitting next to me in the passenger seat, wearing a baseball cap and tapping his fingers on his knee along to the radio's song. He was unusually casual, and oblivious to the fact that he had just knocked the breath out of me.

We'd set out on this trip because a few months prior, my mom had mentioned in passing that she thought my dad was depressed. "He isn't acting like himself," she'd said. "He is unusually quiet when he gets home from work. He seems sad." Though my mom had shared all of this nonchalantly, the weight of her words had still hit me like a ton of bricks. The word *depressed*—or any term even remotely referring to mental health—wasn't used in my household. And *depressed* as it's commonly thrown around by many people could depend on a situation and any given person's understanding or assumptions around mental health.

Was Papa depressed, or was he just stressed at work? Was he tired? Was he in a stage of reflection and transition in his own life as his children became increasingly independent? Why had my mom used *this* specific word to describe his behavior? Did it reflect *her* fear over his changed behavior or her own inability to understand his thoughts and feelings? I was overcome with questions, but as per usual, I knew that it would be up to me, the family mediator—a burden I embraced and am still unlearning—to do something. I decided that spending some time with my dad in a neutral environment where we could get to know each other better without other people and without pressure would make for the best opportunity to get to the bottom of things.

You're probably thinking, *Um, he's your dad—don't you know him?* Well, no, not really, sadly. At that point, I knew that my dad liked collecting suitcases and luggage, specifically of the Tumi variety. He liked driving his Ford pickup truck on the backroads of Virginia, where he had purchased a plot of farmland and played out his wildest dreams of being a cowboy, as inspired by the Westerns he grew up watching. I knew that as a teenager in India, he had snuck away from home one afternoon to watch *Cleopatra* with his best friend, both giggling their way through the nudity. I knew he believed that a strong work ethic should always be a priority, especially in youth. *You can play later in life.* Beyond that, my dad's earlier life experiences and inner thoughts were a mystery. Like teeth, they needed to be extracted carefully and slowly.

Conversations with my dad had always centered around school or work, the news, religion, and, until 2019 (when I married my now husband), my future marital status. In other words, as I have found similarly among friends, he was a typical immigrant parent: laser focused on the future rather than the past. For most of my life, my dad had exerted control and stability by keeping his kids at arm's length: far enough that we couldn't see his vulnerability but close enough that he felt like he was taking care of us. For that matter, I had never talked with my parents about anything emotional, let alone things that were heavy and terrible. This meant that aside from the basic facts of my life, they didn't really know me, either. We put our energy into keeping up appearances within our community and our family.

And so when I floated the idea of this trip to my dad, I was surprised that he responded eagerly. In fact, he found it brag-worthy that his adult daughter wanted to get time alone with him, a rarity in his own circle of friends. He never knew that the catalyst for my initiating the trip was worry and concern about his well-being.

And now we'd be driving up and down the coast of Maine together, sharing a hotel room and every meal. We'd have approximately seventy-two hours to fill, and I had no idea what we'd talk about. I had plans to ask him about his own emotional wellness and to learn more about his life before I was born. I was excited by what I might learn but equally nervous that this trip would somehow worsen our relationship. I felt pressure to plan our trip down to the minute, so as not to allow for any unaccounted time. I feared any lull would lead to a sudden realization on either of our parts that this trip was a big mistake. I researched different things to do in Maine's coastal towns, coming up with multiple activity options so that I could defer to him and allow him to retain a sense of control. I came fully prepared with a list of questions jotted down in my Apple Notes app, but never in a million years did I imagine that we'd discuss *my* trauma, and for the first time in nearly five years at that. My whole life, I had been accustomed to hiding from my parents fragments of myself that could be considered "bad" or "unacceptable" in my family or culture, leading me to live a double life. I questioned my cultural and religious identity in secret. As an adolescent, I snuck onto AIM at night to gossip with friends and flirt with chatroom strangers in secret. I learned to explore my body and its needs in secret. I giggled at inappropriate things in secret. I struggled in secret. I was used to it, but now my dad was slowly opening a door between us that had been shut throughout my life. This trip—the first of many we would take—was meant to be about him, but he demonstrated curiosity and an interest in my life experiences that was so novel I didn't know how to respond.

Sure, I had a desire to know my papa better, but I also feared him getting to really know me. I worried about being able to maintain my own facade and his idea of who I was—an amenable, morally proper Indian daughter. And I worried he would only be reminded of what a disappointment I was to him.

FOR AS LONG as I can remember, I have felt on a daily basis that push and pull between who I am around my family and who I am alone with my friends—a feeling ultimately rooted in something called bicultural identity straddling, which is defined by researchers as an "ongoing process of adaptation resulting from living within two different cultural influences." I know firsthand the suffering, the questions, the inconsistencies, and the inner torment that come with trying to occupy two spaces at once, with having no sense of belonging to one or the other and needing to chart a path forward anyway. And I know I'm not alone. Children of immigrants are often constantly straddling (at least) two cultures, two value systems, and two sets of usually differing societal expectations. Many of us are walking a tightrope, trying to steady ourselves so as not to get devoured by the abyss below.

In truth, this identity straddling applies to anyone trying to adapt under more than one cultural influence. I, for example, am multicultural. For my first eighteen years, my mom, siblings, and I spent most summers in Kobe, Japan, where my mom grew up and lived until her marriage at age eighteen. So although both my parents are Indian, raised by Indian parents themselves, and although I grew up in the United States, I am often nostalgic for my childhood summers in Japan, where I would freely play with my cousins, who were around the same age as me.

My mom identifies as a third-culture kid; her Eastern values are rooted more in Japanese cultural norms than in South Asian ones, and she's always been more open-minded and accepting of other norms and cultures (in part, I think, because of the international school she attended growing up). My dad, who hails from Patiala, was the first in his family to permanently move away from India, first to the United Kingdom with my mom and siblings and then to the United States. Unlike my siblings, I was born in America. My older brother, Ajay, and older sister, Chandani, were both born in Punjab and spent a few years of their childhoods in England, before my family moved to the United States, making *their* immigrant childhood experiences slightly different from mine, despite our growing up in the same household.

If you played back home movies from my childhood in the suburbs of central Virginia, you'd see that I did have some semblance of a quintessential American upbringing—school dances, league sports, Friday-evening binges of *Nick at Nite*. (Binge watching did in fact exist before Netflix.) But along with my adoption of the American lifestyle came long, and recurrent, discussions and arguments with my parents over the fact that I was "too American"—that I was losing my traditional Indian values. They felt that sleepovers and school dances were threats to my focus on education and community obligations. Male friends, meanwhile, were a threat to my purity: discussions about love weren't even on the table until I was old enough to suitably marry.

Despite my parents' best efforts, I did attend those dances and sleepovers, where friends and I—including other immigrant kids in the Sikh community—spent our nights talking about boys and eating fast food. We had dance parties in front of our dresser mirrors, swaying unabashedly to the American music we were usually discouraged from listening to. I even experienced first love and devastating heartbreak in high school—all behind my parents' backs, of course. We were all unified in our secret rebellion.

Regardless of these explorations on the fringes of my parents' boundaries and expectations, I remained constant in my role as a family caretaker. I cared too much, and in hindsight, I believe that the motivation behind that care was an innate fear of being declared unworthy and unlovable by my family. Maybe this stemmed from the pressure I felt to fit the roles expected of me, or maybe it was a personality trait I embodied. Either way, it made sense when my mom handed *me* the top-secret information about my dad's wellness many years ago. She knew that she could unburden herself onto me and that I would likely do something with it.

The Need to Write This Book

We children of immigrants are navigating a new landscape and making different choices than our elders and our family members because we *can*. Yet we are often inundated with overt and covert messages about who we need to be in order to be accepted by our communities. We're often chasing belonging and acceptance, seeking social reward for acclimating into both cultures, even though the sets of expectations might be diametrically opposed. Rather than exploring our own values, we begin to respond the way we think others expect us to—developing a performative identity from a young age.

Growing up, I didn't know this was happening, much less have the words to express the internal conflict it was generating. I felt defensive and resentful, without being able to communicate why. Rather than feeling American or Indian, I was left feeling like I wasn't enough of either one. I'm the first person in my family to be born in the West, to go to therapy and openly discuss my mental health, and to marry outside my race and religion. Being the first to do anything is incredibly daunting. I never knew if I was doing it right or making tremendous mistakes. There's excitement and gratitude, but there's also no one to look to for advice or help. There's no road map. Yes, access and privilege come with being the first, but being the first can also perpetually feel like a burden. I didn't have a close relationship with my much older siblings until later in life, which meant that I was further isolated in my own family, navigating a lot of my childhood and adolescence solo. But just as my immigrant parents don't know what it's like to grow up in this country, I don't know what it's like to move here alone. They experienced firsts, too. We all lived through trial and error. We all figured it out as we went. We all have made a mission of creating communities for those like us. Our stories are different, but our purposes are very similar—seeking betterment and belonging.

Growing up in a family and cultural system that valued traditional success and binary thinking made me hungry to learn how to be accepted and loved. At an early age, I began to devour self-help and personal-development content. I held on to every word in the Chicken Soup for the Soul books and then, later, the words of Paulo Coelho, Zig Ziglar, Elizabeth Gilbert, Cheryl Strayed, and Brené Brown. I greedily grabbed at any bits of information that would help me become my best self. Even Bollywood movies were sources from which to learn what it meant to be a "good daughter," a "marriageable girl," and a future "good wife." Even more, I craved ways to understand if the feelings of inadequacy I stumbled over every day were *normal,* or something I could fix. The books I read helped me in some ways, giving me tools to dive deeper into my own psyche and emotional experiences. They granted me the language for how I related to the world around me, and they allowed me to explore my own motivations and desires. But in other ways, they failed me. The self-help sections in bookstores are often overstocked with white and therefore culturally individualistic perspectives. While these are important and can be helpful, they also neglect and so often invalidate the entire bicultural or multicultural experience. I often failed to find my collectivist culture or values represented in these books. I was being told how to set goals, how to be more mindful, how to have healthier relationships, and even how to explore my motivations as they fueled my *individual* desires. In theory, these are wonderful topics, but in practice, they didn't seem to address how to navigate the lack of personal agency I felt over my own life. Even more, these well-intentioned messages often assumed that the individual had the access, power, or ability to *do* these things, disregarding systemic barriers altogether. It was like being handed the keys to a car despite not knowing how to drive. I learned some things, but I was usually left with a distorted sense of self, and I felt pressure to figure it out myself rather than tap into community and culturally informed levels of care. Now I know that this was simply due to a lack of representation, but at the time, absorbing these messages reinforced my feelings of inferiority—in turn increasing my feelings of shame and making me believe that I was not *enough* or that it was a *me* problem. Eventually, my love of books and my devotion to writing—an important outlet for me from a young age—led me to a career as an editor at *HuffPost.* There, I was always drifting toward subjects/stories that explored our relationships to our intersectional identities and our mental health, which inspired me to go to graduate school to become a therapist. I've learned so much, and it's been an eye-opening journey, not least because of all the ways in which the field is full of gaps for people like me.

As a mental health professional, I am simultaneously frustrated and energized by the lack of representation and the lack of understanding about working across different cultures—especially when it comes to children of immigrants. The work is Eurocentric and colonial in nature—using techniques and modalities historically created by white folks—and generally posits that healing is similar for all people. Of course, there are community and systemic barriers and issues with all forms of self-care and mental health care. Some people are withheld access to health care or can't financially access therapy. Additionally, children of immigrants may be generally discouraged from pursuing certain forms of self-care within their family systems and cultural communities. Just as I noticed these parts of my identity missing from the self-improvement content I gravitated toward growing up, in my graduate studies, I observed a lack of representation of different cultural narratives—like collectivism, focus on community, and interconnectedness—in mainstream Western self-care. Wellness has been co-opted to suggest that independence, individualization, saying no, and cutting out anything that doesn't serve you or feel good to you is the answer. But for many children of immigrants, this is not applicable, useful, or even desirable as the outcome—and for some, it's not even safe. We tend to prioritize community care, as we were raised in collectivist households; we must have more conversations about how community care is a form of individual self-care and individual self-care is also a form of community care. Collectives are made of individuals, and we can't be our best selves within those collectives and in those roles if we are not also taking care of ourselves. Yet we can't be our best selves as individuals without considering the collective and our communities.

It wasn't until I started seeing clients who sought me out for my work on cultural negotiation, bicultural identity development, and acculturation issues that I realized how narrowly we define mental health, self-care, and self-improvement. For me and many others who grew up with collectivist values, self-improvement centers around improving ourselves *for* familial and community roles and relationships, not simply for personal gain or desire. Both would be ideal, but our approach to seeking personal-development care or content is to integrate our cultures and communities, not ignore them. In one culture, as children of immigrants, we are often encouraged to prioritize others at the expense of ourselves. In another culture, we may be encouraged to prioritize ourselves at the expense of others. Neither feels totally right, and this is what has propelled me into my work. What does authenticity look like? How do we hold our multiple identities at once while being well? I have also come to learn that my desire to fit in—like that of most children of immigrants—has always been a product of the systems in which I live. What we see depends on what lens we're looking through, and I've spent most of my life viewing my own personal conflict through the lens of whiteness and through the lens of someone who lacked a sense of belonging—in the outside world and at home.

A study utilizing data from the 2015–2016 California Health Interview Survey found that second-generation immigrants—or children of immigrants—in the U.S. have almost a twofold greater prevalence of psychological distress than their immigrant parents. Not to mention that as of 2021, one in four children (eighteen and under) in the U.S. is a child of an immigrant. Seeking therapy and working as a mental health professional has been instrumental in helping me create a tool kit to communicate and explore my own experiences—overlapping and differing cultural factors and all. I strongly believe that everyone deserves personal growth, healing, and the option to explore what taking care of oneself means, even if they've never been encouraged to do so—whether because no one modeled it for them or because they didn't have access to the resources.

BROWN GIRL THERAPY grew out of my attempt to find community and to bridge the gap that Western self-care methods and discussion had been unable to traverse. It originated from my own personal and professional identity crises around my South Asian American identity and blossomed quickly into the first and largest mental health community for adult children of immigrants living in the West. Through this work, I aim to democratize mental health, promote and destigmatize therapy, and encourage bicultural/multicultural competency for honest living. I want to raise awareness of ways in which we can decolonize therapy and mental health care—or center community, culture, family, and ancestral knowledge in our work while addressing historical and colonial trauma. For many of us, it's hard to believe that we deserve quality care when the care doesn't figuratively or literally speak our language, or when the people providing care are unable to see us wholly within the multiple systems in which we exist. We deserve healing, too.

Since Brown Girl Therapy's birth in 2019, I've found ways to marry my passion for mental health advocacy and storytelling through consulting with media organizations, creating original curricula for workplaces, and training clinicians on working with children of immigrants. I have spoken across many Fortune 500 companies, higher education institutions, nonprofits, and mental health agencies to discuss social activism and the need for culturally inclusive mental health conversations. I even founded a newsletter, *Culturally Enough*, to address everyday issues and provide tools and education for anyone who holds more than one cultural identity. My work has always centered community and accessibility, and unlike the mental health field at large and many of its institutions and systems, I continue exploring ways of removing the barriers to essential knowledge that underrepresented folks deserve access to. I've been able to expand the way I address these issues across different terrains, and in 2021, I became a weekly advice columnist for *The Washington Post*, where I answer the kinds of questions about cultural and mental health struggles that I so desperately wanted to see answered when I was growing up.

Coming from community members, employee resource groups, DEI initiatives, faculty, and my fellow mental health colleagues, the ache for this knowledge has only hardened my resolve. This is my calling. And, truthfully, every time I can have a meaningful conversation about the bicultural experience, a part of me is healing, too.

Children of Immigrants Are Not a Monolith

You're likely reading this book because you are a child of at least one immigrant parent or know, love, and/or work with one. Regardless of who you are, I want to clarify why I use certain terms or language in this book.

The U.S. Census Bureau, Pew Research Center, National Alliance on Mental Illness, and international researchers use the terms *second-generation* and *second-generation immigrant* to describe a child of at least one foreign-born parent. For the sake of consistency, I will use the same labels of second-generation/second-gen immigrant and child/children of immigrants all interchangeably. I also want to acknowledge that some of you may identify as one-and-a-half-generation immigrants, which means you were born in foreign countries and are technically immigrants but moved here before or during early adolescence, so a lot of your social, cultural, and relational experiences may overlap with those of second-generation immigrants born in their host country. Others reading this may be immigrants themselves or third-generation immigrants—grandchildren of immigrants—and may also share in some of the struggles and expectations rooted in different cultural norms and values. With all of this said, I want to note a few important things. First, of course you're not an immigrant if you were born in the U.S. or a new host country; however, the terms *first-*, *second-*, and *third-generation immigrant* are used more genealogically to relate to past and present family members, and they offer context more widely to broader diasporic patterns within our families and communities—further allowing us to distinguish between generational status. Second, I have observed that different people use the adjectives *second-gen* and *first-gen* interchangeably to mean the same thing. In some cases, it is simply colloquial language that is picked up in our communities without considering the technicality of the terms. In other cases, these may be used to establish host-country generational status (e.g., first-generation American). Finally, for some, labels can be empowering. For others, they can feel suffocating or reductive in expressing how we relate to our cultures or our identities. These terms are meant to be empowering, but you do not have to label yourself if it feels oversimplified or inauthentic. You're allowed to explore and choose how these terms serve you. This is all part of a larger discussion and of a reclamation of our own agency to take up space however we choose. We are *not* a monolith, despite having an overlap of shared experiences.

I never want to reduce the members of our diverse and unique communities or groups to one and the same. Sometimes, highlighting an unpleasant truth about our culture(s), our communities, our larger systems, or our families can feel wrong. I intentionally attempt to highlight specific and common struggles within these communities while holding the reality that we are not a monolith. However, I am fully aware of the ways I am trying to straddle between being honest about my own lived reality and observations *and* the stereotyping of our communities. I hope you'll carry this truth and intention with you, too, as you read.

Being a child of immigrants is a unique experience, and there are myriad factors compounding individuals' struggles—including but not limited to acculturation, parental immigration journeys, citizenship status, geographic location, language acquisition, race, and ethnicity. Even in my own family, my brother, my sister, and I had varying life experiences and family struggles due to our genders, birth orders, diasporic histories, and acculturation experiences.

According to the 2020 *World Migration Report*, more than 40 percent of all international immigrants were born in Asia, while nearly 20 percent primarily emigrate from India, China, Bangladesh, Pakistan, Afghanistan, and the Philippines. The same report found that India was the largest country of origin for international migrants, followed by Mexico and then Russia.

The United States has been the number-one destination for immigrants and has more immigrants than any other country. In 2019, Hispanic immigrants living in the U.S. made up 44 percent of the nation's immigrants. A quarter of the U.S. immigrant population is from Mexico alone, far more than any other country. And one in five Black people living in the U.S. is an immigrant or a child of immigrants. Also as of 2019, Asian Americans made up the fastest-growing racial or ethnic identity group in the United States. The six origin groups to which 85 percent of Asian Americans in the U.S. belong are, in order, Chinese, Indian, Filipino, Vietnamese, Korean, and Japanese.

That said, the Brown Girl Therapy community spans across six of seven continents, with focus points in major cities throughout the United States, Canada, Australia, Western Europe, and, most surprisingly, India, which highlights that generational differences can become cultural differences. In late 2020, when I polled the Brown Girl Therapy community, asking where everyone's parents are from, I received responses from over one hundred countries. It shocked me that children of immigrants from over one hundred countries relate to the content I create and the content in this book. I repeat, WE ARE NOT A MONOLITH, but we are collectively experiencing similar struggles and hardships, regardless of where our families are from.

Our experiences are going to differ in innumerable ways. My experience is going to be different from that of someone whose heritage and genealogy can be traced to another part of India, or South Asia, or Asia—let alone someone who grew up in a different geographic location, or had a dissimilar family system, childhood experience, diasporic history, or gender, sexual, racial, religious, or cultural identity than I do. There are infinite ways in which my story and experience may vary from yours. I'm a fair-skinned cisgender woman who is sometimes mistaken for white in certain spaces. As I write this, I am not a parent, and I reside in a two-income household. I am able-bodied and live comfortably in a big, liberal city. I have generational wealth that was passed down to me by my immigrant parents and my deceased grandparents, who were refugees. They worked tirelessly to ensure that their children and descendants would have more than they did. I share all of this to remind you— regardless of why you are reading this—to consider the intersectionality of your identity—or the combination and culmination of your different identities and how they inform your level of privilege or oppression.

What to Keep in Mind as You Read This Book

As a storyteller, I believe in the power of storytelling to connect with others and empower them to step into their truths, so I approached this book with my own personal narrative as the backbone. However, prescriptive elements and guided reflections/exercises for you to dive into are available throughout and in between chapters. Take what works for you and leave what doesn't. My hope is that you'll return to these pages again and again as you need.

I will also break down general themes as a mental health professional and therapist, utilizing my own story and experiences to frame these concepts. Further, I describe many concepts and terms that are not necessarily unique to children of immigrants, but my goal is to deepen our understanding of how these issues manifest for this underrepresented and overlooked population. What's more, I can't possibly cover *all* the themes that are important and resonant to this community. (Trust me, I tried, but my editors told me my book was getting too long, so those will be saved for future books!) Everything I share here is based on either my own readings and career as a former journalist and current mental health professional; my lived experiences; or what I've learned and witnessed through building Brown Girl Therapy. I encourage you to keep reading and to keep learning, even if you don't see yourself completely represented here.

In some of these chapters, you will find me discussing my work with therapy clients who are children of immigrants. I draw on these conversations to provide real-life examples of issues and concepts I discuss. The same is done with people in my personal life and in the Brown Girl Therapy community. Though all the figures in this book may resemble actual people, I want to be clear: other than in the case of my family members, personal details and all identifiable pieces of information have been thoughtfully obscured, changed, or combined to protect the privacy and confidentiality of my clients and people I know. If you see yourself in these pages, it is likely nothing more than a revelation of our shared humanity and experiences.

Furthermore, while some of these chapters contain evidence-based research (cited at the end of the book), some of the theories and hypotheses I discuss are backed by only anecdotal experiences—mine, those who have shared their stories with me, and the thousands of folks who respond to my polls on social media. Though there's no way for me to vet respondents to these informal online polls, I don't want to gatekeep the responses or stories that deserve to be told from self-identified children of immigrants. So throughout this book, I share results from these informal polls. Formal research, while a valid and necessary means of finding patterns and initiating change, takes years and isn't always created with or by the community it intends to study or serve. Counting graduate school, my work as a therapist, and the writing of this book, I have spent years studying certain cultural issues, and I have tried to find formal research where I can. In some cases, the research is much older than I'd like, but I still share it where applicable. However, this book addresses precise and acute mental health struggles of children of immigrants, and the more particular the issue, the less formal research I found addressing it; in many cases, I found none. By building a rapidly growing community on Instagram—with over 225,000 people to date—I have the community at my fingertips. I don't take that lightly. I claim not that these polls are empirical but, rather, that they have been intentionally performed so community members can feel less alone in otherwise overlooked and distressing struggles. The ultimate goal is to build off these for future research and work.

Embrace the Discomfort

By granting myself permission to write this book, I've had to reckon with my own experiences, misunderstandings, grief, and privilege. Sometimes, being a child of immigrants can feel like you've been set up for failure. Like you've been holding your breath and if you exhale, all the parts and pieces you've been taught to be ashamed of will tumble out. I admit that it makes me uncomfortable and scared to put this out in the world. But I know that my younger self would have reached for this book, and when I think about all the people who will reach for it now, I move past my fears. This book will highlight some of the personal ways in which I have struggled with my own intersectional identities, but it will also convey the many ways I've learned to love where I come from and who I am. My hope is that it can help those of you who share in these struggles to learn to reconcile your identities, cultures, and relationships, too.

I don't believe that I can be a responsible mental health therapist without doing the work on myself, and let me be clear: I am on this journey every day, learning and unlearning alongside all of you. I hope you take this book as an opportunity to introspect as well. I urge you to please remember to digest with context. Take breaks. Process. And hopefully you can engage with others along the way. Whether you are reading this because you can relate or because you want to learn more about how a large portion of our population exists, I hope this book will help you show up with compassion for yourself and for others. Most of all, I hope it will encourage and empower you to take ownership of your own narrative. Your story is a gift. I am rooting for you.

Chapter One

Our Stories Matter, Too

In building Brown Girl Therapy and being a writer, I have been so desperate to share my story with the world that I never considered I wouldn't be able to piece it together for myself. Memories serve as a way for us to make connections and find meaning, allowing us to create an identity by linking what we've been through with who we are today. For me, there are large chunks of my childhood that I can't seem to access.

There is innumerable research out there suggesting that memory is dynamic and fallible, and that encoding and retrieval are impacted by a number of personal, genetic, and environmental variables. How can I tell a story honestly and vulnerably when I can barely put pieces of it together for myself? I've screamed into the void, spent years in therapy, interviewed my family, and tried to re-create situations through music, smells, and revisiting environments. I have searched for paper trails and corroboration to be able to validate why I am the way I am and what I remember to be true. The bottom line is that a significant part of my life just doesn't exist in my brain, which stopped processing certain information because of the ongoing stress I experienced as a child. I repressed details to cope.

In an informal poll on Brown Girl Therapy, about 65 percent of 1,500 children of immigrants who responded reported that they, too, struggle with remembering significant chunks of their childhoods. Through a series of follow-up questions, I found that the common denominator was childhood abuse of some sort, usually manifesting as corporal punishment, explosive anger, and/or stonewalling. In fact, 90 percent of 2,400 respondents agreed that these were normalized as forms of discipline growing up.

This loss of memories from our childhoods, paired with the fact that many of us have been conditioned to question the validity of our experiences, is a recipe for unprocessed trauma and learned trauma responses that we may not consciously understand as adults. Many folks I've worked with talk themselves out of believing that their experiences were hurtful, or negative, because they don't remember them in detail or in their entirety. A lesson I have learned as a therapist is that often the details don't even matter. It's the emotional impact. How our past experiences still sneak into our minds or our reactions, behaviors, and thoughts in the present, sometimes years or decades later. Many of us children of immigrants are focused on collecting every single piece of information before we can make an informed decision about what to do or how we feel. But this I know: deep down, we are just waiting for permission to take ownership of our narratives.

As a therapist, I *know* the effects of trauma on the brain. I know that suppressing memories because they are too painful to face may be a protective mechanism. I know that unprocessed trauma can make it difficult to retrieve certain memories. I just struggle to reconcile this for myself. For many of us, so much of doing this work— of healing from our trauma and pain—is giving ourselves the grace and trust we have so quickly granted to others. When we filter our life experiences and memories through someone else's perspective, we betray ourselves in the name of loyalty to others. When we dismiss our own memories, we dismiss the existence of parts of ourselves. And when we search endlessly for proof or for others to legitimize our experiences and feelings, it may indicate that we are avoiding the painful, honest, whole truth of our realities.

We deserve our own love, too. We deserve to tell our stories. Life stories don't need to be complete and finessed to be real. They're ongoing and sometimes conflicting, and by accepting them, or sharing them along the way, we allow ourselves to grow beyond them.

Identifying Our Narratives

I have always been drawn to stories. As a kid, I could be found buried in a book, trying to make sense of or simply escape the world around me. As I got older, I yearned for connection with other people through shared storytelling, mutual listening, and empathy. I have made an entire career out of gathering and analyzing stories, as well as sharing my own. As a narrative therapist, I firmly believe that we are the sum of all the stories that we've been told about ourselves, the stories we tell ourselves, and the stories we've lived through—on personal and systems levels. We all have different and uncountable stories, but we tend to give more power and weight to some over others, creating what is known as our "dominant narratives." It's these dominant narratives that pervade our everyday lives and relationships, informing the way we perceive ourselves and interact with the world around us.

For many children of immigrants, it can feel like we are characters written into our parents' stories rather than architects of our own. We are not taught that we are on our own individual journeys, in which directions can change and avenues we never considered might actually be available to us. Instead, it can feel like things are "just the way they are"—discouraging agency and reinforcing rigid expectations. This internalization of our societal, cultural, or familial standards and beliefs becomes our dominant narrative. Sometimes these storylines are born out of our need and desire for survival, belonging, emotional validation, and so on. *To be a good Indian daughter and woman, I should be more amenable to others.* Other times, they are imposed on us by either those we love and respect or those who take advantage of us and cause us harm. *To be successful, I should assimilate into Western culture, rejecting parts of my heritage culture.* Regardless, we internalize these narratives, and they become part of our sense of self. Narrative identity is defined as a person's internalized and evolving life story. Basically, we construct—and sometimes reconstruct—meaning from our different experiences. We accumulate stories and restructure them to fit into our dominant narrative, then build our self-concept and identity around this larger, overarching narrative.

Many of the clients I have worked with sought therapy because they started to question if their dominant narratives were helping them or hurting them—meaning that they were ready, without consciously realizing it, to pay attention to their alternative narratives. These alternative narratives offer a *different* way to exist in the world, one that is an empowering reclamation of our truths. It's a privilege to reach this point of self-examination that many of our parents or elders may not have had or refuse to entertain at later ages. It can take practice to recognize that this mindset—this refusal to interrogate—might be rooted in survival for our immigrant parents.

Our immigrant parents and elders carry their own internal and external stories of marginalization, inequity, and/or acceptance from gatekeepers in their new country. Every immigrant's narrative varies and is often superimposed by larger systems that define the "good immigrant"—or the hardworking, self-sacrificing, assimilating immigrant who "deserves" to be here—and the "bad immigrant"—or the resistant, ungrateful, "undeserving" immigrant. Immigrants are often negotiating their identities and their cultures in a new country, and this process is ongoing.

Our parents' narratives—founded in their own generational and situational norms—affect our own narratives. Many of us are our parents' legacies: we are who we are because of their sacrifices and hardships, as the story goes. And so many of them rely on our success, not only as an external investment that they can fall back on later in life but also as an internal investment to continue the narrative that their sacrifices and choices were "worth it." Those who chose to move to the West, like my parents, may race against the concept of regret, externalizing their fear and imposing it on us. They're often afraid and in need of control, and if we don't stay close to or on the paths they created for us, then we risk shattering their internalized narratives. They may not know how to handle this. (And, frankly, we may not know how to, either.)

Our narratives are personal to the way we perceive and experience our lives and relationships. However, because relationships and family—or, more specifically, our caregivers—play a significant role, how we create our personal narratives may be closely tied to our family dynamics. For instance, different types of family interactions, like collaboration or varying power dynamics, can inform the way we conceptualize ourselves, other relationships, and the world. Narratives are unique, but a commonality for children of immigrants is the imposition of our parents' desires, needs, and expectations onto our own life stories. As such, I have theorized four common narratives that children of immigrants struggle with—or move between, depending on where they are in their own journeys:

- The **aligned and dutiful narrative** is applicable for children who stay on the path expected of them, *and* this aligns with their own needs and wants, allowing everyone in the family to feel happy and fulfilled by the chosen path. For example, one community member grew up with parents who ran a family business. They always expected him to take it over, and he had an interest in doing that, too, so when the time came, he not only fulfilled a *duty* but also undertook an endeavor *aligned* with his own desires and pursuits.

- The **resentful and dutiful narrative** is applicable for children who accept and internalize the narrative imposed on them despite it being different from what they really desire, causing their parents to feel fulfilled but them to feel resentful and unhappy. For example, one child of immigrants was expected to study engineering because her parents believed it to be the most stable and secure career field. They didn't budge when she told them she wanted to pursue nursing—an equally reputable career choice. She decided to do what they wanted, partly because they would help her pay for her schooling if she listened. She fulfilled her *duty* but felt *resentful* about it. It's important to note that this feeling of resentment may not be permanent, and many children of immigrants have come to accept and find contentment in the paths imposed on them, even if they wouldn't have chosen those paths themselves. A common example I often hear about is the modern-day arranged marriage, where one marries someone to whom they were introduced and who is "family approved," only to find that they discover love with this person, too.

- The **redeeming and fulfilling narrative** is applicable for a child who extricates themselves from an imposed narrative to pursue something of *their* choosing. Though it's not something that the child's parents or family members wanted for them, or could even conceptualize, the elders came around to supporting their kid. As such, the child was able to maintain—or restore with mutual effort—a relationship with their parents. For example, I have heard from fellow immigrant-origin therapists whose parents were not supportive of their choice to go into the mental health field, because they did not understand it. Eventually, though, they were able to teach their parents (who were also willing and curious) about the pride they have in their work, evolving the relationship. This one usually requires parents to do work to prioritize their kid's happiness, regardless of their own expectations and desires.

- The **separate and fulfilling narrative** is similar to the redeeming and fulfilling narrative arc in that it is applicable for a child who extricates themselves from an imposed narrative. However, in this narrative arc, the parents don't come around (or haven't yet), creating a separated and detached relationship within the family, even though the child has chosen something that is *fulfilling* to them. For example, I have heard several stories from people in the community who chose same-sex or racially different romantic partners whom their parents didn't accept. I have also heard stories about people who willingly chose to leave their family systems because of abuse—a difficult decision that ultimately is for the well-being of the person making it. This is a particularly painful narrative that can be initially destabilizing, and may lead to emotional and physical cutoffs in familial relationships or even temporary or permanent estrangement.

Our dominant narratives are composed of specific life experiences, or stories (like those I mention above), and they enforce certain core beliefs, or beliefs that we internalize as factual based on our lived experiences. *I'm a bad son for choosing a creative career. I'm a selfish sister for not checking in more. I'm an ungrateful employee for taking this much time off. I'm a weak person for being on mental health medication.* Our dominant narratives are not necessarily permanent entities, though. Instead, they are dynamic and change and evolve as we—and our relationships with others and our cultures/identities—change and evolve. In fact, we can take any experience, or story from our life, and through the pursuit of growth, curiosity, and self-awareness, we may change our perspective of it, ultimately shifting our dominant narrative. Paying attention to these narratives—where they come from, and why—can empower us to reclaim our agency. It can plant a seed of possibility for something different—nudging us to step into the gray and embrace the reality that two things can be true at the same time. This is how we begin to accept ourselves, complexities and all.

Reflection questions for you to think about your past, present, and future narratives:

PAST

Imagine your life up until now as a book.

By reflecting as a storyteller on your own life, you give yourself authorship over the arc of your narrative. You can then reflect on the following:

- What "chapters" or storylines would be a part of your life book so far? Consider which experiences or events summarize your life or your evolution as a person. Be specific and take your time with this.
- After you have some chapters noted, reflect on if, and how, they come together to align with any of the narrative arcs I mentioned above.
- If you don't identify with one of the four I describe, what would you call the dominant narrative of your past?
- What are themes that arise in the narrative arc? Are you struggling with the same thing over the course of many years? Is there one major focus across these experiences?
- What do your overarching narratives indicate? Negativity or positivity? Struggle or triumph?
- Take a few days or weeks, and then return to this exercise. Are there stories you left out that could have changed the arc of your dominant narratives? Are there life events that you haven't given yourself credit for? Why do you think you forgot them initially? This allows you to start considering alternative storylines that you want to give power to.

PRESENT

If you had to sum up your current dominant narrative in three to seven words, what would they be? Reflect on what's coming up for you. What feels especially salient for you right now? What is impacting the narrative you are living through? It can be a particular struggle—maybe something you've been navigating for a long time and can't shake—or a particular success. Now ask yourself:

- Is your current dominant narrative positive, neutral, or negative? Why?

- How does this narrative fit into the bigger context of your life story (think about the PAST exercise)?
- Are you aligned with any of the four narrative types mentioned above?
- How is your current narrative internalized from other places, people, or sociocultural expectations? These may be related to a narrative imposed on you.
- Are you content with this dominant narrative? If not, what—and how—would you want to change?

FUTURE

You meet your future self. You can decide how far in the future. Now consider:

- What are they like? How would you describe their sense of self, their character, their priorities?
- What are their relationships like?
- What's important to them?
- What are they struggling with? What have they learned?
- How have they evolved?

By considering these questions, you imagine an aspirational narrative. What does this mean for the present you? How does this future narrative compare with or differ from past or present narratives you have subscribed to or currently subscribe to? What core beliefs may be holding you back from reaching this aspirational narrative? What alternative storylines do you want to imbue with power in order to align with this aspirational narrative?

Confronting the Reality
of Our Narratives

By the time I was ten, my family had moved to our third and final home in suburban Virginia, and because of the significant age gap between us, my brother, Ajay, was out of the house in college and my sister, Chandani, was about to be. I felt a lot of emotional distance from each of my family members, especially my siblings. In part, this was because my parents didn't nurture our relationships with each other, but it was also because of our age differences. At ten years my senior, Ajay was more of a fatherlike figure—often mediating cultural and generational discussions between my parents and me—and Chandani, seven years older than me, was in her own world; though I wanted to be included in her life, I felt like I was just an annoying little sister for much of my childhood.

I was often made to feel bad for not being more like my brother, outwardly confident and obedient, or my sister, outwardly carefree and low maintenance. I was emotional, sensitive, and hyperaware of my surroundings. It's easy to show the physical and physiological needs that were met—and I am grateful for these!—but I also felt emotionally bereft. I'd been consumed by obsessive thoughts and fears and sadness for most of my young life, and I wished I could make it clearly visible to my family. I wanted to arrange it all on a platter and say, "See! This is what I mean. This is what is happening to my insides. Acknowledge it!"

I can't speak for my brother or sister, who are closer in age to each other, but for me, it was very normalized to be living this separate life. I didn't know what was happening in their lives, and they didn't know what was happening in mine. We joke now as adults that we had different parents growing up. From my perspective, they had the more attentive, joyful, present father, while I had the more absent, controlling, volatile father. Though my siblings spent a few years of their childhoods living in India with extended family present—and going through more similar life stages together—I spent my childhood solely in a new country, and it seems likely that our parents' relationship and mental health statuses changed as they navigated being new immigrants. All of this likely affected the differences in how we were parented. Regardless, we had, and still have, very different relationship needs—something that has never been explicitly acknowledged in my family. Of course, as an adult with a different and more intimate relationship with my siblings, I have learned that they, too, struggled in their own ways with our parents, and that we are all on our own journeys of exploring what emotional safety looks and feels like. It's easy to filter our relationships with our siblings through the lens of how *we* were parented (rather than how they were) and how we perceive their experiences (rather than how they actually experienced things).

Looking back as a therapist, I know that kids are intuitive and internalize the stress in their homes, even if it's not explicitly directed at or communicated to them. As such, they usually need extra attention and nurturance, especially because they will naturally blame themselves for the distress or conflict they are noticing. I wasn't emotionally needy—I was emotionally neglected. Now, I don't blame my parents for their lack of attention to my personal and individual emotional needs. I know that they did the best they could. I know that I will always be endlessly grateful to them. I also know that I wish things had been different for me. Being loved is different from being nurtured or accepted.

The way I processed my neglect was by retreating to my room often, by default spending as little time with my family as possible. I often felt like I only had myself. I learned how to entertain myself, but I craved intimacy and hungered for emotional nurturance in ways that I didn't get and didn't know how to ask for. My family members all describe the younger me as some version of aloof and indifferent. It made them feel bad when I'd retreat, and I remember that I, too, always felt bad—like something was wrong with me— for not wanting to invest in my familial relationships growing up. But I understand now that it shouldn't have been my responsibility to initiate or sustain those relationships as a kid, especially as the youngest. I didn't know—and couldn't have known—what I know today about the role of a parent and the needs of a child.

In fact, in my work, it's very obvious that many children of immigrants are dealing with the fallout of not having their emotional needs met when they were growing up, and many still don't realize this is something they struggle with. For a child of immigrants, it can be incredibly hard to discern between different needs. You may reflect and realize that some of your childhood needs were met, while others weren't. Here are some examples for you to consider:

- Maybe you were fed, clothed, and monetarily provided for (which is huge, by the way!). But were these needs also used against you through guilting or shaming to secure obedience, submission, or deference?
- Maybe you were protected from external harm (bullies, strangers, and harsh environments). But were you also given safety and protection within your family system when a family member acted in harmful ways?
- Maybe you were praised when you hit milestones and achievements, but were you also encouraged to simply try, do your best, and have fun?
- Maybe you were provided with stability through holidays, religious community, and honored traditions. But were you

provided with stability in terms of communication and access to connection with your parents/caregivers?

- Maybe you were loved and supported through endeavors that were acceptable and respectable in your parents' eyes. But were you shown curiosity and support when you had different desires or opinions?

- Maybe you had the physical space to attain some privacy and attempt to work through your own struggles. But were you also encouraged to talk through your struggles openly, and/or were you comforted when you were sad?

- Maybe you were told stories about your ancestors' resilience and strength to fortify your identity and connection to your roots. But were you also encouraged to explore what identity means to you and express it in ways that felt authentic to you?

- Maybe you were rewarded and validated when you performed well or played a certain family role. But were you also punished severely when you made an honest mistake or given no clarity on why consequences were imposed?

We can honor, acknowledge, and show gratitude for all the ways we were loved and provided for as kids, *and* we can recognize that there were limitations on how other needs were, or weren't, nurtured and met. Both can exist at the same time.

Repeat after me: *I am not needy. I am just someone with needs that may not have been met.*

My sister recently apologized for not always being there for me growing up. We talked about how my reputation as the "problem child" is deeply embedded in our family narrative. I was called naughty and did not know how to emotionally regulate when things got hard, often leading me to lash out. When I would try to turn to my siblings during times of intense conflict between me and my parents, their first question would often be: "What did you do?" My sister admitted that sometimes it was easier to consciously agree with this dominant family narrative than question it. All I ever wanted was for my family to recognize and acknowledge how alone I felt as a child and as an adolescent. I know that my sister and I were able to have this conversation because of the work we have mutually done on our relationship—as sisters but even more as chosen friends. By revisiting our separated and personal relationships with our parents as adults, and our lived experiences as kids, we have been able to acknowledge each other's struggles. We agree that not being more involved when we were younger was a missed opportunity, but we're here now.

A few months ago, my mom found some old files that included a letter I wrote to her when I was probably in my late teens. It was an apology for "being a bad kid" and "never being able to do anything right." My mom laughed it off. "You were such a problem child!" she exclaimed heartily. I got off the phone and cried. My parents' inability to tend to my emotional needs had created a narrative that I carried with me well into adulthood—one that is still painful, though no longer paralyzing, for me to revisit. Now, through my mental journey and as a therapist, I know there's another side to that coin, and I have new language to express that alternate narrative: "Or maybe I didn't feel safe. Or loved. Or wanted. Or secure," I wanted to say.

As a child of immigrants, I have been loved fiercely, but I have also come to learn that like many other second-gen kids, I was loved in pieces. I was fed, clothed, and monetarily provided for, but manipulation, guilt, and shame were inflicted to command obedience and submission. When you are loved in pieces, you are taught that parts of yourself are unworthy and unlovable. That sticks with you. My parents measured my goodness and judged my intelligence through a particular frame of reference. They (consciously or not) focused on the parts of myself that they believed would make me stronger, smarter, and more successful—all in the ways they understood these qualities based on their own experiences. Their hope was that they could ultimately steer me to the three *s*'s that drove their thoughts, fears, and decisions: security, safety, and stability.

As an adult, I've had to learn how to tend to those neglected parts of myself, nurturing them as I wish they were nurtured when I was a child. I didn't have access to books or education or social media that captured my intersectional experiences when I was younger. I didn't know that what I was thinking or going through was shared by others. So I continued to swallow the pain and the discomfort, convinced that I was the problem.

What Is Normal?

I always perceived how my parents treated me and each other as "just a part of my culture"—probably because my parents have defaulted to this excuse when I try to speak up about something that feels unhealthy or unhelpful. More recently, I asked my mom if she remembered throwing *American* at me like a bad word when I was growing up—hurling it at me whenever I went against the culturally approved expectations that came with being an Indian woman or daughter. I was outspoken, not easily controlled by my parents—no matter how hard they tried—and I was emotionally expressive, hard to keep quiet. "Sometimes there just seems to be a cultural differ-ence," she responded, as if defeated.

I asked members of the Brown Girl Therapy community what normalized aspects of their heritage cultures or families they person-ally perceived as harmful and dysfunctional. Out of hundreds of re-plies from folks with different backgrounds, the most common were machismo, or masculine pride and patriarchal norms; not talk-ing openly about problematic issues in order to maintain a facade that everything is fine, good even; being forced to respect unde-serving elders; the expectation of duty to the family at any cost; and maintaining abusive familial or spousal relationships to keep the peace.

In considering what is normal within a family, we must question how this impacts the family's functioning, and in considering how a family functions as a system, we must also be willing to explore how it *doesn't* function. In the mental health field, family dysfunction is categorized by different traits. Common examples are role confu-sion, rigidity, lack of emotional cohesion, control, conflict fraught-ness, perfectionism or unrealistic expectations, secrecy, harmful communication patterns, instability, and conditional love. Function/dysfunction of a family is also compounded by chronic illness, sub-stance use, domestic violence, addiction, emotional neglect, and/or abuse.

What may be considered dysfunctional for one person in the fam-ily may actually be functional for another. For instance, if you have a family member who continuously starts arguments, feels attacked, and/or gets defensive, this can feel incredibly frustrating to other members who are interacting with that person. *Other* members who interact with that person may feel this is a dysfunctional aspect of their relationship, but for *that* person, the behavior serves the function of avoiding vulnerability and exerting some semblance of control (even if it's false control). We also have to explore how power is perceived, experienced, or regulated in the family system. For instance, in many immigrant families, power is reserved for elders and men. As such, it's these members who can often "get away" with certain unhealthy or harmful behaviors.

When I asked members of the Brown Girl Therapy community if they would label their upbringings or family dynamics as dysfunctional, 57 percent of 6,491 said "yes," while 33 percent said "somewhat." I wish I were surprised, but I'm not. Many community members, clients, and children of immigrants are constantly navigating the line between toxicity or dysfunction and what has been normalized in our own families and cultures. Dysfunction is how *you* define the impact of your family dynamics on yourself, but as I have come to observe in my work with children of immigrants, some of the most common forms of dysfunction in immigrant families are rigidity; clearly defined or differentiated hierarchies and rules/expectations; hypercriticism; corporal punishment; emotional neglect; and substance abuse by a parent. In fact, when I listed these in an Instagram poll, 91 percent of 6,007 said their families of origin—or the family units in which they were raised—include at least one (if not all) of these types of dynamics.

If these dysfunctions are commonplace in many of our immigrant families, that begs the question: Where does culture end, and where does trauma begin? Or more so, in which ways do culture and trauma live in their own lanes that sometimes intersect? And when does culture become a scapegoat for toxic behavior? *It's the way it has always been done, after all.* Early in graduate school, I gravitated toward feminist therapy, which accounts for how power dynamics, marginalization, and inequity inform our realities. This is not just through the lens of gender but, more generally, through our intersectional identities, such as sexuality, race, ethnicity, socioeconomic status, and so on. We all exist in a paradigm that is informed by white supremacist ideology, patriarchy, colonialism, and capitalism, and whether or not we have been able to consciously address our own internalized biases or relationships around these structures, they exist and manifest in different ways. This may be the immigrant choosing to give their child an anglicized name, or the child of an immigrant purposefully mispronouncing their own name for the benefit of others. Or it may be the way we talk, fix our hair, or dress at work in the name of "professionalism" or what is considered "modest and appropriate" in our cultural communities. This may be the pressure many women feel to defer to elders, or men, even if they don't agree with them. Or it may be the beauty standards we subscribe to—or that are imposed on us—through the lens of femininity and masculinity. Or it may be more subtle, like the prickling sensation on our neck when we realize we are the only person of color in a room. Regardless of how we engage, or not, with the larger systems in which we exist, the truth is that "normal" is based on norms created within these systems. Just because things have always been done one way doesn't mean they should continue to be. And this is true for the way a family functions, as each family system has *its* own culture informed by larger systemic or heritage cultures. As Resmaa Menakem, author of *My Grandmother's Hands*, said: "Trauma in a person, decontextualized over time, can look like personality. Trauma in a family, decontextualized over time, can look like family traits. Trauma decontextualized in a people over time can look like culture."

Normalized Trauma

I spent much of my life ignorant of the term *trauma* and convinced that the things I had witnessed or experienced in my life were just *normal* (i.e., experienced by everyone) and also "not that bad." After all, I love my parents, and they love me, and all the stories I have heard or read about childhood "trauma" convey blatant or extreme scenarios—physical signs of abuse or physical abandonment. I never allowed myself to explore the possibility that my parents could love me *and* I could experience trauma because of them. Once again, it's been black or white: if you love someone, you can't possibly perpetuate harm that can be defined as "trauma." However, our understanding of whether we are struggling revolves around what it means to be normal, and things that are normalized and commonly performed and accepted are not necessarily healthy. To simplify it: when things are considered normal, we get used to them. So what happens when *normal* is defined differently in the home environment than it is outside the home? And what happens when we finally start to accept that the "normal" we've known for our entire lives is rooted in oppression, patriarchy, and colonialism—always on a systemic level and sometimes within our own homes and families?

It's important to note that not everyone who experiences something negative will perceive it as traumatic. More so, two people can have the same experience and subsequently be impacted very differently—one considering it trauma and the other not. And "healthy" itself is also subjective: what feels good to one person may not feel that way to another person, regardless of background or culture. No matter, though, these experiences shape the ways we tell our stories—or avoid the *whole* truth of them, picking and choosing the chapters that fit into the narrative we *want* to be true.

I've worked with many children of immigrants who seek support because they are significantly functionally impaired due to the experiences and trauma they've been subjected to at the hands of their own families. Families whom they love—and who also love them, they would likely argue—and families who use culture as an excuse not to change. Many clients will discuss a parent's emotional and verbal abuse—stonewalling, invalidation, and unfiltered and explosive anger—and defend it as normal and cultural. Here's the thing: abuse in the guise of love is still abuse.

Via my *Washington Post* column, one child of Turkish immigrants reached out to me about her mom's silent treatment, which she still experiences today in middle age. "I am realizing this is emotional abuse," she wrote. It had taken her decades to acknowledge this, and many of us may never fully believe that our experiences were or are harmful enough to label "traumatic," let alone "neglectful" or "abusive," *because* our parents love(d) us. Another reader wrote, "What is the line between Indian family dynamics and emotional abuse?" These questions are common and arrive in earnest, with many people struggling to understand how to conceptualize their lived experiences and cultural values congruently.

In an Instagram poll, about 89 percent of 2,300 respondents said that their emotional needs weren't met when they were growing up. We are expected to survive off minimal nurturance, and yet research shows that emotional and affectional neglect can have a significant effect on a child's development and ability to thrive, self-regulate when navigating difficult emotions, and build a strong self-concept. Several of the people I have worked with have defended their parents to me when discussing the pain and ruptures they feel in their relationships with their parents (or a parent). "But they loved me" and "I feel bad making them look bad" are commonly expressed refrains. This immediate need to defend them only highlights how insidious and unseen emotional neglect can be.

Let me be clear: emotional neglect is not necessarily abuse. While neglect may be an intentional disregard, it is usually a failure to even recognize a child's need. As Dr. Jonice Webb highlights in her book *Running on Empty*, well-meaning parents may not know better. Of course, some folks may have experienced both neglect and abuse, but the former does not automatically lead to the latter. It's important to explore the nuance between neglect and abuse, power and fear, and a need for control and manipulation. What's more, emotional neglect is not specific to children of immigrants, but I have observed that we especially fail to recognize the impact of our experiences, because we deny them or avoid them to preserve our family dynamics or cultures. This complicates our ability to recognize dysfunctionality, much less heal from the effects of it.

Regardless of knowing where our parents may be coming from—and the possible intent (or lack thereof) behind their behavior—it doesn't change the effects that their behaviors have on us. Our parents may have done the best they could, or reverted to cultural norms they grew up with, *and* they still may have caused us harm.

The earliest memory I can conjure up is from when I was four or five, and I know this much to be true because we were living in the first of our three houses in the United States. I remember my mom taking me upstairs for bedtime, but I stopped on the landing of our staircase and refused to go to bed until my mom and dad hugged after an argument they were having. I couldn't go to sleep until I had proof that things were okay between them. I can't remember why my siblings weren't there or what the argument was about, but it would be one of many that composed the soundtrack of my childhood.

When I was growing up, it was normal for my parents to fight, loudly and unfiltered. It was also normal for me to mediate their marital conflicts. It was normal for alcohol dependency to have a huge presence, both in social gatherings and at home. It was normal to feel anxious in the back seat during car rides home from these weekend community gatherings, eyes darting back and forth, anticipating if or when a fight would erupt between my parents. It was normal to be asked as a young kid to keep secrets for and between family members. It was normal for me to feel hurt or sad and bottle it up inside, and it was normal not to receive comfort or emotional support from my parents or siblings. It was normal for the people I loved to have different thresholds for bottling up their own feelings, and it was normal for the pressure cooker to eventually overfill and release—pressure cookers don't boil over!—often explosively and randomly. It was normal to be on the receiving end of these outbursts—sometimes physically and other times emotionally. It was normal to have to get over it, without an acknowledgment or apology, and pretend the next day that it never happened. It was normal to mislearn that communication is the act of trying to be louder than the other person, and that conflict resolution is a competition to see who can be more hurtful and ultimately shut the other person up. It was normal to walk on eggshells. It was normal for me to call my brother at university, crying about the chaos at home, and for him to invite me to stay with him and do crafts and watch movies with his friends. It was normal for power to be hoarded by the men in my family and in my community. It was normal to wake up one day and not know for sure whether my parents loved each other, or themselves . . . or me. It was normal to lie to my parents about where I was or have to constantly account for my time and whereabouts. It was normal for me (and my peers) to be paraded around like a show pony at community events when I was succeeding, and it was normal to hide, lie, and pretend when things didn't go quite as expected. It was normal for extended family and community members to discuss my weight, body, grades, and marriageability. It was normal to believe that I was overreacting if I had feelings that were different from those of my parents or my siblings. It was normal to be called an old soul as a young kid. It was normal to be pitted against my peers. It was normal for me to be constantly compared with my brother and sister. It was normal to always put family first—even at the expense of investing in good friendships—and it was normal to mislearn that being loved also means being mistreated, as they are one and the same. It was normal to accept pain and to offer my loved ones unconditional tolerance, regardless of how it harmed me.

Because all this was normal, I did not question any of these experiences. For many children of immigrants, pursuing growth and healing means reconciling with what we've believed to be normal. When someone experiences certain types of trauma for so long, it can become second nature—albeit numbing—to live amid the chaos, avoidance, or conflict, and it can be hard to distinguish what is okay from what is not.

Norms in our own family systems are created because of various factors—cultural standards and values, as well as intergenerational patterns and experiences. Examples include spanking/hitting as a form of discipline; *how* respect and communication are modeled or expected; and the ways in which food or substances are prevalent, centered, or used in the home environment. "Normal" in one family may be abnormal in another. Norms are not necessarily "bad." We may learn to celebrate and honor traditions—like religious holidays or Sunday dinner at your grandparents' house with the whole family—and through these norms, we may learn the importance of community and family care. In all cases, we must acknowledge these norms and, even more so, get comfortable with questioning them.

The stories that frame accepted, or expected, behavior within our own families can determine the larger narratives we are inclined toward as individuals. Like culture, family norms/values are not static, and yet many of us grew up in households where our parents or elders tightly grasped on to rigid values, norms, and expectations. There's an understood social contract, and it may not be explicit. As individuals, we develop our identities, senses of belonging, and senses of security through these family narratives. Cultural norms become family norms. Family norms become individual norms. Again, just because it's always been done this way doesn't mean it isn't harmful.

Many children of immigrants feel guilt or shame for "talking poorly" about their loved ones, or they feel that it reflects badly on *them*. Others may believe that no one else can possibly understand because they are so isolated within their own families. Identifying how your family functions without labeling it as negative or positive may be the first step to exploring the reality of your family dynamics. Here are some questions to help you reflect on how your family functions and what is considered "normal":

- What are the power dynamics in your family? How does this impact the way your family functions as a system?
- How and when is love freely given or withheld in your family?
- Has anyone ever gone against what was considered "normal" in your family? What happened, and how did other members react?
- What is missing or lacking in your family system or, specifically, between certain family members that you wish existed?
- Have you ever talked to anyone in your family about how your family functions? If so, what was that like?

- Do you feel safe being vulnerable with your parents, siblings, or other family members? Why or why not?
- How do you contribute to how your family functions or dysfunctions? Be honest with yourself.
- Whom did you live with growing up, and how does this impact the norms in your family?
- How—and when—do your family members communicate with one another?
- How are fear, shame, anger, and guilt utilized in your family?

Interrogating Our Narratives

My mom and dad came to America at twenty-nine and thirty-five, respectively. They had enough money from the sale of their previous house, no credit cards, and an onslaught of obstacles. My dad was trying to take his medical board exams and get his unrestricted medical license (that would be valid in the States), while my mom was adjusting with two young kids, alone in a new country, and pregnant with her third: me. My dad was battling immigration issues and the imminent threat of having his visa denied while also navigating housing and banking in a new country. He'd taken a risk moving even deeper into the West from the UK, away from family, social capital, security, and norms he was comfortable within. He was building a new life, and in doing so he realized that he could not afford to make any mistakes. He needed to trust himself to figure it out at any cost: his family—my mom, my siblings, and I—were depending entirely on him. I theorize that his lack of a support system, a safety net, or a road map, as well as how he learned to trust his own intellect above all else, distorted his views of his own abilities and knowledge.

I imagine that a lot of things contributed to what I have perceived as my dad's self-righteousness: Being born a boy in a particularly patriarchal country celebrative of boys simply for being boys. Being the eldest child, and son, in a family with parents who encouraged traditional filial/male roles. Being the sole financial provider of a family of five in a new country. Being a doctor with a lot of accolades and needing to make split-second decisions about other people's lives. When I was growing up, there wasn't much engagement or curiosity; rather, his statements, opinions, and beliefs were the last word. I learned to accept and respect that he knew everything and never question him. I learned to feed his ego with platitudes. This was built into the way I was expected to view him as an authoritarian parental figure who knew best. I was taught to fear my dad. My mom was in charge of managing the day-to-day activities in our household, and my dad was mostly pulled in only when there was a serious family matter or when I was in trouble. His presence would be weaponized: *Just wait until your dad comes home.* Or it would be deemed too scary, and my mom would thus be relegated to acting as a buffer: *Don't worry, I'll talk to your dad.* Or, worst of all, he was considered a last resort: *Your dad's busy; don't bother him with that.* I never went to my dad first, and I learned over the years not to go to him at all.

Don't get me wrong—he's humble. He'll never correct someone who mistakes him for the other Sikh doctor who works at the same hospital. He doesn't need recognition for his work or his faith. He's always been motivated to provide and set his family up for success and security. But his narrow-minded views about what was right or good didn't allow for an expansion or expression of self that I desperately ached for growing up. My mom adopted these values in more insidious ways. She was as protective as a mama bear, but she, too, lacked the capacity to fully understand, process, or communicate emotions. I often felt like I was too needy or too much when engaging with me didn't feel easy for her. I was reminded often how tiresome I could be, so I learned to deal with my own emotions through crying—so much so that my mom told me on a number of occasions that I would make a good actress given how quickly and often I could cry. I was convinced that something was wrong with me because I responded to the world differently and more intensely than my family members. I learned that being impenetrable and unaffected meant being strong and that being vulnerable meant being weak.

Eventually, I came to model these beliefs internally through self-rejection and self-shame. Many children of immigrants I've observed through my work do the same. When things have always been a certain way, it can compound this belief many of us have that maybe we are just making it up. *Maybe it's not real. Maybe I'm not strong enough. Maybe because other people had it worse, I should stop complaining. Maybe it's not that bad. Maybe they didn't actually mean it to be hurtful. Maybe if I were stronger, it wouldn't feel so bad. Why am I so upset about this?* We carry the invalidation we received in our own homes and start to turn it inward against ourselves, questioning our own experiences.

IN MY WORK, I've talked to grown children of immigrants who have histories of childhood abuse or trauma and as adults can't reconcile with the reality of their experiences. They'll contort themselves every which way to justify what they went through, forming narratives in which it's their fault rather than accepting their own family members' culpability, for fear that doing so would be a betrayal.

Here's the thing: when you were a child, your parents or caretakers had the power. Many children of immigrants struggle to understand this because they learned from a young age to act like adults or take on adult-like responsibilities due to family or parental circumstances. This is known as parentification. Maybe you were the only one who could speak English or your host country's language, and you had to translate or help with paperwork and bills. Or maybe you were a latchkey kid who had to take care of yourself after school when your parents were still working. Maybe as an older sibling or cousin, like my brother, you had to help care for younger children in the house/family or mediate cultural and generational differences between family members. Or maybe, like me, you mediated family conflicts at a young age and were expected, as the listener, to allow your family members to emotionally unburden themselves and their struggles onto you. Whatever it was, this parentification—whether emotional or instrumental, meaning practical but not age appropriate—caused you to develop a self-concept embedded in caretaking. Most children of immigrants whom I have worked with or talked to were parentified children.

We are taught to tie our senses of self to the needs of our parents and elders, taking care of *them*. This mental and emotional gymnastics contributes to our lack of self-trust, and we measure our worthiness against our ability to anticipate others' needs. Research even suggests that parentification—to a certain degree—can be a form of emotional neglect, yet many of us have inserted this experience into our narratives as a nonissue.

Growing up, I was always called an old soul, usually by an aunty or uncle who was impressed by my wisdom. In reality, I was wise and empathic for my age because I was expected to know more than I developmentally should have, and I lived in constant fear of upsetting my parents. And I know I'm not alone; when I asked children of immigrants in an informal poll if they had ever been called old souls or mature for their age when they were growing up, 79 percent of 6,119 said yes. Though usually meant to be a compliment, this characterization may not always feel positive, because it is often a consequence of having to grow up too quickly, and it usually results in not getting *your* needs met.

A few years ago, when I was talking more openly to my dad about this and about how neglected I felt growing up, he asked me point-blank if I had ever asked for what I needed growing up. "Did you reach out for it?" he said, expressionless. His obliviousness shocked me. I told him that it shouldn't have been my responsibility to ask; it's a parent's job to tend to their kid's needs and protect them physically and emotionally. "How were we to know that's what you needed?" he responded. It's not a concept that he understood, and it certainly wasn't a need that was fulfilled for him when he was a kid, either.

The attunement—or awareness of and response to someone else's emotional needs—that a child deserves from their parents or caretakers is fundamentally important. It's less about intellectually *knowing* that our parents love us and more about *feeling loved* by our parents. This requires our parents to want to know us as individuals rather than as extensions of themselves. It requires their willingness to create space for needs beyond their own. And it requires them to not constantly neglect themselves, too. For our parents, a narrative of self-sacrifice combined with a young age of marriage and/or a lack of emotional support or attunement from *their* own parents led them to neglect themselves, impacting their access to the emotional depth we required of them.

At any point, for all of us, there are multiple narratives that we may be subscribing to, and the ways in which we frame these stories are monumental to how we will build our identities, relationships, and self-concepts. We can blame ourselves. We can blame our cultures.

We can blame our parents. But the narratives that will actually serve us aren't about blame. We need to discover new and evolved, albeit imperfect, alternative narratives that allow us to explore the wilderness of the gray—where things aren't clearly marked but we have more agency to decide: *Well, what now?*

> Your parents are not meant to be the antagonists of your story, but remember, they are also not the authors. By writing and owning your own narrative, you are not betraying or rejecting where—and who—you come from.

Changing Our Narratives

Questioning and critiquing the narratives to which we subscribe can help us engage with the parts of ourselves that are still hurting and can help us learn new ways to reauthor our narratives for our healing.

If we wait for the people who ruptured something within us to repair it, we give away our power and agency for healing. For better or worse, walking away is not the goal for many of us. We end up thinking that the only alternative is sticking things out and accepting what we are given—even if it's harmful or not enough. But we have agency over microchanges and microhealing that can build healthier relationships and lives. Doing the work—the healing, the growing, the forgiving, the recognizing—requires active effort and reconciliation.

With the tools I have today, as a longtime active therapy-goer and a curious daughter of immigrants, as well as with the skills I've developed through my graduate program in clinical mental health counseling, I have been able to facilitate change within these relationships, rewriting—and owning—my narrative along the way. I have faced my own story—the good, the bad, and the ugly. The things I never wanted to admit and the things my parents wanted to pretend never happened. I have been radically honest with myself about what it means to be a child of immigrants and what took me way too long to learn or unlearn. I have also learned that I do not have to prove that my trauma is real. It's not a matter of figuring out who was right and who was wrong. It's not a matter of seeking vengeance or humiliating those who hurt me. It's not about receiving external validation. It's about speaking my truth, and sharing myself so vulnerably and honestly that I eviscerate my internalized shame.

On that first trip together in Maine in 2015, my papa and I began to shatter a wall, and thus the narrative in which I felt separated from my parents, that is too often built between immigrant fathers and daughters. I started to share more about what I had been going through when I was depressed years prior, and he listened earnestly. He may not have fully understood, but he also didn't deny me my reality. He recounted stories about living in India, stories about his dad, whom I don't have any recollection of, and stories about his early years in America. I learned that I fear disappointing him and worry that everything I do might be a burden. We talked about the concept of happiness and some of my dreams as we sat by a fireplace sipping whiskey in Kennebunkport. And in Acadia, I observed that he's not very outdoorsy and doesn't like to be out of his element. I also witnessed his impatience (even in waiting for the best lobster in town), his restlessness when he doesn't have anything to do, and his penchant for happily adding crispy french fries to just about any meal. While my dad exudes power, he's a softy who's terrified of losing control. He has spent most of his adult life navigating unprecedented situations and experiences, and even though the situations I have faced are different, that challenge of the unexpected and unprecedented is something we have in common. In Bar Harbor, he bought a new baseball cap that he still wears today, a reminder of the first time we spent intentional and mutually invested time together. Though the trip to Maine brought us closer, I left feeling like there were many things that I still didn't understand and, further, that there were many, many more I'd have to realize on my own as I pursued my generational healing and reflection. But first I had to start by making room to trust myself.

Communication tips for
healthier conversations

When we haven't been taught how to communicate with our families, it can be difficult to know where to start. We often all fall into a pattern or cycle that has been consistent for years but may not be healthy or totally working. Here are some strategies for approaching communication in ways that will allow you to connect more deeply with your family and loved ones.

- When we think about gaining exposure to uncomfortable or new experiences, it can feel daunting to jump all the way in. So instead of changing the way you communicate all at once, consider what would feel safe to "test" on your loved one. Maybe it's practicing using I-language or setting a small boundary. Maybe it's being vulnerable or asking for something you need.
- When you feel yourself getting overwhelmed, try to build in a pause. This can look like stepping away, not immediately responding to something, or asking for time before continuing the conversation. This allows you to consider what your immediate reaction would have been and whether or not you want to stick with it.
- Oftentimes, folks in the community tell me that their parents are always contradicting themselves: *We support you, AND*

we want you to prioritize this other thing. I'm glad you're happy, AND I just don't understand why you couldn't have chosen X. In these moments, a double-sided reflection may help you encourage them to get clear about what it is they actually feel or mean. This can look like: *You say you support me, but you also feel like I should prioritize something that takes away from what makes me happy.* This highlights a discrepancy without sounding confrontational.

- Our reality is influenced by language, and we create narratives about ourselves through words, usually forgetting to cocreate this language with our loved ones so that we are all on the same page. Make sure you are using language or words that are relevant and comprehensible throughout the conversations. For example, if you use a word like *boundary* with someone who has no understanding of what it means, then you may lose them before you even get past the word. This is also helpful when you hit resistance; consider finding a different way to ask or say the same thing.

- Change the method or environment in which you have bigger and deeper conversations. My parents dubbed one of the rooms in our house the War Room because it was where we had some of our worst fights. Now I try to avoid that room when I want to talk to my parents about anything meaningful because I feel like the environment has primed us all for conflict. Instead, I will try to go on walks—I don't know what it is about walks and immigrant dads in particular!—or change the setting. Similarly, if you are always fighting with a loved one over text message, stop texting about things that lead to conflict! Call them, or wait to meet in person. And if you are always fighting in person but can't seem to express yourself fully, consider writing a letter or an email to give the other person space to digest and respond in their own time.

- Get clarity on explicit terms. If a loved one keeps complaining about or highlighting a certain *behavior* or *feeling* that is upsetting them, try to get clarity on what they want and exactly how they would know they are receiving it. This will help address any subjective definitions of feelings and behaviors. For instance, if your mom is always telling you that you don't help her out around the house, and yet you feel like you do, ask her *what* she wants you to do, in explicit terms, for her to know/feel that you are helping.

- Reflect and validate their feelings *before* asking for what you want or sharing your own feelings. Oftentimes, when we are feeling attacked or getting defensive, we totally dismiss or overlook what the other person is saying. In these times, it's easy to reply with "Well, I . . ." Try to take a second to reflect what you heard—this will allow them to correct you if you're wrong—and validate their feelings. (You do *not* have to agree to validate their internal experience.) And *then* say what you want to say as a response. For example, if your sister is annoyed that you never call, and she starts naming all the things *you* aren't doing that she expects, you may start to feel attacked. Pause, and address the emotional component: *I can understand that you expected me to call, and I didn't, and now you're frustrated with me.*

- Redirect the conversation. If there are certain people who tend to be more triggering or unhealthy for you than others, have handy some talking points *about them* that you can use to redirect the conversation. For example, if an aunty always talks about the fact that you're not married (or that you're getting old, wasting your time, etc.), instead of responding to

this, immediately redirect: *How's [grandkid's name] doing?*
Or: *I heard you and [uncle's name] recently went to Italy;
how was that?*

- Be mindful of when you are "matching" others. If they are
  yelling, you don't have to yell. If they are attacking you, you
  don't have to attack them back. This may require
  disengagement (e.g., walking away, going to the restroom/
  another room, or asking to call them back in a few minutes).
  Healthy conversations are not about having the last word.

- Practice! Prepare for upcoming conversations by preemptively
  playing out scenarios and noting how you can handle them in
  ways that feel good to you and allow you to care for yourself.
  This looks like writing out what you will say and imagining
  potential response scenarios, then different responses to those,
  and so on. This isn't perfect, but it will help you build up
  confidence and intentionality around word choices.

Chapter Two

When Things Don't
Go According to Plan

I t took me twelve years to graduate from college with a bachelor's degree. This has been my biggest hoarded secret, one that fewer than ten people know (until now). In writing this book, I observed myself still trying to skirt around having to write about this fact. I know that the very things we avoid or deny are usually the very ones we have to confront. Revisiting this part of my life has reminded me that we can't skip chapters in our life narratives. We must own *all* parts of our stories, and often the only people who think of our less pretty truths as shameful are our own worst critics (i.e., ourselves).

In 2006, I was starting my college career at seventeen, fresh out of high school, where I was a top student, a star two-season athlete, and the youngest trained EMT in my area. My life choices and experiences had all been guided by a compass leading to a destination marked "the Good Indian Daughter." Sure, I rebelled and challenged the narrative here and there, but I was ultimately driven by these kinds of questions: How can I make my parents proud? How can I give them things to brag about to family and friends? How can I make their sacrifices worth it? How can I exceed their already high expectations to prove how worthy I am? Like many children of immigrants, I wanted to be *aligned* with my *duty*.

Consciously or not, I carried those questions with me to college, where I immediately declared myself premed, convinced that I wanted to be a doctor like my dad—not a cardiologist like him but a neurosurgeon. I used to say, "Together we can cover two of the most important organs in our bodies!" and he would smile. It's not lost on me now that I've found my way back to the brain—just not in the manner I would have expected.

The pressure to be a doctor wasn't explicit in my household the way it had been in some of my peers' households. My brother, Ajay, initially chose law before circling back to medicine, by choice, later in life, and my sister, Chandani, decided halfway through college that she wanted to pursue fashion. My parents were encouraging, and in fact, they supported her in spending summers at New York's Fashion Institute of Technology and going to Milan for about a year after graduation. My mom has always believed that if you're going to choose something, then "you should go for it and do it with a bang!" The irony here, of course, is that exceptionalism was still expected: do the nontraditional thing, but make sure you are perfect at it! So it wasn't that I wouldn't have gotten support otherwise—I just never considered that I might not yet have known what I wanted to do, or that it would be okay for me to take my time to figure it out.

There's a reason why we are mandated to take general electives in college. For many of us, this can feel like a waste of time: *I know what I want to do! Let me do the thing already!* Laser focus on a singular goal is not necessarily a bad thing, but at seventeen or eighteen, there are also many of us who either have no idea what we want to do or, like me, haven't thought beyond an expected path. I blindly jumped on the straight and narrow, right into taking biology and organic chemistry classes during my first year. It didn't take long for me to realize how wholly unprepared I was. Very quickly in the first semester, I discovered that the laissez-faire attitude I'd had in high school, where I'd easily aced my classes, wasn't going to cut it. Almost immediately, I began floundering. I struggled in my classes. I struggled when I tried. I struggled when I asked for extensions. I even struggled when I stayed up until the college library closed every night, headphones in, trying with all my might to grasp the most basic concepts. And for as long as I could, I didn't tell a single soul. I became an expert at pretending—at making things look good on the outside, no matter how I was really doing. After all, the act of going to and succeeding in college was a given in my family, much like breathing. When it didn't go as expected, I was convinced that there was something wrong with me, but I had nothing concrete to point to. I had done well in high school, so why couldn't I do well in college? My brother and sister (among other peers of mine) were children of immigrants and had learned how to balance their familial and cultural expectations with success, so why couldn't I?

Chasing Validation and Praise

Looking back, it's like watching a B-rated horror movie. You *know* that someone needs to intervene, that with one conversation, one admission, things could turn out completely differently. I didn't have this "Aha!" moment in which I got an F-graded paper back and realized I needed to get my act together. Instead, it was a slow burn—Cs turned into Ds turned into Fs. I avoided it at first, certain that things would miraculously get better. *I have always been good at school.* I was in denial. The further I sank into my hole, the less I tried to get out. Acknowledging that I was struggling felt worse than avoiding it. I knew neither how to struggle nor that struggling wasn't a core failure. I started to skip classes altogether. I would still make a point of going to the library to study—er, socialize—with friends, but I would sleep in during the mornings and sometimes through the afternoons. I would lie and use studying and classes as an excuse to become even more distant from my family. *Can't talk—I'm so busy with schoolwork!* In fact, I would go out of my way to discuss all the extra activities I was doing to compensate for my academic failures. I was captain of the bhangra team my freshman year. I was treasurer of Students Helping Honduras. I joined the field hockey club. I believed that the busier I could make myself look, the more I could pretend like everything was okay. I had no idea that I was sinking into a depression, paralyzed by my learned all-or-nothing mindset. I was drowning, and my every decision or action was a leap into an extreme—either do it all well (or pretend to) or don't do anything at all. I transferred my energy from actually doing schoolwork, or seeking support, to creating a facade that I could hide behind. I know now that even small steps, any steps, are important. That doing anything would have been helpful.

I'm reminded of different clients who all struggled to perform as well as they wanted to—or as well as their immigrant parents wanted them to—in school. One quickly lost motivation after getting a bad test score back. To her, the bad grade wasn't just a small step in the wrong direction; it immediately overturned her sense of self. Another client told me that she started lying in high school even though she was doing well. When I asked why, she said she felt the need to continuously stretch the truth so that things always sounded *really great* even if they were just *good*. Good wasn't good enough. Things could always be better. How much we valued ourselves was directly tied to how well we were perceived by others.

In one of my corporate workshops, I have attendees reflect on who or what they are motivated by. While it's very rare for an attendee to have their own happiness, passion, or enjoyment marked as a motivator, in almost all cases, parents or family elders are a top motivator. It's common for children of immigrants to depend on external feedback and praise—primarily from our parents and elders—in order to feel *worthy*. Many of us learn that love is earned.

When I was a child, praise was my love language. I learned to hunt for and collect accolades and achievements; the more I had, the more I could cash in to feel loved by my parents. To continue receiving the love I needed, I would work tirelessly to outdo my previous achievements. Until college, I had been exceptional at most of the things I did. Captain of my soccer team, regional awards for field hockey, president of the French National Honor Society. I never learned how to *learn*. Instead, I learned how to *achieve* and how to stay within the confines of my natural abilities and strengths. Even in high school, rather than actually learn—or enjoy learning—about the topic, I studied the material that I would be graded on. I didn't learn discipline, not even when my mom put me in years of dance and piano lessons. My parents expected me to know how to practice and how to enjoy the process of building a skill, but instead I dreaded these classes (and often lied to get myself out of them) because I was naturally bad at them.

Garnering praise made my world feel safe. I learned to people-please in order to control how others perceived me and potentially treated me; by manipulating the way I was viewed, I could receive the love I needed. This is a form of impression management, or self-presentation, as conceptualized by Erving Goffman in the late 1950s.

There are different techniques for impression management, including conformity, flattery, excuses, self-promotion, association, and acclaim. This can look like hiding parts of your personality that

you feel don't fit in to be accepted by a larger group, or compliment-
ing someone and subsequently seeming pleasant, or associating with
certain people to promote your own self-image. Generally, though,
it's as it sounds: impression management is filtering and controlling
how others perceive us and thus managing the impressions others
have of us. It's not always a negative thing; it can benefit relationships and be important in professional settings—like making sure
you look good in a job interview or getting the compensation you
deserve when you make it a point to highlight your accomplishments. We all engage in impression management to some degree, but
research has suggested that people from collectivist cultures are
more prone to engage in impression management. This is unsurpris-
ing, given that people from collectivist cultures value interpersonal
harmony and unity; they are often conformity oriented and driven
by a sense of belonging and acceptance from others. When I was
growing up, praise taught me that I was constantly being evaluated
by the measurements and standards of other people—starting with
my mom and dad. In college, when I talked to my parents, I used
self-promotion and excuses to leave out the reality of what was actually happening, and I ingratiated myself with them. I maintained
control over how I was perceived by others, but I failed to grasp the
enormity of my deception.

What I didn't know was that I was further isolating myself from
connection. In fact, researchers in China found that impression
management was positively associated with loneliness and negatively
related to life satisfaction. The more I hid my reality, the more I felt
disconnected. The more I felt disconnected, the more I felt shame,
and thus the more I hid my reality. It was an ugly negative feedback
loop, and I didn't know how to escape it.

I have come to learn that encouragement, not praise, was what I
actually desperately needed. Encouragement can look like being

celebrated for trying, honoring progress and growth, and being present in the process. Encouragement can build confidence and self-esteem, whereas praise may actually *decrease* self-esteem, according to one study, as the recipient's senses of self and security become entirely dependent on success and achievement. The same study found that when kids were praised for their personal qualities rather than their efforts, they were more likely to feel shame.

EVEN THOUGH I HAD physical distance from my parents when I was at school, I was still tethered to them. I was expected to talk to them every couple of days, if not every day—not an unusual expectation for children of immigrants. I've heard from many who feel obligated to account for their whereabouts and be readily available to their parents at any point. I've also experienced and witnessed how this can increase levels of anxiety around productivity and utilizing time in efficient and effective ways (as defined by our parents). In high school, I was expected to constantly account for my time: When was I in school? Where was I going after? What did I do with the spare twenty minutes I had in between school ending and field hockey starting? If I didn't answer my phone on the first round of rings, I would have ongoing missed calls from my mom until I did. My promise or my words never felt like enough—and I still struggle with this today. In fact, of 6,025 children of immigrants polled, 89 percent said they have struggled, or still struggle, with guiltily feeling like they have to account for their time when it comes to parents, colleagues, bosses, or even themselves. In college, I no longer had a rigorous schedule, and with the freedom to decide when I would go where and for how long, I felt even more anxiety. On some level, the need to be accountable to my parents had been a crutch that I could no longer rely on.

Though I would stay in touch with my parents regularly while on campus, my university was only about an hour and a half's drive away, which meant that my dad would come visit me off campus for dinner at a local Carrabba's Italian Grill every month or so. These were our first experiences in spending time together one-on-one, and I always dreaded them. I knew that it would take a lot of emotional and mental energy to pretend like I was okay and to make sure my dad left believing me. At this same time, my dad was pursuing his own master's degree in hospital administration, and because he could barely type, I would type up his assignments while he dictated. Between doing his homework and taking bites of our meals, he would ask how school was going. I would always say that it was going fine. During our dinners, my dad was blissfully unaware of what was trapped in the spaces between those few words. The moments in which a million thoughts about letting on to my reality would rush through my head. My heart hurts at now knowing that neither he nor my mom really had any inkling that they should question or challenge what I told them. That I would lie to them in this way. They didn't push to know more, because it didn't occur to them that I wouldn't just tell them, just as it never occurred to me that I could. I don't know what it would have been like if I had told him at the very first D that I couldn't do it. That I needed to take time off. That I needed to change course. Back then, I had no reason to think they would have supported me.

They never asked how I was doing; rather, my dad would ask if I needed anything, and my mom would ensure that I was eating well. They always checked in to make sure that my physical and physiological needs were met, as they had done throughout my childhood, but they didn't tend to any mental or emotional ones. None of us knew how. And since I didn't initiate a conversation or share anything more, they assumed that I was fine. Why wouldn't I be? Why would I be struggling when their life's work had been to set me up for success?

My dad has always told my siblings and me that education is *the most* important thing we can pursue; it's one thing that no one can ever take from us. Though I agree with the sentiment—any pursuit or attainment of knowledge is important—he always referred to education strictly in terms of traditional degrees. This further cemented my narrative that smartness meant accolades and academics, and anything else was inadequate.

As I was struggling in college, I was overshadowed by my brother's master's degree and law degree, and by my sister's successful post-university career in fashion. I saw their hard work paying off. So when I didn't achieve good grades despite hard work, or coast on my natural abilities, I felt like I had let everyone down, and I didn't know how to dissolve the edges of my shame—or that internalized shame was the very thing keeping me from getting the support I needed. Instead, it hardened into glass shards that kept other people at a distance.

When I talk to my parents about these years now, they often share that *they* just wish I had told them, but they are not the same today as they were then. I'm not even convinced that I would have told the truth if they had asked. A part of me was in such denial that I genuinely believed if I could pretend like it wasn't happening, then maybe it would magically go away or I could fix it before anyone found out. I didn't know how to tolerate disappointing my parents. And I didn't know who I was if I admitted my failings. It never even occurred to me that there was an alternative path.

I knew, too, from past experiences that I couldn't really turn to my parents as a resource. When I was caught going to the movies with my (secret) high school boyfriend, or when I was told that I needed to get on birth control for medical reasons, or even when I had a stalker in high school, which ultimately led to my getting phys-ically hurt, my parents didn't talk about it. Nothing was explained or processed. There was no shared space to think, or ask questions, or feel emotions. Everything was ignored or swept under the rug. So I learned to read my cues—I knew what I was expected to say, what they were expecting to hear. I built off this reality and my under-standing of my parents and their expectations of me, and I contin-ued to play my part and say my lines. I didn't know how to face the fact that I could no longer fill that role myself, let alone tell them.

Now, as a therapist, I feel deeply saddened for the younger me. I also feel frustrated. I had no conception of what support or help looked like on campus; I didn't know that a counseling center, or an option to take a leave of absence, existed—much less the research I know today about college-aged students, identity, and mental health. One in three freshman college students (worldwide!) struggles with mental health issues. Some data suggests a higher prevalence of men-tal health issues among students of color in college samples, and other data points to students of color statistically accessing mental health treatment less than their white peers. I have had extensive conversations with colleagues who work on campuses or with col-lege students, and they have shared similar stories of isolation, fear of speaking up, and lack of access to resources. I wish I had known what these colleagues and I often tell our clients who are struggling: no matter how isolated you feel, you *are not* alone. Even more, our worthiness, likability, existence, and enoughness expand beyond the very particular and specific struggles that we often get trapped within. Yes, we are products of our past experiences and condition-ing, but we are also products of what comes after, and we get to de-cide what comes next. We can decide how our experiences define and factor into our own narratives. When we struggle or sink further into darkness, it can feel impossible to recognize that we may have a sense of agency. It's not always obvious, and it's not always immediate. But it's there.

The Three *E*'s

As I look back on this time in my life, I can pinpoint that my struggles were due to a combination of what I call the three *E*'s—the need for external permission, emotional immaturity, and an expectation of exceptionalism.

Need for External Permission

Growing up, I would put everything second to what my parents expected of me. Even now, permission is a driver of my day-to-day interactions. I am always asking versus telling: "Is that okay?" "Would you be okay with that?" "Does that work for you?" I was taught and socialized to believe—especially as a woman—that someone else, preferably someone older and more respected, must grant me permission to do anything in my life.

As a result, I never truly developed a sense of self, and I lacked a sense of self-direction. The compass guiding me was built by my parents. In high school, I had lived in a protective bubble made up of my parents' structure and routine, built and maintained around their expectations. Sure, I detoured in secret here and there, but overall, I never had to develop a sense of responsibility or direction. The path was laid out for me. I didn't know *how* to be responsible for myself; I didn't even know how to be *aware* of myself.

Emotional Immaturity

In college, I became self-indulgent. Free from my parents' reins, I finally had the autonomy to do as I wanted, but I lacked the emotional maturity to handle the responsibility that came with this freedom. It wouldn't be until years later that I learned to build discipline and understand the importance of doing things you don't necessarily want to do right now in order to attain the things you want for your future. I didn't know that sheer *want* wouldn't be enough. I struggled with a fixed mindset: *I am smart, and that will be enough.* This fixed mindset—or this notion that my individual traits could not be changed—was compounded with the praise I depended on, creating a core belief that if I messed up, failed, or didn't get something right the first time around, I was a failure. I have hypothesized that many children of immigrants struggle with a fixed mindset because they're expected to fit into a mold rather than given room to expand and contract in ways that feel the most authentic to them.

Simply put, I was unequipped to handle my failures in college. It was never explained to me that sometimes we try and fail. I was never taught or modeled an openness to learning (rather than just doing or achieving). If they ever had any struggles, my siblings never let me in on them. I learned a lot of life lessons through trial and error with relationships outside my family, many of which early on involved a lot of error and a lack of knowledge of understanding or managing my own emotions. Or I learned these lessons by watching family shows like *Boy Meets World*, *The Fresh Prince of Bel-Air*, or *Gilmore Girls* on television where the characters learned to deal with hardships through the support of family, friends, and mentors.

Since I had never truly had these pillars of support, I didn't know how to find or create them. Instead, I remained trapped in a cycle of sadness, depression, and ultimately failure that I was convinced I couldn't get out of. I felt powerless and like everything was out of my control, and without the language to communicate what was happening, I deferred to the worst-case scenario: worthlessness.

Expectation of Exceptionalism

When I did finally receive advice, I didn't take it. Months into school, I met with a professor who was the premed adviser, as all premed students were required to do, and she told me, in no uncertain terms, that this may not be the right path for me. She was frank about my poor academic performance in classes that were foundational to getting into medical school. I ignored her and doubled down on my denial: I was on a path, and it was expected of me, and nothing or no one was going to get in the way. If I'm being honest, I think that on some level I felt entitled to success. My parents were part of the wave of South Asian immigrants (thanks to Black and Indigenous freedom fighters) who were given permission to immigrate to the U.S. because of the value they were able to prove they could offer to this country. Within such immigrant families, meritocracy, or the idea that hard work pays off, has evolved into praise as a primary method of parenting, bringing us full circle.

This country put us all on a pedestal, and my parents put me on a pedestal—and I liked the way it felt way up there. I found myself subscribing to that model minority myth: I should succeed because I am Asian American, because I am Indian. Growing up, I went to a diverse high school in that it had a large Black population. However, during the majority of my time, I was one of only three Indians, all of whom were bracketed together (and often called by each other's names). We were very much "exotic others" compared with the rest of our classmates, in a school that more or less allowed us to move between the different groups via osmosis. I didn't have language for the racial triangulation I experienced then—I was closer to whiteness than were Black people but still not white. Add to that the model minority myth, which further pitted me against Black people and other ethnic groups as a South Asian woman. It also further compounded my reputation as the smart one, the respectful one, the exemplary one. This was reinforced by the many times I was celebrated on the morning announcements or offered up to a class as an example of how to do an assignment correctly.

According to the Pew Research Center, despite in-group disparities between Asian Americans, this population is still achieving higher levels of educational and economic attainment than the overall U.S. population. My own parents were South Asian immigrants who worked hard and were successful at accumulating wealth in this country, so I felt as if I was meant to carry on that generational excellence. And because I had my physiological needs met and financial privileges that others lacked, I didn't feel like I was allowed to struggle. *I come from people who succeed.*

In 2022, the Pew Research Center conducted dozens of focus groups on Asian Americans living in the United States. In the analysis, many Asian American children of immigrants discussed how harmful the model minority myth, or the myth of exceptionalism, has been for them. Teachers may expect a certain standard from us academically, only creating more obstacles to our reaching out for support. Parents may internalize this narrative and reinforce these expectations at home. I have had this conversation many times with various South Asian and Asian friends or clients, and we all have felt the pressure to succeed in traditional ways and to live up to the expectations that are placed on us in school or at work. These expectations seep into how we see ourselves, and they feed the pressure that so many of us place on ourselves.

Achievement and Identity

As children of immigrants, many of us are taught that there is a "right" way, a "right" time, and a "right" order when it comes to living life. We are expected to obey our parents and elders, listen to their advice, and follow the paths they lay out for us. Many of us are expected to go to college, then pursue a career that can ensure security, then meet a family-approved partner, and then have a family. In my work with children of immigrants, many folks feel shame for not staying on these preapproved paths or for being on completely different timelines. I've talked to second gens who didn't study in the fields expected of them or opted out of academia altogether—by choice or because they struggled, too. Many have shared that they were groomed from young ages to be in the same prestigious fields as their parents, while others have said that they were expected to be on certain education and career paths as retirement plans for their parents, who didn't have the same opportunities. What's more, women in the community have revealed the repercussions they faced for not wanting kids at all or wanting kids *later*; for wanting to prioritize their careers over marriage; or for being divorced. One male client discussed wanting to pursue a more creative career that would actually make him happy, even if it involved a pay cut, but he felt too guilty to follow through because his parents considered creative pursuits hobbies, not viable career options. Many immigrant parents may not understand having choices or exposure to different pathways. This enforces a narrative that we internalize: anything off the beaten path is bad and shameful, even if it feels necessary, good, or right to *us*.

Even more, the shame that many children of immigrants feel for *choosing* different paths is similar to the shame that others feel for situations they didn't choose. One second gen has shared that she is unable to have kids and has been advised by family members not to talk about it publicly. Another said that she carries her dad's shame over her learning disability, and that he believes *he* is being punished. Instead of commendation for the strength and courage it takes to walk new or different paths, there's an unmovable standard, and either we meet it or we don't. Looking back, I have come to learn that while I was struggling in college, I created and internalized what we call in narrative therapy an identity conclusion: *I am a failure.* I wrapped my entire being and self-concept around these core beliefs: *I am not enough. I am not smart. I am not a good daughter.*

A new story about myself was born, one in which I was not enough in any aspect of my life. It's easy to feel inadequate when we measure ourselves against anything—or anyone—other than who we really are. This may be a sibling, something you didn't choose for yourself but that someone else wanted for you, or something your peers have attained that you haven't.

I know now, all these years and all this healing later, that I am not a failure. I know that mistakes, slipups, and mental health struggles are not indicative of failure, nor do they define me. They are a messy part of life that all humans encounter. But this story of failure would become my dominant narrative for years, one that would return again and again. I could only start to truly change it once I confronted my narratives around achievement and worthiness.

Reflecting on your achievement behavior

Do you agree with any of the following statements?

- I feel like I have to do X or Y, or else my parents/caregivers won't be proud of me.
- I was raised in an environment where social perception was emphasized.
- Success isn't a goal; it's an expectation.
- My emotional needs were met only when I reached a milestone or did something *well.*
- I feel like my worthiness is tied to my ability to achieve.
- As a child, I was not encouraged to be independent, creative, or curious.

If you said yes to any of the above, you're not alone! Many children of immigrants are motivated by achievement, and we pursue things because we've been taught that we need to chase the next level or goal, and there's a timeline for when and how we can do things. We've also been conditioned to believe that we are lovable as long as we are good at things and as long as we achieve things. This reinforces negative achievement behavior.

Negative Achievement Behavior	Positive Achievement Behavior
• Pursuing something because you've been told it's the right time or you have to—even if you don't feel ready. • Feeling loved or validated when you have something tangible to show for your time. • Avoiding high-risk tasks or endeavors to minimize your chances of failure. • Needing to share your achievements with others or on social media for external validation, praise, or respect. • Using peer comparison as a way to measure your success. • Powering through obstacles as a show of your worthiness. • Forming an external identity around certain achievements and feeling unable to change course. • Pursuing a career, materialistic purchase, or activity because it will increase your social status or build your résumé. • Internalizing your parents' expectations as your own needs and pursuits.	• Validating your own competence and work ethic. • Gracefully accepting failure or mistakes as part of pursuing achievement. • Recognizing achievement as a possible by-product of pursuing your goals but not a requirement for happiness. • Recognizing your own limits when goal setting. • Celebrating your own achievements regardless of others' reactions to them. • Identifying what characteristics, and strengths, you have to celebrate regardless of their potential to help you "achieve." • Having clarity on why a goal is important to you beyond how it will be perceived by others.

As you unlearn your achievement behavior tendencies, consider the following questions about your goals and pursuits:

1. Why do I want this?
2. Who am I doing this for?
3. How will I feel if I do pursue this?
4. How will I feel if I don't pursue this?
5. If no one can know that I achieve this, will I still enjoy/want it?
6. Who actually benefits from this achievement? In what ways?
7. How does taking this step help me achieve a bigger goal of my own?

Chapter Three

But What Will People Say?

Content warning:
mentions of sexual assault and
references to self-harm

M y time masquerading as a successful college student came
to an end after a year and a half. Unable to meet the requirements to maintain good standing at my university, I
was academically suspended. I'd finally run out of options. No more
pretending. So before the end of my last semester, when I was on a
visit home and overcome with guilt and shame, I woke my parents
up at 3:00 a.m. to tell them. We were sitting in the Florida Room
(now called the War Room because of all the arguments and tough
conversations that have happened there). My parents were half-
asleep, scared and confused in response to my sense of urgency.

"I'm failing school," I blurted out. As soon as the words left my
mouth, I wanted to reach out, grab them, and shove them back inside. Mom and Papa didn't respond at first. They didn't yell, which

scared me more than any lecture or punishment would have. Instead of being angry, they were bewildered and disappointed, which only made me feel worse.

"Go to sleep; we'll talk about this tomorrow," Papa said, resigned, before heading back to bed.

The next day, there was no discussion. There was no moment in which they asked me how I was doing, or if I wanted to keep going; even I didn't think to take a beat, gain some support, reexamine my life journey. There was only one clear path forward, and they grasped on to it tightly: I could be reinstated if I successfully completed a year of community college classes. That was that. There was too much internal and external pressure to do anything other than pick myself up, quickly and quietly, and keep moving forward. I know now how important it is to give ourselves permission to reevaluate *why* we are making the choices we are, and to interrogate if they are still serving us. Looking back, I didn't know that I could step *off* the path, and that this may have been the change in narrative I needed to set myself up for success. I genuinely believed that if I didn't uphold my parents' expectations (or at least try to), then I didn't deserve to be a part of the family. I had been reduced to the achievements that could be emailed, and later WhatsApped, among extended family and community members. I felt like my parents had set conditions on their love—stay within the limits, or face the threat of being removed from the system altogether.

I continued to build my inner life around my identity as a failure while also continuing to lie. This naturally created a barrier in my other relationships: I was too ashamed to tell the truth and couldn't tolerate the breakdown of my own understanding of self, let alone share that breakdown. So I lost touch with many of my college friends, frequently telling vague half-truths about why I was really back home and almost always omitting the fact that I had gotten kicked out. Some friends disappeared entirely, only reinforcing my belief that there was one way to do life and that anything else would mark me as an outcast. Additionally, my parents enlisted my brother and sister to "speak sense" into me. I felt like my whole family was teaming up against me, so I continued to ice them out, too, furthering the distance we would have to go to bridge real mutual relationships with one another.

DURING THE FOLLOWING couple of years, I was in and out of school. Some semesters I did better than others, but I always got pulled back into a shame spiral for not being able to cut it. At the same time, I speed-dated career options and jobs, jumping around like a pinball, doing everything from scribing in an emergency room to coaching a high school field hockey team to shadowing a physical therapist *and* a family physician. I even applied to work at ESPN and volunteer at a youth residential treatment center. I was trying to do everything—once again falling into the trap of "busy equals successful"—and I was desperately trying to take back my life, but doing none of it with my whole heart.

Unsurprisingly, nothing stuck. When I wasn't at school or at a job/volunteer site, I locked myself in my room, where I spent my time making goal lists and creating vision boards. I printed out affirmations and famous inspirational quotes, then plastered them all over my bedroom walls. I surrounded myself with reminders of dreams that I was too depressed or too tired to chase, without pausing to wonder if they were really *my* dreams.

In 2010, during my second stint back on campus at my original university, one of my friends could sense that I was struggling and gave me information about the university's counseling center. I don't know what finally prompted me to ask for help, but after years of feeling trapped with no escape plan, I decided to try counseling. It was free, and my parents didn't need to know about it. Nothing else seemed to be working, so I figured it was worth a shot. In retrospect, I think there was a part of me that also believed that going to therapy would make me look good to others, or at least serve as a testament to my own efforts to understand why I wasn't living up to the expectations I placed on myself—and my family placed on me. *Hey, I'm trying everything here! See!* Yet another way I engaged in impression management.

I was assigned a therapist at the counseling center, a white woman I'll call Mel. I spent our few sessions together talking about my academic struggles and the general angst that suffocated me daily. I didn't know what to even make of therapy at the time. I didn't have language to articulate how culture was impacting my relationship with success and happiness and productivity and belonging. Moreover, I hadn't yet developed enough of a sense of self to acknowledge that the constant dull ache in my body was a symptom of external pressure and feelings of inadequacy—and probably also depression. Talking to her helped me feel less alone, but I am not sure if I learned anything substantial beyond that.

Now I know: therapy isn't just the therapist doing the work. They don't simply wave a magic wand and figure it out for you. Instead, a good therapist will meet you in the trenches and sit with you, allowing you to begin to feel "seen" before excavating at the wound site with you. To do that, you need to be open and honest. But I didn't take off my mask with Mel; instead, I ingratiated myself, much like I did with my parents. I needed someone, a third party, to corroborate my story—to stand witness to my pain. But I didn't let her. My need to people-please was so insidious that I was not even aware I was doing it. Just as I tried to be the perfect Indian daughter, I tried to be the perfect counseling client—something that I now know actually creates more barriers to change and help. This also meant that I relied on Mel to show me the way without giving her any sense of which direction I needed to go in.

There's a difference between *being* willing to address what is happening and *thinking* that you are willing to do so. The former requires a readiness to look inward and outward—yes, to hold yourself accountable but also to recognize and accept what may not be in your control. The latter reinforces a false sense of self.

The late Dr. Donald Winnicott, a renowned British pediatrician and psychoanalyst, suggested that our true selves are authentic and knowing, especially when we need support and assurance. This stems from our childhood years, during which we theoretically learn to trust that our needs are acceptable and that we have people who can meet them. I didn't learn that, and so I didn't develop a true self.

When I look back on this time in my life, it feels like I split in half. There was the me I projected to others and the me I really was. This incongruity began a journey of self-loathing and shame that I struggle with even to this day. I sometimes wonder what different set of circumstances, what different inputs, might have created a scenario in which I could have admitted that maybe I was not ready for college. But I know that for a different path and a different narrative to have been accessible to me, my entire existence up until that point would have to have been different, too.

Then I faced a traumatic event that would alter my life forever.

Avoidance Is No Longer a Coping Mechanism

In the spring of 2011, I was sexually assaulted. It changed everything. I no longer worried about how things looked to others or what I needed to do to get my academic life back on track. The assault transformed my internalized shame into self-disgust. I became numb. I wasn't even sure I'd make it to my next birthday. For years after my assault, I struggled to look men in the eyes, to be in crowded spaces, and to watch certain movies. I already didn't have the tools I needed to process my emotions, and now I also didn't know what my triggers were or how to handle them.

At that point, I was in a relationship with someone—I'll call him Seth—who was the only person I told and who ended up being my saving grace during the aftermath of my assault. I decided to spend that summer of 2011 in New York, where he was living. My parents were on board because I would stay with my sister—who could look after me—and they thought I was going to be working. While I intended to volunteer as a hotline advocate for an Asian American domestic violence agency, I quit after the first shift because I couldn't handle how triggering it was. Even volunteering in the first place was a testament to my need to turn anything bad that had happened (to me or because of me) into something positive. And, regardless of it all, I still felt pulled to "keep busy."

I didn't tell my family that I had quit the hotline. It felt like another failure on my part. Instead, I would get up with my sister as she got ready for work, only to go back to sleep once she left for the day. Most days, I would lie in bed until Seth was free to hang out. This continued for the rest of the summer, but as August rolled around, I knew that I would be expected to return to school that fall. I felt it was time to at least inform my sister about my assault, so I summoned the courage to tell her before she was going out one night. In some way, my timing served as an avoidance tactic. She was naturally caught off guard and didn't respond. When I look back, it's clear that I wasn't so much asking for help as I was desperately trying to give my pain away. We never talked about it again until very recently. At the time, I was frozen in disbelief that she didn't respond, but her response, or lack thereof, fed my belief that no one in my family really knew how to care about me. I also felt like a burden, further cementing the narrative that I was indeed a problem child. When I talk to my sister about this today, we are both at a loss for words. Our relationship has changed shape, and the idea that either one of us would divulge a deep, vulnerable truth with no reciprocity is unimaginable to us both. It wasn't that my sister didn't care about me; it was that we didn't have a foundation for a relationship, and then here I was throwing this significant trauma at her. *I know we don't have a relationship, but catch.* It was a plea for help, but I didn't know *who* to ask, and she didn't know *what* I needed.

Talking to Family About Mental Health and Trauma

When the summer came to an end, I moved back home with my parents. I could no longer pretend that getting my bachelor's degree was the most important thing for me to focus on, and I knew that they wouldn't accept this unless I told them why. At that point, it had been three months since my assault, a year and a half since I half-heartedly attempted counseling, and five years since I first started my college career.

I decided to tell my family members one by one; something about approaching it individually felt less threatening than telling my parents together. I started with my mom. She was so worked up about my asking her to go outside with me to talk that the worst thing she could imagine I had to divulge was a pregnancy. To this day, I still wonder if that would have been worse news to her than my getting assaulted. It would have been visibly harder to hide from the world.

My dad was angry and wanted to go to my college town to find the men who hurt his baby. My brother, who was visiting, approached it as a physician. "Do you need to get checked out or tested?" he asked matter-of-factly, giving a glimpse of his kind yet pragmatic bedside manner. I cannot for the life of me remember most of the subsequent conversations, but I do know that I was never asked how I was doing. That no one validated how hard the experience must have been for me. That I didn't feel better for having told them.

I had been terrified to tell my family about my assault, and their reactions and responses only confirmed that fear. Instead of feeling unburdened by sharing this trauma, I was left buried under the weight of their lack of sensitivity, incessant curiosity, and need for control. They asked: "Were you drinking? What were you wearing? How late was it?" I heard: "This could have been avoided if you were more responsible." Their tendency to think in black-and-white terms exacerbated my already existing feelings of self-disgust. I felt blamed and humiliated.

Sexual assault and violence, unfortunately, are common across the world. According to the Rape, Abuse & Incest National Network (RAINN), every sixty-eight seconds, an American is sexually assaulted. And according to the CDC, women and ethnic and racial minority groups experience higher rates of sexual violence. Cultural context is important: fear and shame are key barriers to seeking support for sexual assault, as it is compounded by our generational, social, and cultural understandings of gender superiority in patriarchal systems, or by how we are conditioned to "accept" what is "normal" versus what is considered violence. One much older immigrant woman shared with me how in her circle of friends, women were expected to have sex with their husbands even if they didn't want to. This was considered their duty and therefore not necessarily categorized as "marital rape." Furthermore, research has found that survivors of sexual abuse within cultures that prioritize family honor and female modesty may struggle with seeking support and experience higher levels of social stigma. In these cases, sexual violence may be perceived as worse than death. Even when I received the support that I needed years later, the ways in which culture shaped or informed my experience of sexual assault were never discussed. Yes, from an individualistic vantage point, I—an individual—felt like I lost my dignity and experienced levels of shame because of what happened to me. However, in my collectivist culture, I felt humiliation over how my assault caused my parents and my family pain. And how even though it wasn't my fault, it was something that might affect my reputation and "purity." My shame and self-disgust had so many layers, but only the surface was explored in my sessions with a white therapist down the road. Admittedly, I was able to keep her at a distance by using the fact that I felt shame because of my cultural values.

The conceptualization of sexual abuse is further complicated when the perpetrator is someone within the family. Many folks in the Brown Girl Therapy community have confidentially shared stories with me about sexual abuse at the hands of family members, as well as about the expectations placed on them to keep their abuse secret for the sake of maintaining relationships. In one case, a threat of deportation was on the table. It's absolutely heartbreaking.

Cultural beliefs around chastity extend into many different religious communities and households, across races and ethnicities. I've worked with first-generation and second-generation immigrant clients who have struggled with rigid beliefs around sex because of the cultural narratives that were enforced in their families of origin. These include beliefs and messaging about abstaining from sex until marriage; not explicitly discussing sexual health or healthy reproductive/sexual development; and gender stereotypes around sexuality, masculinity, and femininity. I never had conversations about sex or sexual health with anyone in my family—not even my older sister, who presumably also had no one talk to *her* about these topics. After an event last year, I was sitting around with a group of South Asian women who were all swapping stories about having their periods. One shared that when she's on her period, she can't be around the men in her family, while another shared that she is still unlearning the narrative that having your period is "dirty" or something to be secretive about.

So now here I was, going from never touching with my parents the taboo topic of sex to sharing that I was sexually violated by unknown men. After the assault, my parents didn't have anything to offer except worry and fear. I know now that their worry provided them with a false sense of control. It doesn't change that what I needed then was support, patience, and acceptance. I lacked the language to express those needs and my feelings. Instead of giving me the comfort I needed, they asked, "What are you going to do instead?" My parents continued to process only what was happening to me as an educational derailment. They needed to latch on to an action that could be taken to comfort them and distract them from having to actually sit in this trauma and pain with me.

When I look back, my heart still aches thinking about everything the young me didn't know, and everything she wasn't equipped to handle, and everything she didn't have the language to name. It pains me that many children of immigrants out there are pretending to be okay for the sake of their parents' reputations or sanity. Or to make those around us feel more comfortable. So many of us grit our teeth and bear it because that's what our parents did, and as a result, we are unable to pursue success, happiness, or safety in the way that feels right to us. Maybe it's a gap year. Maybe it's individual or group therapy with others who have gone through similar experiences. I didn't have access to anyone else who openly discussed experiencing an assault, so it became natural for me to compare myself with my younger self or with younger versions of my siblings (who, to my knowledge, haven't shared in this experience).

Living at home without support caused me to sink deeper into a dark depressive episode I call the Disdain for Sunshine. I continued to take classes at a local community college and worked toward an associate's degree—conversations about completing my bachelor's were temporarily on hold. During this time, whatever friendships I had left after already shutting people out were cut off. It was easier to do than to talk to people about my assault or my academic time-line, especially since those I started university with had graduated at this point. I would often sleep during the day and stay up at night. I wouldn't get out of bed for days at a time, except on the days when I had classes, or to use the restroom and occasionally get a glass of water. Once in a while, I would get the urge to make boxed cupcakes—Pillsbury Funfetti—and would usually do so late at night while my parents were asleep. I wouldn't bother to shower or change out of my baggy dark-blue sweatshirt and oversize dark-green sweat-pants with "Club Field Hockey" imprinted on the right thigh, a daily reminder of the college I was kicked out of. I had a consistent dull ache in my head and an overwhelming sense of hopelessness. I had also started struggling with suicidal ideation and self-harm. On the days I would go to class, I would cry for the entire thirty-minute drive to school and back—often hoping I would get into a car acci-dent. I don't think I actually wanted to die; I just wanted what I was living through to be over. I was desperate for connection, and the driver behind my suicidality was shame.

The only person I felt a connection to was Seth, who continued to be my only anchor but now lived halfway across the world on a Ful-bright fellowship. Try as he did, he couldn't save me from my rock bottom. Like anyone who is drowning, I unintentionally started to take him down with me. He repeatedly encouraged me to consider therapy, and finally, it felt like that was the only option I had left.

WHEN I TOLD my parents that I needed to see a therapist, they perceived it as their own failure. *But what will people say when they find out? What will we tell them? Are you sure you need to see someone? You'll be fine. We can help you. Why do you need to talk to someone else when you have us? Just give it time. It will be okay with time. Just fight it. What does it say about us that our own daughter needs to turn to a stranger for help?*

No matter their good intentions, the sudden onslaught of questions and fears distanced me from them. I wished they would have asked: *What can we do to help you? What do you need from us?* I wish they would have approached this with: *We don't understand, but we're willing to try.*

I know that my struggles translated to my parents as a reflection of their love and parenting skills. After all, our culture stresses our roles in the context of the *whole*. I was born a daughter, a granddaughter, a niece, a sister, a participating member of our community. I was all of these selves for others before I was Sahaj Kohli—the individual. Sure enough, even though I could barely shower every day, I was expected to continue to be all those things. I was still asked to babysit my newborn nephew, which often consisted of me crying in the corner of the room while he sat in my lap confused. Even when I asked for what I needed, it wasn't given to me. I would ask my family not to leave me alone at home, because I was having really bad episodes and thoughts about hurting myself, but they didn't listen. In trying to help me, they inadvertently took my agency away from me, too. They thought they knew better; they believed that giving me responsibility would help me. Instead of trusting in a system with which they were unfamiliar, my parents tried everything else, including breaking their own rules and stepping out of their comfort zones. My mom took me on a trip to Europe in hopes that a change of scenery would help get my mind off my trauma (spoiler alert: it didn't). My parents, who were very against the idea of me dating, supported me in visiting Seth abroad because they recognized his role as my lifeline.

Looking back, I can understand the desperation my parents must have felt over wanting to protect me and save me from enduring ongoing pain. I know now that they were unable to handle these emotions because they didn't have a frame of reference themselves. Again, *I* experienced the repercussions of the fact that emotions were never part of their vocabulary, neither when they were kids nor when they were parenting me.

The thing is, there isn't a reason to change things that seem to be working—until something breaks. I was the first in my family to want (and need) to discuss my trauma. I was the first in my family to openly present with signs of a mental health crisis. I was the first in my family to advocate on my own behalf for professional mental health care. My parents didn't know how to process this. Often, since I consistently spent days in bed, they would come to my room and rub my head affectionately, all while saying things that they thought were supportive but only added to the pressure I felt: *Focus on your career. Try to be happy. The worst is over, so you should be okay now. You don't need to tell anyone about this.* They truly believed that if they thought positive thoughts, the negative things would dissipate. They only believed in what they could *see*. That the "bad" could be overcome by focusing on the "good." This behavior denied my reality and added a new layer to my shame: Why couldn't I be grateful it wasn't worse?

Gratitude shaming, or shaming ourselves into feeling grateful rather than what we're actually feeling, is a common behavior in children of immigrants. It's also known as toxic positivity or spiritual bypassing and is used to avoid unresolved or even difficult feelings. On the one hand, your parents may have done so much for you, and many of them may have lived through trauma and suffering to get you where you are today. On the other hand, when gratitude is expected and serves as an integral part of a relationship's functioning, it can lead to feelings of indebtedness or feeling like you're not allowed to make mistakes, disagree, struggle, or advocate for yourself.

Gratitude shaming can trivialize someone's individual experience of struggle, reinforcing isolation and silence, and perpetuating the idea that we must "save face" in order to honor or respect our families, communities, and cultures. Having parents and grandparents who have lived through wars, genocide, abuse, and so on can lead to an underlying belief that someone will always have it worse and your own suffering is thus invalid or a product of weakness. This kind of mental health impostor syndrome can erode a person's sense of self-trust, resulting in self-dismissal and therefore not seeking help.

REMINDER: Pain and suffering are not a competition. It may be true that your parents or family members have experienced hardships and suffering, and your mental health struggles are valid, too.

I know now that other people could have it worse, *and* I could still struggle. My parents could be doing their best, *and* I could need more than they were capable of providing. I still wrestle with the all-or-nothing mindset that so many in my community and culture contend with. When we have expectations for there to be *one* right path, we invalidate all other experiences, distancing ourselves from the very connection and support we might need.

AFTER A FEW months, my parents reluctantly agreed to allow me to see a family friend—I'll call her Preeti Aunty—who was a psychiatrist. Because she was like a second mom to me growing up, the intimacy of our established bond didn't nurture the professional relationship I was eagerly in need of.

Culturally, seeing a therapist is discouraged in many immigrant households and communities of color because it can be equated to "airing dirty laundry"—even though there are confidentiality standards in the field and it's a private endeavor. Seeking help is seen as countercultural or as a betrayal to our communities. Many of us, especially those in Asian households, have internalized the concept of saving face, or preserving an outward reputation. For children of immigrants, it's easy to become very skilled at compartmentalizing. We have been conditioned to believe that anything that could even remotely spur judgment or disrespect within the community should be kept within the family unit, or disregarded altogether. These "negative" experiences or "bad" needs build up and leave us to climb mountains in our own homes—separating us even more from connections that can help us, heal us, save us.

The irony is not lost on me that my parents didn't understand therapy, or even support it, as they subscribed to the notion that things should be handled internally within our family system, and yet they were more comfortable with someone in the community helping me rather than someone who wouldn't have any influence over the community knowing private information about me or us. Their need for control and for the familiar trumped logic.

I recently interviewed Preeti Aunty because I had no idea what my dad had told her, what I had told her, and how she had perceived me or my mental health. I wanted her to fill in some of the blanks for me.

As I was sitting with her at her dining table, I couldn't believe that in the decade since our unofficial therapeutic relationship we had never talked about it. She shared that I was shut down and detached in our interactions, often avoiding eye contact and providing monosyllabic answers in response to her questions. She wanted to understand the severity and acute nature of my depression, but all she had to go by was that I had experienced sexual trauma and was having "dark thoughts." Apparently, neither I nor my dad ever gave her any more details or information. Of course, knowing it had been a few months since my trauma at that point, Preeti Aunty advised regular treatment for what appeared to her to be post-traumatic stress disorder (PTSD).

I didn't know she informed my dad of this. I remember going to her house after community college classes and hanging out with her mom, whom I called Nani. We watched Zee TV shows together. Nani knew that I didn't speak very good Punjabi, so we would often sit in silence, laughing at the shows and holding hands. I felt comforted. Preeti Aunty said that I would often eat dinner with them but wouldn't really talk about anything, and she respected my silence. I told her that I remembered her being intentional about not trying to be intrusive, and we both nodded, because as therapists we understand that sometimes the best way to build a relationship and support someone through crisis is to just be an undemanding presence. A safe space is usually a judgment-free space where folks feel respected and valued; it's also a space where the people involved feel comfortable in their own boundaries. My parents should have been a safe space, but they weren't, because they had expectations about what needed to happen, when it needed to happen, and how. Though they loved me, they didn't quite believe that I knew what was best for myself. They wanted to depend on their own instincts—the same ones that had brought them to the U.S. and led to *their* own attainment of success and security. And, unfortunately, I played into it, knowing what I needed to say to make others happy and still unable to deviate from the narrative that I couldn't trust myself.

Preeti Aunty told me that she often thinks about what her role was during that time. Now, as a therapist myself, I know that there are ethical considerations around seeing family friends or having dual relationships with clients, which is why our work together was never formal therapy. Instead, we would meet at my dad's office or her house "to chat." Preeti Aunty agreed that she had a sense I wouldn't really talk to her because she was under an implicit social contract to report back to my dad. We didn't have the confidentiality I needed between therapist and client. Preeti Aunty could recognize the manifestation of my trauma in ways that my parents couldn't. She was the stepping stone in allowing me to sit with what I was experiencing rather than try to avoid it or push through it without intentional consideration.

Interviewing her gave me some closure around the second-guessing I have done over the years, a direct result of the self-distrust I developed as a child. *Was the depression that bad? Did I rewrite history to make it worse than it was? Was my trauma real?*

Four Trauma Responses

There are several different types of trauma responses, known as the four *F*'s.

- Fight, categorized by varying degrees of irritability, aggression, control, and conflict.
- Flight, categorized by varying degrees of anxiety, avoidance, or escapism.
- Freeze, categorized by varying degrees of dissociation, numbness, detachment, and decision or analysis paralysis to stall.
- Fawn, categorized by varying degrees of placation and people-pleasing.

These are automatic reactions to triggers that may indicate a threat. While these are survival coping mechanisms, some people who experience trauma may build up hypervigilant and overreactive nervous systems that (because of past experiences) perceive threats even when they may not be present. Pete Walker, author of *Complex PTSD: From Surviving to Thriving*, notes that people who experience trauma—singular or ongoing—are more likely to over-rely on one of these responses. I have struggled with all of them. Because of my childhood, I use fawning as a way to pacify a situation or my parents, thereby avoiding discomfort and distress. Like many children of immigrants, I have an inclination toward flight that is rooted in denial. I grew up in an environment where the usual response when faced with something perceived as negative was to turn away and ignore it. I learned that if you keep your distance from something negative/terrible, you protect yourself from inviting it into your life. Over the years, I have been able to identify my behaviors and reactions to my assault as freeze responses. I was so overwhelmed that my nervous system shut down, and I dissociated and detached from my reality.

Though most people engage with all of these to some degree, I have noticed in my work that many children of immigrants lean toward fawn responses. These responses are rooted in a lack of boundaries, codependent behaviors, and people-pleasing to pacify the very person/people who have caused us harm/pain. This further reinforces a lack of self-trust. Many of us also learn to be conflict avoidant in order to keep the peace, since many of us were modeled conflict, not conflict resolution. When this is the case, any kind of open and honest communication can feel foreign and countercultural.

We must also take into account how certain behaviors that are correlated with different trauma responses can also be passed down generationally. For instance, people from racial and cultural groups that have experienced historical and systemic trauma may be more hypervigilant, with a readiness to fight, appease others, or retreat for the sake of survival. Gender and sexuality can compound or complicate these inclinations, too, in a society, and different cultures, where men may be encouraged to fight and women encouraged to fawn due to systematic definitions around masculinity and femininity (and the extremes of each). The intersection of our identities is always in play.

The Mind-Body Connection

Research has suggested that Asian American clients might be more inclined toward problem-solving in therapy and wanting practical advice because this aligns more with Asian values of self-improvement, education, and deference to expertise. I saw this in my work with children of immigrants across several ethnicities beyond Asian American. I was consistently asked for homework, reading assignments, or outside work that they could do to "get better." In some cases, clients would tell me they were frustrated that they weren't making progress fast enough. Healing is a journey not a destination. The urgency to fix a problem can tie into the narrative that for as long as our problems exist, we are problems that need fixing. Of course, you do have to do the work outside the room, but it's not a process that can be rushed or expedited like many of my clients would want. I had one client whose family member got in touch with me to tell me that I was "giving her room to be weak" because she hadn't been improving in the three weeks we'd been seeing each other.

My parents subscribed to this belief as well: for as long as *something* was wrong, they needed to try to fix it. Around the same time I began unofficially "seeing" Preeti Aunty, I started struggling with migraines and an intense melancholy that my dad was certain had to be attributed to vitamin deficiencies. I couldn't just be depressed, because depression doesn't make sense in a world where my parents had tirelessly worked to give me everything. As such, my migraines were taken to my family physician (the same doctor I had previously shadowed, so she was trustworthy and in our inner circle). I was put on antidepressants and given a prescription for sleep medication, but my migraines and melancholy persisted. The medication made me more depressed (as some have that effect on people), and I resisted the drowsiness from the sleep medication—possibly my feeble attempt at maintaining control. The quick fix was proving to be not such a quick fix after all. As a mental health professional, I now know that medication is necessary for some, but for others, although it allows for the valleys we may feel trapped in to be shallower, it doesn't take away the relational dynamics or the root causes of some of the behaviors and beliefs that contribute to the mental health struggles. That's why research suggests therapy as a complement to medication. Therapy encourages behavioral modification, the learning of positive coping skills, and the unlearning of negative and harmful beliefs.

Eventually, I got some blood work done that showed high levels of prolactin, which called for an MRI just to be safe. Once again, I was subjected to being probed and prodded by yet another close family friend, a neurologist whom "we could trust to keep things secretive." He found a benign pituitary tumor. My parents started to use my tumor as a way to cope with my depression. When they would talk to Preeti Aunty, they would update her on when my next MRI was or on my latest blood work results. They were using this physical manifestation, something literally seen in my brain on an MRI, to connect the dots between my struggles and my current symptoms. *Oh, Sahaj is struggling because we recently found a tumor, and it was scary!* It was scary, and yet it was merely one of many factors contributing to my depression.

I have seen clients who present with symptoms of depression, sometimes so debilitating that the most basic day-to-day functions are difficult for them. Still, they can't conceptualize that they are struggling. Instead, they share wishful thinking that something physical will happen so they can feel validated. Likewise, I struggle with validating my own invisible pain—something many of my therapists and close friends have pointed out. Much like I felt on the drives I would take to and from community college, depressed, crying, and hoping to get hit by another car, I sometimes desperately want there to be a tangible physical representation of what is happening internally. If I could outwardly "show" my internal pain, it would be validated and cared for.

I've grappled with this for my whole life. Yes, my depression was valid because I did go through something that is universally understood as traumatic. But my body and brain's inclination toward depression started much earlier than that. Even as a child, I always had headaches and migraines. Often, someone in my family would think I was faking it, but I have come to recognize that a lot of my childhood at home was chronically stressful in ways that it didn't need to be. I shouldn't have had to be hypervigilant about my parents' mercurial moods. I shouldn't have been brought into their marital problems. I shouldn't have been responsible for knowing how to communicate my needs as a child—especially without the modeling or education to do so.

I also spent the entire beginning of my college career battling physical health issues while ignoring the mental health struggles I was experiencing. At one point in my first year of college, I was diagnosed with temporomandibular joint (TMJ) syndrome because I would wind up with debilitating and chronic headaches, jaw pain, and toothaches as a result of persistent grinding and clenching from stress. At another point during my years on and off after my suspension, I wound up in the hospital for what I thought were kidney stones but what actually turned out to be a ruptured ovarian cyst. I had also been diagnosed with severe mono, which took months to recover from. I ended up in the hospital once or twice and realize now that I may have clung desperately to my mono diagnosis. While it was chronic due to not taking enough care of myself to heal from it, it was also, I believed, a more viable illness to point to than "I'm mentally struggling." Sure enough, I was told that my recovery would have been faster had I taken better care of my body and rested. On some level, these medical issues brought me relief: *See! Something is wrong!!!* They allowed me to get the sympathy I was looking for. And on another level, I somewhat perceived these physical ailments as another way in which my body and brain were failing me and thus causing me to be a failure.

Of course, I know now that my body and brain are connected, and many of the somatic and physical symptoms I experienced were directly associated with mental health struggles, such as depression, anxiety, and stress. They were both valid, with or without the presence of the other. People in immigrant households/cultures are more likely to seek support from medical doctors than from mental health clinicians, and as such, they usually wait until there are physical symptoms to tend to. Moreover, mental health issues may be somaticized as physical symptoms, especially for Asian Americans. Part of this is a lack of understanding about mental health care, but needing somatization—or the presentation of physical symptoms of psychological or emotional issues—to validate mental health issues further stigmatizes those issues: the physical manifestations are more likely to be perceived as "fixable" rather than as symptoms of deeper, or less understood, problems, creating yet another barrier to digging to the roots of these issues.

Learning Self-Compassion

During my years in and out of college and community college, as I struggled with this need for a visible manifestation of the invisible, I found myself drawn to people who were also confused and hurting. I helped friends navigate their own mental health struggles. On one random Thursday, I hung out with a friend and stayed up all night at their place because they mentioned having suicidal ideation. For many, I was often the first person they called, because they knew I would drop everything to be there for them. I didn't recognize it as such, but I was useful in a crisis—not much different from the way I was at home when there was conflict between family members.

If I couldn't figure things out for myself, then at least I could help someone else figure things out. Though I struggled with recognizing my own pain as valid, I never wanted someone else to hurt in that same way. Self-compassion researcher Dr. Kristin Neff defines self-compassion as "the ability to notice our own suffering and to be moved by it, making us want to actively do something to alleviate our own suffering." I am moved by others' suffering and, in fact, usually anticipate it so much so that I act in ways to ensure I do not contribute to it. But I have never considered my own suffering to be as important.

In Maine, on our first father-daughter trip, my father and I had a very heavy conversation about what I had needed during this period of my life, when I was in the throes of my depression, and how inadequate his intentions were. In the car as I drove, he kept saying that he wanted to just make things right. He wanted to report what had happened to me. He wanted to move quickly so that we could move past everything even quicker. It reminded me of how my mom would often say, "Do you know how this is affecting me?"

Her reaction reinforced that my personal struggles, or "failures," were, by extension, my family's struggles and "failures." I had to manage my parents' feelings about what had happened to me before I could even take the time to manage my own. I know now that my depression seemed like a massive failure to them, not because they think I'm a failure but because they thought that they had *failed me*. In many immigrant cultures, a kid's actions, success, and state of being in the world are considered a direct reflection on their parents. My sadness translated to their sadness. My Disdain for Sunshine translated as their inability to successfully bring me the sun. Today, years later and thanks to pursuing my own long-term therapy shortly after I moved out of my parents' house, I've come to understand that my parents did the best they could with what they knew. It's taken a lot of hard and long conversations to get them to understand that their moving to this country granted me not only the opportunities they expected but also the privilege of tapping into a resource they never had. And, yes, sometimes they still wonder about the validity of professional mental health care. To my immigrant parents, the

concept of sharing deep, personal feelings with a stranger (and paying for it!) is nonsensical. Mental health stigma is ingrained in every
one of us in some form or another—from how we were raised to
how strength and health are portrayed in the media we consume.
We challenge stigma by confronting stigma, and for many of us children of immigrants, it can often feel like we're talking to brick walls
when we share things with our parents that they don't necessarily
understand or support.

I've heard time and time again in my work how hard it is for children of immigrants to feel like therapy is even an option. There's so
much guilt, and often the struggles we face may feel privileged or
trivial in comparison with what our parents have endured. For children of immigrants, I have coined this "thriver's guilt," or feeling
guilt or remorse for growing, healing, and accessing resources and
opportunities that our parents didn't or don't currently have. While
my parents might have felt like they failed me, I felt deep shame for
feeling like I failed them. I felt shame for not being strong enough to
"get over" what happened to me, even though, rationally, I knew it
wasn't my fault.

I realize that my parents' starting point for understanding mental
health care was a lot further behind the starting point of someone
who grew up in the West. They risked making their own lives harder
when they moved here, but no way in hell would they take any risk
to potentially make mine harder. I've had to remind myself of this,
and I want to remind you that if your parents feel shame or failure
over your wanting to seek therapy—ultimately choosing growth and
healing—then that is not a direct reflection on your goodness as
their child but a likely indication that they are fighting a battle with
themselves and their own cultural conditioning. By speaking up and
sharing your own stories, you may be starting a new, healthy cycle in
your family—one in which all experiences are worthy of attention.

When my dad moved to this country, he was in survival mode, with little access to time or resources to do much else. I understand now that this hindered his capacity to access and explore emotional security or even understand the need for it. It was never a norm for generations before him, so why should he need it? By creating in his new country a space and a home marked by financial and physical security and comfort, my dad gave me more access and opportunities to attain and explore emotional security and mental health. And, ultimately, he worked himself into a place where he can begin to understand how worthy an endeavor that is. Recently, I asked my dad if he would consider going to therapy, and without hesitation, he said yes. He told me that after witnessing all the ways it has served me, he can see how therapy is important work. That, for me, is the true marker of success.

Tips for talking to immigrant parents about mental health

Telling anyone that you are seeking or in therapy is a personal choice. It's important to find what feels right to you when it comes to your pursuit of healing. Whether you feel the need to have a *big* conversation and formally sit down with your parents, or whether you just want to normalize therapy and mental health in your household, here are some tips:

- Reflect on what you hope to achieve by having this conversation. This can help you start preparing for how to have the conversation, what you can expect, and responses to different scenarios.
- Prepare for resistance, and plan for ways you can self-care before and after having this conversation. Do you have a go-to grounding exercise you can resort to? Do you have someone you can call afterward to debrief?
- Consider if you have other allies in the family whom you can bring into these conversations or ask for support from while you navigate this topic with your parents.
- Many immigrant parents may feel like *they* failed if their kid is in therapy, so it's important to use destigmatizing language

and normalize therapy and mental health care in ways that feel natural to you.

- Use language your parents will understand and/or words in their native language. For example, *depression* can feel like a big and heavy word that doesn't necessarily translate in a lot of languages. Consider how to best communicate with them so that they can understand and relate.

- Address their foundational fears. Are they concerned about what you're sharing? About limits to confidentiality? About how much money you are spending on mental health care? Come prepared with some FAQs to help them understand and learn more about what it actually means to be in therapy.

- If you are talking to *them* about going to therapy, consider focusing on a mutual goal to create a dynamic whereby you are collaborating *with* your loved ones rather than asking them to change, which could make them feel isolated or defensive. For example, you could say, "I want our relationships to be stronger so that we can enjoy our time together."

- With your parents, watch movies or celebrity interviews in which mental health or therapy is a theme or storyline, and then have a conversation with them. A lot of pop-culture institutions, such as Bollywood and K-dramas (or other culturally/linguistically appropriate television shows and movies), are incorporating mental health storylines and being more up front about mental health. This can help you talk about the subject without it feeling intrusive or directly associated with you/them.

- Many people who struggle to understand or grasp mental

health concepts as valid will often refer to physical pain, or tangible somatic symptoms (headaches, back pain, etc.), to describe their stress, overwhelm, depression, or anxiety. If this is the case in your family, you can use it as an opener to educate them about, and normalize, the connection between mind and body. For example, if your mom complains about her back pain and it's associated with being on her feet all day, you could ask her about the *stress*, *validate* all that she does, or *affirm* that she deserves a break, too.

- I have noticed that immigrant parents often respond better to an explanation of functional impairment. How does your depression, anxiety, or stress *impact* your life? Consider framing it in terms of how it impacts things they can understand, like your sleep, your ability to concentrate at work or school, or your loss of pleasure in doing things that usually make you happy.

- Modeling mental health care and being able to express or show how it helps you, makes you happier, and/or keeps you well and functioning may be all your parents need to start their journey of understanding what therapy is. This may look like sharing what you are learning and how you are utilizing these lessons to better your life. For example, you may say, "My therapist and I were talking about assertive communication last week, so I practiced it at work and ended up getting a raise!"

- For some immigrant parents, having science-backed research on therapy, on certain mental health-care practices, on medication, or even on what "anxiety" and "depression" are can help frame the conversation in a way that may be fascinating or feel more "valid" to your parents.

- If it feels frustrating or scary, or like you're going in circles, remember to start small and prioritize your own emotional regulation and self-care during these conversations. Remember that the long-term goal may take a while for some of us, so set more realistic, bite-size goals over a longer period of time.

Chapter Four

What's Faith Got to Do with It?

My mom always says that God will take care of us and that, ultimately, good things happen to good people. When I was living at home after my assault, my parents' lack of control over the situation and my mental health caused them to grasp on even tighter to their faith. This is common in religious communities and households where people conflate faith in a higher power with a lack of autonomy or agency. My parents outsourced their responsibility and opportunity to be part of my healing to God, believing that Waheguru would heal me. This unwavering belief blinded them to the choices we had in facilitating some of that healing ourselves, too. We sent our thoughts and prayers, brushed everything under the rug, and hoped for the best.

I grew up faithful, but my assault cracked my religious identity, causing it to crumble to pieces. My parents weren't sure what they had done to deserve this, and I internalized this mindset as well. I wondered if I had strayed so far off the path as a Sikh that my assault was my punishment. Maybe all the ways I'd questioned and defied my parents, or all the ways I'd lied, had led to my trauma—a culminating retribution. *Maybe I deserved this.*

Acculturation and Identity

When my parents moved to America in 1988, they gravitated toward people who shared their culture, values, and traditions to find
belonging and community. By default, this included religion. My
dad spent a week in the United States before my mom came with my
siblings from the United Kingdom, choosing a small suburban town
in central Virginia because his medical school classmate and childhood best friend was there and helped him get a job. As some of the
first Sikh immigrants to settle in the suburbs of Virginia in the '80s,
my parents and their peers worked tremendously hard to build community and create a foundation for the next generation. This is an
immigrant narrative threaded through several generations of my
family tree: in the 1940s, my great-grandfather helped establish a
gurdwara that still exists today in Tehran, Iran, and in the 1960s,
my grandfather helped establish Kobe, Japan's first gurdwara. This
physical manifestation of their faith created an anchor in new cities
and countries they would learn to call home. It was something beautiful that fostered a safe space for our community and declared, *We
are here to stay.* They aren't alone: in an Instagram poll, 80 percent
of 3,312 children of immigrants said that religion was important to
their immigrant parents in finding belonging and a sense of community in their new country.

A significant motivator for finding this community is retaining a
sense of our heritage culture and religious roots—a strategy that is
part of a bigger process known as acculturation. Acculturation is a
varied process that depends on the extent to which a host/dominant
culture is adapted to or acquired and the extent to which the culture
of origin—or heritage culture—is retained. Though there is not a
one-size-fits-all approach to acculturation, I will use John W. Berry's

model of acculturation to break down the concept. According to his model, four acculturation strategies include:

- Marginalization, or minimal interest in maintaining the heritage culture and minimal interest in connecting with the host culture.
- Separation, or interest in maintaining *only* the heritage culture and minimal interest in engaging with the host culture.
- Assimilation, or minimal interest in maintaining the heritage culture and interest in being fully engaged with—and absorbed into—the host culture.
- Integration, or interest in maintaining the heritage culture *and* acquiring the host culture.

Berry and other researchers of acculturation emphasize that these different strategies are highly contingent on, and varied by, different contextual levels of influence—individual, family, peers, school, political-social context, and global forces. The acculturation process can vary dramatically, and every person or family unit has a different experience of acculturation. Even more, parents—and their choices and expectations—play an essential role in their kids' acculturation processes.

One community member shared how her parents settling in Chinatown allowed her to retain language and exposure to food, community, and tradition in ways that other community members who grew up in predominantly white American areas could not. These ethnic enclaves, where one geographic location is primarily populated by one ethnic or cultural community, create a space for immigrants and refugees to settle down and transition into the host country. Conversely, I have heard stories about immigrants not having geographic access to their cultural or religious communities, forcing them to assimilate into the dominant culture or risk forced separation for not fitting in.

For me, growing up in central Virginia, it was common to hear Japanese TV dramas in the background while being washed over with the smell of Indian spices from the kitchen in our house. For many of my childhood years, we would eat our meals sitting on the floor at a kotatsu, or low wooden table with a heating unit underneath, that my maternal grandfather had sent as a gift to my mom. It was remarkable that my mom had continued to maintain her fluency in Japanese and stay connected to *her* cultural roots, and this was partially thanks to a small store about an hour away from our house that sold Japanese foods and rented VHS videotapes. I'd join my mom on visits there, delighted that the older woman who owned the store would give me some free jelly candy while she and my mom conversed in Japanese and picked out the latest drama for my mom to watch. The experience for many migrants and their children is no different: Our relationship with our culture(s), and with all the things that make it so—language, food, media, history, religion, values—is directly impacted by our access to others like us in the geographic locations where we are implanted. This was especially true before Netflix, social media, and the rise of communication applications. These, by default, can impact the acculturation experiences—and, inevitably, the sense of belonging—of family members, too. If geographic location is a barrier, other intentional choices made by parents can help immigrant families retain access to their heritage cultures. I hear stories about families putting their own twists on American holidays, opting for comfort dishes from their origin countries rather than turkey for Thanksgiving. One community member shared that they were allowed to speak only Russian at home, and because there weren't any tutors around (before remote tutoring), their parents were intentional about creating homemade exercises and workbooks to assist them.

Our immigrant parents are often experiencing acculturative stress and going through identity crises, while we, their children, are going through our own as we develop. Sometimes these journeys overlap, and other times they create barriers between family members. Simply put, many children of immigrants spend their most formative years in the host country, thus more easily adopting the host culture and its values and norms, leading to a difference in acculturation— known as the acculturation gap—between immigrants and their children. Immigrant parents may be slower to learn the dominant language or host country's cultural norms, and they may place heavy expectations on second-generation children to uphold their heritage culture and beliefs. This can create a bifurcated experience for a child of immigrants who is expected to behave in one way at home and in another way outside it. All of the children of immigrants I know or have worked with clash with their parents to some degree on at least one difference in cultural or religious values, traditions, or norms. A meta-analytic review of research based on Asian and Latino American families found that the acculturation gap between parents and their children may lead to increased intergenerational conflict and negatively impact youth mental health and academics. (This is an interesting finding for me personally, when I consider the struggles I experienced in my youth.)

The acculturation gap, and a mismatch of strategies in the family, is further exacerbated by the fact that many immigrant families live in joint or multigenerational households (more than their Western counterparts do). Even among siblings or partners, there may be multiple different acculturation strategies at play. For instance, my brother's wife married my brother and moved from Dubai to America in her midtwenties. She was acculturating at a different rate (and age) than my brother, who at that point had been living in America for nearly two decades. Further, my brother has identified more with

Indian culture than I have—he is a proud Sikh immigrant who lived in India for about seven years of his life, and he dons a turban that physically identifies him as "other" in the West. Meanwhile, my sister assimilated more seamlessly growing up, and she recently admitted that she never really saw herself as a woman of color through her years in a predominantly white school system and college environment—something I don't relate to. I was more integrated growing up, having a pretty strong foundation and belief in Sikhism while living my more Western childhood, but over the years, I assimilated, and as an adult, I am exploring what integration looks like for me, again.

It's important to note that the acculturation process is not static, and it happens internationally, too. My family in Kobe, Japan, belongs to a mighty cultural and religious community of Sikhs, Punjabis, and Indians. This community allows its members to retain Indian and Sikh values and norms while also acculturating into Japanese society. Whenever I visit India to see family, I am always surprised by how Westernized some of my extended family members are—sometimes more than I feel I am. They are up to date on Western music, American fashion trends, and English slang. Thanks to technology, tourism, and globalization, remote acculturation—or exposure to cultures that are geographically separate from one's heritage or host culture and subsequent engagement in acculturation without physical immigration—is not uncommon.

Cultural Assimilation

The constant negotiation of two or more cultures involves the looming threat of cultural assimilation, or absorption into the host culture. While cultural assimilation usually indicates a rejection of the heritage culture, there are varying degrees to which an individual or family accepts or resists assimilation. But it's hard to discuss this without acknowledging that *something* is always sacrificed in all forms of acculturation. Assimilation is a survival tactic for many, a defense mechanism in a hostile culture. It has toxic roots in colonization and reinforces problematic beliefs about hierarchical racial orders, othering, and worthiness. Of 5,455 children of immigrants who replied to a poll on Brown Girl Therapy, 37 percent shared that they were encouraged to assimilate growing up; 38 percent reported that their parents were resistant to the dominant culture; and 25 percent were not sure. I have theorized four common reasons for experiencing cultural assimilation in the immigrant community that are not necessarily exclusive of one another:

Forced cultural assimilation can happen because there simply isn't another choice. The flexibility with which a family or person can adapt to the host culture may also be due to their heritage country's history with colonization and colonial rule. Due to British rule, my dad was mandated to learn English growing up. My mom went to an international school, which happened to also be a Catholic school, in Japan where she had more exposure to Western culture. I have heard other examples of folks who have parents or ancestors who grew up in countries where their religious liberties were limited. It's also important to note that this forced cultural assimilation is, historically, the experience of Indigenous folks everywhere.

Default cultural assimilation may involve more of a choice, and due to the exposure of certain cultural values or beliefs, it's often more "accepted." For example, the British introduced India to cricket, but India has since welcomed being a leading nation for this sport. Another example is the celebration of the host country's holidays. If you live in the West, where Christmas is usually a big societal holiday/season, you may celebrate the holiday culturally, too, either to feel a sense of belonging with your peers or out of joy and festivity. This may not lead to a rejection of your own religious or cultural holidays, but it is something you do by default as an addition to—and separate from—your own foundational cultural identity. There may also be internalized cultural ideas and values that are nods to cultural assimilation, such as living together before marriage, intermarriage, a change in parenting styles to mirror the host country's norms, and loss of an ancestral language that is no longer prominent. These become a default because they may start to match *your* beliefs and values in the new country and/or express a loss of access to your heritage culture, causing you to fill in the gaps with what is readily available.

Survival for ease as the motivator behind cultural assimilation can happen when internalized ideas and everyday choices revolve around making life feel easier. This may look like immigrant parents learning the host language to navigate society—or employment—in their new country, or acquiring a taste for certain sports, recreational activities, foods, or clothing because they are accessible. Maybe your relatives stop wearing the traditional clothing of their origin culture because it's harder to find and purchase where they live. Ease as a motivator can be insidious, too.

Survival for safety as the motivator behind cultural assimilation can lead to real or perceived safety concerns that are often internalized. For example, I have worked with children of immigrants whose parents took vocal lessons to unlearn their accents, or whose parents moved to the West and chose to give them anglicized names, believing that these would reduce the likelihood of bullying or racism. I also know many Muslim and Sikh families who put American flags outside their homes to feel safe and accepted in their neighborhoods—especially in the aftermath of 9/11. Of course, for many, the physical dissimilarity to the host cultural group may still lead to experiencing racism and discrimination. This is known as the perpetual foreigner stereotype, which posits ethnic minorities, specifically Asian Americans, as "others" and never truly "American," even if they are born in the United States, naturalized, or identify as such.

Even in the face of discrimination or racism, many immigrants and their children still resist assimilation and continue to claim and retain their cultural and religious values and identities. My brother was living in New York City when 9/11 happened, and a few weeks later, when he was at a bar, he got beaten up by a stranger for being a "terrorist," his pagri pulled off his head. My mom even suggested that he wear a baseball cap to lie low, but he refused to let the experience define or diminish his own religious beliefs. How we experience and respond to discrimination and racism is personal, yet these are very real issues for many of us—from workplace discrimination and pay inequity to hate crimes and racial and religious profiling. The statistics bear this out, and in recent years, political rhetoric has inflamed animosity and increased hate crimes and police brutality. An important contextual part of experiencing a sense of safety is how welcoming and accommodating—through tolerance and policies—the host community is to immigrants.

Assimilation is not always the goal, or desire, in immigrant families. The ultimate fear for my own parents, I have come to learn, was cultural erasure. Many immigrant parents try to avoid cultural erasure by speaking their native language at home to their U.S.-born children, or by teaching their kids a foundation of religion and culture and holding them to certain expectations, even if they are not in line with Western cultural norms—like arranged marriages, traditional gender roles, and collectivist beliefs. My parents came to this country not because they wanted to leave their roots and identities behind but because they wanted to build a more promising future. For earlier generations, when immigration was inextricably tied to service and contribution to the economy, assimilation was often favored or encouraged. Of course, this still exists today, but I have come to understand that my parents—Papa especially—measured their own worthiness and success as parents by how well their kids were maintaining their culture. However, no matter how hard my dad tried, Western cultural norms and values trickled into our daily lives. For example, even though I was born in the U.S., Punjabi was my first language. By the time I got to preschool, I didn't understand basic English commands, such as "Sit" or "Raise your hand," and my parents would have to translate certain words, such as *bathroom*, for my teachers so that they knew what I was saying. Eventually, my teachers told my parents that they needed to stop speaking Punjabi to me, or I was going to fall behind. So my parents did what they thought they needed to and started speaking English to try to help me have an easier life in America. Now, I can't really speak Punjabi, an unintended consequence that makes me feel disconnected from my roots—and something I scramble to remedy as an adult.

MY ACCULTURATION PROCESS has undoubtedly been impacted by the way I was raised. My dad's conservative religious values as a Sikh didn't mirror the strict religious beliefs of my extended family in Japan, where my dad was known to be the "strict" parent/uncle. He encouraged religious curiosity yet expected a strong identity rooted in Sikhism. I know now that children are meant to challenge and question things in order to build a strong and stable foundation for their own beliefs and senses of self.

My dad had two house rules for us growing up. The first: marry a Sikh. The second: don't cut your hair. Sikhs believe that to exist in the way God created us, we should maintain our appearance the way it was created. Some Sikhs believe that cutting the hair is akin to figuratively cutting off one's roots. I grew up with long, thick, un-shorn black hair that grazed my ankles. As an adolescent, I would find ways to throw my hair up, usually wearing it in a braid and folding it at the bottom with a couple of hair ties. I didn't under-stand *why* it was so important to keep my long hair, and I don't have memories of my mom or sister (neither of whom had hair as long as mine) helping me learn to love and take care of my beautiful long hair. Without learning about meaning, retention of heritage culture or religious values can feel burdensome. I just felt annoyed by how difficult it was to take care of my hair. So I started resenting it. I often dreamed about cutting it all off; I would stand in front of the mirror creatively playing with hairstyles that made my hair look shorter. I started to desperately want a "white girl" ponytail—you know, like Cher Horowitz or Lizzie McGuire. I was always jealous of the way white women could just throw their hair on top of their heads, undemanding and bouncy. I conflated the ease with which these women were able to wear their hair—effortlessly and conveniently—with the freedom of independence and choice. In college, at twenty, I finally decided to cut my hair while I was traveling in Australia over spring break. I didn't tell anyone in my family except a Japanese cousin and travel companion who had been cutting her hair for some time. I came to learn later from my parents, who were doubly upset and betrayed, that my sister had also dabbled in cutting her hair at the same time. We were both trying to figure out our own religious identities, and the hold religion would have over our choices, in parallel—but in isolation. My siblings and I have since shared inti-mate stories about our relationships with Sikhism, but because our relationships with one another didn't develop until much later, I con-tinued to navigate my own acculturation journey alone.

My confusion and frustration over my identity extended into my cultural and racial background, too. When I was growing up, my mom and I would spend Sundays bleaching our faces with whitening creams; in both my Indian and Japanese cultures, whiteness is considered beautiful and superior to darker skin tones. I spent most of my high school years wearing hazel contact lenses because I thought they made me prettier. Often, aunties and uncles would take it upon themselves to comment on my skin color and how pretty it made me, strengthening my belief that because I was fairer skinned, I was worthier.

For a majority of my life, I subscribed to the belief that to be "American," I must reject my origins—and all the cultural and religious values that came with them. That to be of value, I must reach for whiteness. That I must "fit in" in order to be good, worthy, accepted, or successful. As people of color in this country, we have been taught that our acceptance or deservingness is directly correlated to how comfortable white people are with what we look like and how we act. After all, identities are social constructs that help other people feel comfortable in knowing what they can expect from us. I am actively and continuously unpacking and unraveling my own internalized racism and colorism, my own privileges, and how the systems in this country to which I have for so long desperately wanted to belong are unjust, problematic, and in need of complete dismantlement. I'm not alone: when I asked members of the Brown Girl Therapy community if they struggled with, or are still unlearning, internalized racism or colorism, 88 percent of 5,546 children of immigrants who responded said yes.

In a letter to my *Washington Post* column, one white reader related that she is married to a brown Zoroastrian immigrant from Iran. She went on to share that he has made comments about how happy he is that their kids are white passing and have fair skin. She also mentioned his stories about being hyperaware of his "otherness" growing up and how that led him to feel embarrassed over his parents' accents, food, and music choices. The truth is, internalized beliefs about skin color and race are insidious, and many folks may not even realize they are subscribing to them. I've had community members and clients share that they just "prefer" white romantic partners, or they make biased comments about other immigrant groups or marginalized communities without realizing that accepting these negative stereotypes is, in itself, a product of assimilation.

If you're reading this and feeling cornered by these revelations, remember that our learned behaviors and patterns are rooted in larger, intentionally created systems that do not serve us, and we have just learned to live within them. Internalized racism/colorism is founded in shame. And that's where we have to start. It's important to question norms, embrace discomfort, and, ultimately, welcome transformation. Here are a few starter questions for you to consider for critical self-reflection:

- When was the first time you felt like an "other"? What happened? How did this reinforce certain assimilation behaviors?
- Reflect upon recent times where you felt inferior to others. What happened to make you feel this way, and how did you subsequently behave or handle it?
- How do your cultural and racial backgrounds impact your experience of the different relationships you currently have? How do they impact the way you "show up" in the different systems you live, study, or work in?
- In what ways do the racial or cultural backgrounds of those surrounding you on a day-to-day basis impact your experience or your behavior?
- In what ways do you feel shame toward your racial or cultural identity? Where is it rooted?
- Who benefits from your acting in "certain" ways?
- As you heal your internalized racism/colorism, what do you want to embrace?

The Importance of Religion
in Acculturation

Acculturation cannot be discussed without addressing how intertwined religion and culture are for so many of us. Some would even argue that religion and culture are inseparable, since practices, beliefs, and traditions tied to religion meld into a group's or a person's culture—or norms and values and way of life.

Though I had various Japanese influences in my childhood, my parents' relationships with others often centered around Sikhism and Sundays at gurdwara. And for me, being Sikh and being Punjabi and being Indian bled together over the years. There is a reciprocal relationship between religion and culture, and I, too, struggle to distinguish between the two, often conflating one with the other. Being exposed to my Punjabi culture, language, and food meant attending religious gatherings and community events that were organized through the Sikh community. And going to community events where aunties and uncles spoke in Punjabi (or Hindi) and danced and sang to Hindi and Punjabi songs (old and new) often meant being around other Sikhs. Even my local annual Punjabi Mela—an all-day festival to celebrate and share the culture of North India, including food and clothing/jewelry stalls and Indian dancing and music—was organized by the Sikh Association of Central Virginia. (My dad spearheaded this festival when I was sixteen years old because of a hate crime he experienced; it led him to want to educate the community.)

For me and many others, religion is intertwined with culture, and these two essential features generally create the household traditions, expectations, values, and norms that a child of immigrants is raised with. In an Instagram poll, 85 percent of 4,345 children of immigrants who participated agreed that religion and culture are so interconnected that it can be hard to discern between the two. This is particularly significant when immigrants' cultures or religions are considered a minority in a given country—maintaining one or both can be an act of resistance.

Though religion pertains to faith and belief in God, and culture pertains to practices and traditions, there is much overlap. But they *are* different. They are each practiced or incorporated into people's lives in different ways. For example, while Indians may practice a wide variation of religions—such as Hinduism, Sikhism, Buddhism, Jainism, Christianity, and Islam—the majority religion of Punjab is Sikhism. Therefore, a religious community is often also a cultural community (e.g., in the way the Sikh community organizes the Punjabi Mela), but a cultural community does not necessarily involve a specific religious community (e.g., though Hindu Punjabis are culturally and genealogically from Punjab, they practice Hinduism, not Sikhism). Even more broadly, there are Indian cultural values, or South Asian cultural values, or, as I have noticed in my work, immigrant values that extend beyond a single race, ethnicity, culture, region, and religion.

Cultural values that may be imposed by larger systems of colonization and patriarchal ideas may impact the way religion is practiced or accepted throughout a community. They can even impact how an individual relates to their own cultural or religious identity. One attendee of a community workshop I facilitated on bicultural identity shared that his parents divorced when he was young, and moving between their houses when he was growing up always elicited a sort of culture shock for him. He would have a certain level of freedom in one house, where the parent was European and Catholic, that he didn't have in his other house, where the parent was Arab and Muslim. He further shared that there was some overlap, with guilt, especially as it related to God, being used by both parents as a weapon of choice. When asked about how culture and religion shaped the other

for him, he said that he doesn't identify with either religion but respects his parents' cultural values and choices when he is with them.
Another Brown Girl Therapy member who identifies as a Christian
Indian shared that she often feels like she doesn't belong in either
community. She feels as if she's not Indian enough because of her
Christian values, and not Christian enough because of her Indian
values. Her disconnection is intensified because America's understanding of Indian culture is centered around movies, language,
music, and food that don't represent the specific South Indian region
where she is from. This is another reminder that the practice of religious and/or cultural values is not monolithic. Not all Arab or Muslim women wear hijabs, and not all people from Latin America speak
Spanish. Punjabis are known to enjoy partying and drinking alcohol, but not all Punjabis partake in this cultural stereotype.

We all create meaning through our beliefs—and often through
the family narratives imposed on us growing up—which are informed by religion and/or culture. These may involve things like
birth, marital, and funeral practices; dress or clothing; and dietary
requirements or restrictions. There's overlap, and yet the history or
reasoning behind these choices may be different.

Religion	Culture
• Religious scriptures and stories. • Specific beliefs and values about God and goodness and morality. • Gender norms/expectations. • Restrictions on substances or diet.	• Cultural parables, superstitions, and stories. • Gender norms/expectations. • General beliefs and values around community and communication. • Fashion norms.

- Religious requirements or expression through attire/clothes.
- Birth, marital, funeral, and age-related traditions and rituals.
- Hymns, prayer, meditation, and other expressions of religion (singing, etc.).
- Religious terms and language utilized during religious practices.
- Place of worship and other religious sites.
- Religious community bonded by religious orientation.
- Religious symbols (e.g., cross, Khanda, Star of David, etc.).
- Holidays and significance.

- Cultural celebrations or traditions (e.g., quinceañeras, with or without religious context).
- Cultural institutions and buildings of significance.
- Cultural symbols (e.g., flags).
- Specific recreational activities that are culturally paraded (e.g., cricket, football, afternoon tea, etc.).
- Dance, music, media, and cultural crafts/arts.
- Language, cultural slang, dialect.
- Cultural community bonded by shared culture.
- Holidays celebrated culturally (without religious connotation prescribed to them).

Individualism versus Collectivism

Religiosity—and its relatives: faith, prayer, and morality—may carry a lot of weight in immigrant households because it may intersect with the values of a collectivist culture. Where individualism encourages a person's independence and personal growth and views people as distinctly separate from one another, collectivism encourages group cohesion and collaborative growth and views people as interconnected with others. This focus on community, and especially on the feeling of being part of something bigger than oneself, can be paramount to healing and wellness.

My parents' involvement in the religious and cultural community of central Virginia, one that has significantly grown in size since I was born, has given us an extended family nearby, though our actual blood relatives live across oceans. They bonded with other families and created strong social networks and support systems, which are known to have benefits to well-being. The generosity and love go well beyond niceties and extend into real consideration and care. On any given day, my parents can be found visiting this aunty to drop off food because she hurt her foot or meeting with that uncle to check on how *his* father abroad is doing. This is in direct contradiction with the Western concept of "every man for himself." In fact, this orientation toward a community combats feelings of disconnection and isolation, which can be imperative for immigrants and their children who are building lives abroad with little to no established support. Not to mention that this kind of social support is beneficial to our well-being and helps manage psychological distress.

From a young age, I would often ask my parents why we had to go to gurdwara every Sunday. I was chronically cranky and wanted to sleep and be lazy, and as I got older, I wanted to devote my weekends to my friends and social events. Why did our faith need to be witnessed to be valid? Going to gurdwara felt like a social event, but it wasn't until much later that I recognized that religion for many children of immigrants is mainly experienced in a social environment—a way to commit to our faith and to our community.

Like our family systems, each social system has rules and expectations that maintain its functioning. In collectivist families and cultural systems, people are generally evaluated by how well they can harmonize with other group members based on shared values, expectations, and norms. Conversely, in an individualistic culture, people are generally evaluated by how self-sufficient, independent, and driven by personal goals they are. While focus on the collective may come at the expense of the individual, or focus on the individual may come at the expense of the collective, it's important to note that extremes in either context can be detrimental. And no context is without its flaws.

AFTER MY ASSAULT, while I was living at home and trying to figure out how my life would move forward, my parents wanted to go about their lives and maintain the status quo, showing others that things were okay. So we didn't tell community or extended family members the truth about what I was experiencing or going through. This has been the hardest thing to forgive my parents for. When I truly needed care and generosity—the very reason we had built community—I was deprived of it, and by default so were they. During these years of navigating my failures, my depression, and my trauma, I witnessed and experienced the *other* side of religion and collectivism; it was rife with judgment, fear, and harmful norms. To my parents—and, indeed, to many in collectivist contexts—social perception seemed more important than personal struggles.

I, too, felt that fear. My parents had always been active leaders and revered members of the Sikh community, and I was terrified of tarnishing my parents' reputation. It was my duty as a daughter to do as they said, even if it was hurting my well-being. I was taught to always pretend like I lived in a glass house: people could come and go as they pleased, peering into nooks and crannies, seeing what might be messy and taking what they wanted out of context and passing it on to others. So I learned to hide things better. If you go into my parents' house, it'll appear spotless. Every surface shines, and it's a shock to learn that the food filling the fridge to the brim is cooked in the same kitchen that looks like it has been prepped for an open house. Bedrooms are meticulous, and the living room doesn't seem lived in. My mom has always feverishly cleaned every corner of the house every evening before she goes to bed. But if you're brave enough to venture a little deeper, you'll find mismatched Tupperware overflowing from kitchen cabinets when you open them and junk boxes shoved into the backs of closets. And you'll realize that the house is a perfect metaphor for how we wanted to be perceived by others.

Social-Oriented Perfectionism

While I often felt like I had to be perfect in order to receive validation growing up, it wasn't until I started working with clients in graduate school that I realized there were actually different types of perfectionism—self-oriented (demanding ourselves to be perfect), social-oriented (feeling pressure from others to be perfect), and other-oriented (expecting others to be perfect).

In a lot of conversations around perfectionism, you'll hear it coupled with labels like "type A," "controlling," "demanding," and "high-strung." This might be true for some, and this kind of perfectionism is usually categorized as self-oriented perfectionism, but culture plays a role in how we adopt or learn perfectionist behaviors. Social-oriented perfectionism, or the experience of feeling like others expect you to be perfect, can be compounded by social media use, but more specifically, in a collectivist culture, it may be tied to the value of conformity or interpersonal harmony. In fact, social and cultural stigma are a major barrier for people of color and immigrant communities when it comes to seeking mental health care. Their reluctance is tied to saving face and protecting family and community reputations.

When children of immigrants were polled, 92 percent of 3,124 said that they, too, struggle with perfectionism, and 70 percent of 2,827 said that they feel like both culture and family imposed perfectionism on them. (Only 8 percent said neither did.) Research suggests that self-oriented perfectionism—or merely striving to do well—can be adaptive. This can be due to its correlation to traits related to motivation and success. However, the same research suggests that social-oriented perfectionism can be maladaptive and harmful, increasing anxiety and decreasing confidence.

I have worked with several children of immigrants who came to see me for general anxiety or depression, and we eventually uncovered that they struggled with severe self-oriented perfectionism, being hypercritical in the ways they evaluated themselves and their behaviors. Through our work together, it became obvious that this self-oriented perfectionism was modeled through social-oriented perfectionism in which my clients felt pressure from their parents, family members, and/or community members to perform or achieve to a certain standard. When asked whose voices they heard in their heads during times of self-criticism, they oftentimes responded that they heard the voices of close family members or caregivers. My mom has never minced her words, and when I tell her that she has hurt my feelings or isn't being very nice, her reply will often be that no one is as honest as a mom and that it's a sign of love. While I understand the sentiment, the execution of it, I have come to believe, conditioned my own voice to be hypercritical. I learned to be critical of myself, and I not only assumed that others were just as critical of me but also started to become hypercritical of others—all in the name, I thought, of "love." It is something that I am still, to this day, trying to unlearn. Children need safe spaces to make mistakes and learn from them. This is how they build self-efficacy, self-compassion, and tolerance for the discomfort of growing pains. Instead, many of us have built our self-schemas around the criticism we received in our childhoods and adolescence. If our parents can model acceptance of mistakes and failure, then we can strive for high standards without that striving becoming maladaptive. But if standards are unrealistically high and we're taught that our inability to reach them indicates personal failure, then perfectionism becomes a problem. After all, there is a difference between wanting to excel and wanting to be perfect.

"Tough love" became the primary method of parenting that I experienced. My parents were so intertwined with their community that it started to feel like my failure was not just an extension of them but also an extension of my community. I began to believe that I wasn't just letting down myself or my parents or my extended family—I was letting down my Punjabi and Sikh community, too. After all, regardless of whether or not we want to, many of us serve as representations of our entire communities, exacerbating the pressure we feel to attain a certain standard.

The internalization of high standards alongside extensive criticism from caregivers can also lead to pervasive feelings of shame. It's an ugly cycle: We're criticized, so we pursue unrealistic standards. We can't attain said unrealistic standards, so we feel like failures. And feeling like failures feels shameful, as though we are letdowns to both our families and our communities. We learn to build our identities around shame. It makes us feel like we can't speak about our struggles. This cycle intensifies disconnection between people, regardless of how "close-knit" or "insular" our families and communities are.

Some religious and cultural communities may even prioritize performance over behavior or outcome over intent. Not to mention the immigrant parents' need to "show" family back home that their family in America is successful and that they have maintained their culture and religion abroad. In my community, "negative" life experiences have been talked about in hushed whispers, as if they're contagious: *So-and-so got divorced. So-and-so got laid off. So-and-so is in therapy. So-and-so had a miscarriage.* It has gotten to the point where aunties and uncles exaggerate details or fib to their friends so that the truth about whatever struggles they're experiencing won't get out. There have been so many times that my mom has told me about something a peer is doing—based on what their mom told her—and I will know, from social media or from talking to my peer, that this information is incorrect. I don't betray my peer by sharing the reality with my mom, but often, the conversation carries a "be like them" tone that just becomes a bitter pill I have to swallow.

Perfectionism perpetuates impression management as a family system and a culture. One study examined how perfectionism evolved for college students over twenty-seven years between 1989 and 2016, finding that across the U.S., Canada, and the U.K., perfectionism had steadily increased. So despite the cultural and religious layers, the issue is more common and generalized, not just limited to immigrant communities. And given that perfectionism has been linked to depression, I'm left wondering how many others like me have also been struggling in silence.

I grew up in a community where whispers of domestic violence and alcoholism and infidelity were frequent, but then on Sundays at gurdwara or at community events, families gathered together to pretend like everything was fine. Being religious doesn't make you a good, kind, or honest person. Having faith doesn't automatically make you strong. Praying doesn't release you from your own role in situations. Bringing food to your sick neighbor doesn't absolve you of mistreatment in your own home. If anything, as it goes in most hierarchical systems, those in power often get away with more than they should for the sake of perception and interpersonal harmony.

I'm reminded of a Sikh community on the East Coast that was the focus of gossip when I was younger because a person in power had been accused of sexually abusing a child. Even though court records had been made public, this man had been given continued access to the local community sangat and its children for another twenty-five years. The shock and disbelief rattled my family. *How could someone we knew and respected in our community be guilty of this?* Let alone someone who lived and breathed religion and held a recognized position for his knowledge and his passion in spreading Sikhism.

Living at home as an adult during this time helped me start to understand the hypocrisy that often prevails in our immigrant and religious communities. Not only do we fail to show up for those who don't feel safe or comfortable giving voice to their trauma, but we also fail to speak out against our own families or communities, ultimately upholding systems and situations that are incredibly damaging to people's psyches. We often do this to support the veneer of religion and culture—though it's those very religious and cultural values that have been broken. Religion can even be weaponized against children of immigrants: in fact, 70 percent of 4,579 children of immigrants who responded to one of my Instagram polls admitted that religion had been used against them to enforce control or to instill fear or obedience.

To simply choose to leave home would be a form of assimilation, and for many of us, it's not a viable option. Instead, we would risk our families, our communities, our names. There's so much more weight to mistakes, to risks, to wrong choices, conditioning most of us to feel like we have to be absolutely perfect to be worthy of it all. Yes, there are people who would sacrifice their families, communities, and names for the sake of mental health, but when these are the sole elements on which someone can hang their identity and the main way they have been validated as a human being, this is much harder to do. In my work, I have found that for many, the battle is often between striving for the unrealistic to maintain important relationships and retreating from important relationships to protect mental health.

One of my therapy clients had been held hostage by what others thought about her choices, regardless of how unhappy she was. She was navigating trauma at the hands of her own mother, who was revered within her cultural and religious community. My client would report how her mom often told her that she was "not a good enough Hindu" or that "a good Hindu wouldn't do . . ." And often these darts would be thrown at her when she was exercising her independence in any way—whether by going out with friends or spending money she had made. Despite having all that community, she had no one to turn to.

Gender Roles and Expectations

My mom was adamant that no one needed to know about my assault, partially because she worried others would think of me as unmarriageable or unworthy—I would no longer be perceived as a good Indian woman in society. The unfortunate reality is that some people actually would see me this way. The need to have things fit into a culturally and socially approved box can absolutely impact the mental health and well-being of children of immigrants. Then add gendered expectations to the mix. Though Sikhism espouses equality across genders, culturally, the community—as is the case across most religious and cultural communities—still enforces gender roles and responsibilities. And out of almost 4,000 children of immigrants polled, 72 percent agreed that gendered expectations are imposed in similar ways across their religions, cultures, and families.

Though my parents are both well respected in our cultural and religious communities, they play different gender-based roles. In a 2018 study, researchers found that immigrants tend to maintain and uphold the traditional gender norms of their origin countries. My dad has sat on the board of our gurdwara and has been included in decision-making, whereas my mom, along with other aunties, is mostly involved in keeping things running day-to-day or cooking the langar. In fact, I have never personally known a female gyani, or congregation leader, and neither have my parents. Though it's not forbidden, it's rare. These gender biases extend into marital and cultural traditions, which can be patriarchal in nature. Though I am grateful that my family has never subscribed to this, for some, boys are considered worthy of celebration at birth, whereas girls are not. My sister and I grew up celebrating Raksha Bandhan, tying a thread around my brother's wrist every year to appreciate his role in protecting me; it's a beautiful sentiment I still uphold, but it feels invalidating of my sister's role in my life. One African community member shared how bride price, or the payment a prospective groom makes to a prospective bride, is still relevant in her community. One Hindu follower shared how Karva Chauth is where women are expected to fast for their husbands and how only sons are supposed to be able to perform the last rites of their parents. One Muslim woman shared that she has never been to her dad's grave in their home country because he's buried in a cemetery for only men. And, of course, there are more general and common patriarchal practices, such as taking a husband's name at marriage.

On top of gender, there are often caste or class systems in place, depending on what community and religion you come from. Even though Sikhism is a religion that denies casteism, there are, of course, references to the "different" Sikhs depending on their ancestral history and the work they do. These conversations can allude to a hierarchy around who is marriage material within the religion . . . a religion that is meant to be rooted in justice and equality.

The social nature of a religious and cultural community is multifaceted and much more nuanced depending on which child of immigrants you talk to. When I conducted my online polls on religion, I heard from hundreds of folks who wanted to share a bit about their personal experiences. Some common themes included the questioning of religion being equated with being Americanized, an inability to separate religion and culture, and the diverting away from one or both due to the harmful social norms upheld within them.

Religion, Culture, and Mental Health

Religiosity and spirituality have been shown to decrease psychological distress. In fact, utilizing religion or meditative prayer to cope can help many redefine their stressors, attain calmness, or find meaning and guidance during painful or overwhelming experiences. Even in Sikhism, the workings of the mind and the ego are mentioned throughout the Guru Granth Sahib, serving as reminders for followers to slow down and practice humility, gratitude, and detachment. Likewise, many religious communities have a focus on community and advocacy, as Sikhism does with the pillar of seva, or selfless service. Being religious and having strong cultural roots can often feel like a proclamation of the importance of ancestral and community care, which are sadly overlooked in the West. I, for one, have always found myself seeking Sikh spaces, first at summer camps and then, as an adult, at Sikh professional conferences and meetups. Being in these rooms and having access to folks who look like me or my family members, with turbans and long, flowing hair, helps me anchor myself and root into my religious and cultural identity. This is a testament to how my parents' acculturation strategies—centering religious and cultural community—influenced me.

Our mental health issues can also be compounded by religious and cultural identity, due to historical trauma and heightened vulnerabilities related to marginalized status. There are many barriers to seeking mental health care or self-advocating in the West, which can lead to religious folks purposefully avoiding professional care altogether in order to avoid experiencing racism, prejudice, or other harm. One workshop attendee shared how her therapist kept commenting on her hijab during sessions, making her uncomfortable. Many therapists are simply not trained to be religiously or culturally inclusive in their clinical work, and they veer away from the topic altogether, even though it can be a protective factor for our mental health.

Research suggests that members of communities of color—and immigrants specifically—are more likely to seek mental health support from within their communities. What's more, when religion is part of their cultures/families, they are more likely to seek support—or be told to seek support—from a religious leader than go to therapy. Positive religious coping—or turning to religion or God as a useful tool of support—is beneficial. It increases self-esteem as it relates to being part of something larger than oneself, and it can enhance prosocial behaviors in religious and cultural communities. However, negative religious coping—or centering narratives that God is punishing or abandoning us whenever we make "mistakes" or have negative experiences—can undermine a person's sense of self or healing journey. For some, religious coping serves as a complete replacement for mental health care, self-care, or proactivity. In these cases, there can be a belief that solely returning/turning to religion and prayer is enough. Many children of immigrants have been told to "pray" their struggles away or that their hard times are the result of "not praying enough." Religious reasoning is sometimes used to make sense of one's struggles or those of others, in the same way I tried to make sense of my assault as a punishment for withdrawing from a path expected of me. Maybe it is enough for some, but it also has the potential to minimize a person's sense of agency in changing their situation/circumstances, *and* it can invalidate the hard work and efforts of someone who actively seeks out or learns additional/other types of care. One community member shared how she was taught that everything was given by Allah and everything was taken by Allah. This made it difficult for her to trust in not only her own skills and worthiness but also her own agency in life. These internal struggles were reflected in her family dynamics, where "mental health" was nonexistent. All-knowing Allah would handle situations however they needed to be handled.

> Religion creates a sense of accountability and connection to others, *and* we can only be as healthy in that connection as we are in learning to take care of ourselves.

Many of us children of immigrants reckon with religious and cultural narratives that may result in ostracization from these communities. We must understand that taking care of ourselves or seeking out healing doesn't have to mean that we don't have faith in a bigger power, nor does it have to mean that we are rejecting our cultural or religious communities. One does not necessarily replace the other.

For me, it wasn't until years later, when I started down a more intentional path toward healing, that I had the capacity and the desire to return to my faith. I wear a kara every day, and I often recite the Mool Mantar for my own grounding and reminders. Through having Sikh nephews and a niece and meeting other adults who span the spectrum when it comes to religion, I have felt more comfortable exploring what Sikhism means to *me*. My relationship with my faith is deeply personal to me now, and it's something I may continue to have questions about. The strength of my faith may vary, but the underlying tenets and pillars of Sikhism—justice, equality, honesty, and service to others—have contributed to who I am today. I don't take that for granted.

How to reflect on your own relationship with religion and culture

It's healthy to regularly interrogate our own self-concepts and how they are tied to religion or culture. For many of us, it can feel complicated to explore faith in ways that are different from those of our parents. As such, I wanted to provide some reflections on important themes that may help you wherever you are on your journey.

EXERCISE: Identify how you can discern between religion and culture through thematic mapping:

1. List the values, norms, and expectations founded in your religious identity.

2. List the values, norms, and expectations founded in your heritage cultural identity.

3. Reflect on the overlaps and differences between your faith/religious upbringing and heritage cultural identity.

In examining your relationship with faith and culture, it will be important to reflect on the narratives you associate with them and where these narratives come from. Below are general and thematic reflection questions to get you started.

General Reflections

- When were you first made aware of your culture? What about your religion?
- What were some of the first experiences you had with others of a different culture or religion?
- When you were growing up, how did your parents/family enforce (or not enforce) religion and religious behaviors/attitudes in your life? What about cultural behaviors and attitudes?
- Did your parents ever formally talk to you about culture or religion?
- When was the first time you questioned your faith? What about the first time you butted heads with your culture? How has this impacted you?
- What's something you were never allowed to question about your religion or culture?
- What "norms" in your religious or cultural community have had an impact on your own understanding of your religious or cultural identity?

Community

- What does "community" mean to you? What communities were you part of growing up?

- Did you grow up with nearby access to your religious community? How has that impacted your relationship with religion?
- Did you grow up with nearby access to your cultural community? How has that impacted your relationship with your heritage culture?
- How has religious community or cultural community made you feel a sense of belonging or a sense of isolation in your life?
- How has travel (abroad or locally) shaped your understanding of your faith, religion, and culture? Is there a location with religious or cultural significance that you have visited or want to visit? Freewrite about this.
- How does media (songs, shows, pop culture) contribute to your relationship with your religion or culture?
- How does Western media represent your religion or culture? How has this impacted your own internalized narrative?

Tradition

- How is food utilized within your religious practice, if at all?
- How is food important to your culture?
- What kind of food did you grow up with at home?
- What childhood memories do you have about culturally or religiously significant food?
- What traditions did you grow up with? Were they rooted in religion or culture?
- Are there any traditions you maintain on your own now? Are they rooted in either your religion or culture? Why are these important to you?

- Are there any traditions in your religion or culture that you don't know the meaning of? Do some research and reflect on what you learn.

History

- Consider or learn about the history of your religion and religious conflict. What is important to note?
- Learn about your own family's history with religion, including family members who are more or less religious and why, as well as events that may have led to religious persecution or religious conflict. What is important to note?
- How has colonization or war impacted your religious or cultural community's identity?

Chapter Five

Feeling My Way Through

was always an emotional child. (And, let's be honest, I'm still an emotionally expressive adult.) Growing up, I spent a significant amount of time in my room listening to sad songs and crying under the covers. I cried because I hurt, but I also cried in relief. I was always in awe of how others could write lyrics that gave language to the inner turmoil I was never fully comfortable expressing or processing on my own. My mom never understood it. She would tell me that I should cry only when someone dies. I wondered if I would ever grow into my big, big feelings or if I would always feel crippled by them. The discomfort of big or intense emotions is something I see reverberate through many immigrant families. Neutrality of expression is respected and encouraged. Many of us second-gen immigrants witnessed and observed our parents' endurance of hardship without complaint. Stoicism is a survival skill that our elders learned to protect themselves from external sources of suffering. It may have allowed my grandparents and their peers, who experienced displacement because of the Partition of 1947, to overcome adversity and build resilience, or it may have given my parents the capacity to forge ahead when things felt particularly taxing for them as immigrants in the U.K. and the U.S. It's not necessarily, or always, a negative trait. It can involve self-control and an indifference to or detachment from the kinds of emotions that might lead to rumination or negative thought spirals. Stoicism keeps us from dwelling on distress or negative thoughts. However, it can also result in emotional deprivation. It may be the reason why my dad seemed cold and disinterested to me growing up. It may contribute to my mom's lack of patience and tenderness when I feel sad or down. When people embody stoicism, they may lack the ability to tend to others' emotions because they are neglecting tending to their own. In the name of "staying strong" or "powering through," my parents created a wall that disallowed intimacy and emotional closeness with me and my siblings. Being in control of our emotions was highly valued and applauded in my home, as it was in the homes of many other children of immigrants. I often felt guilt for being too happy or shame for feeling too sad; in the former case, I was told that I needed to calm down, and in the latter, I was told that I was overreacting. The toxic positivity that my parents embraced during my depression—and in my childhood—denied me the ability to learn about or embrace my wide range of beautiful emotions. Relatedly, in a Brown Girl Therapy poll, 80 percent of 1,203 respondents said they would call at least one immigrant parent "stoic." One community member wrote to me: "My dad is stoic, and so are all his friends. The one way they deal with this is by relying on alcohol to mask their emotions." Another shared: "My stoic mom expects praise for enduring toxic and unhealthy relationship dynamics rather than leaving." These narratives are passed down, becoming cultural or family norms. Many children of immigrants I have worked with have faced similar struggles. Several, from different backgrounds, often restrained their emotions, even in the room with me; they felt uncomfortable when we discussed something worth celebrating or embarrassed when they showed sadness. Our clinical work during these times required inviting their emotions into the room—unapologetically.

My parents were unable to tend to my emotional needs, and in turn, I felt that sharing anything about my emotions meant I was complaining. I'm reminded of a recent harmless incident with my parents in which we were walking outside on a particularly hot day. My mom and I were talking about how hot we were, and my dad responded: "It's hot. We can't change that, so why complain about something that is already happening or has happened?" In the past, I may have internalized this as shame, but at that moment, I replied: "There's a difference between acknowledging something and complaining about it." He was quiet, usually an indication that his internal wheels were spinning, and I knew better than to push it. I have come to realize that my parents' stoicism and lack of emotional awareness contributed to my inability to truly understand my own feelings.

Managing and Regulating Emotions

Emotion regulation, or emotion self-regulation, is our expression of, and our ability to manage or control, our emotional states. There are different types of emotion regulation strategies, and these can vary significantly depending on a lot of factors, including culture. One study even found differences in regulation strategies between participants from northern Europe and those from southern Europe—attributing these differences to differences in class, culture, and race.

Emotion regulation is a long-term process and a motivated process, in that we are driven to regulate our emotions by end goals that we may set (or that are imposed on us). For instance, learning to regulate feelings of frustration may be motivated by a desire to complete a difficult task. Or learning to regulate anger may be motivated by a desire to be happier in relationships. The goals are not always external. Sometimes they are internal. For example, regulating our guilt or shame may be motivated by not wanting to be so uncomfortable; therefore, we just do whatever is asked of us instead of setting boundaries or saying no. Our parents may be motivated by learned narratives of stoicism or saving face, so they regulate their uncomfortable feelings by simply avoiding them altogether.

Some emotion regulation strategies are associated with better well-being, but others may worsen it. The most common strategy I have witnessed in my work with clients and second-generation immigrants is suppression, or withholding, masking, or restricting emotional expression. This ties back to stoicism, which is often passed down as an internalization that having feelings—any feelings—is a problem. The suppression we learn, and are modeled, prioritizes distraction from and avoidance of these emotions. Toxic positivity—*It could be worse! You'll be fine! Think positive thoughts! Be grateful!*—is a common response and an effort to push these emotions away. But what actually happens is that these emotions get shoved inward and thus suppressed, causing numbness and detachment from all feelings. Suppressing your emotions can cause physical stress to your body and suppress your immunity. When I think back on how many health issues I had in my adolescence, I can't help but wonder if *something* would have been different had I expressed and shared my emotional and mental states.

Suppression of emotions may be a product of patriarchal societal issues, too; many women fear being labeled "hysterical" or "angry Black women" or "too sensitive/emotional." One culturally bound illness called hwa-byung is observed mostly in Korean women; it is a result of anger suppression, which is rooted in certain Korean values, such as filial piety, female submissiveness, intolerance toward mental health issues, and so on. Similarly, men may be gender socialized in a way that discourages them from sharing or discussing emotions. Generally, research has found that greater adherence to certain values, specifically emotional control, is uniquely associated with poorer attitudes toward seeking mental health help. The narratives around emotional expression and regulation are multifaceted and can transcend culture.

The majority of research on emotion regulation still centers Western, European, and white experiences, but how we interact with our emotions varies widely across cultures, and there is an array of ways in which emotions impact our mental health. For example, people in non-Western cultures may be more likely to suppress emotions in support of their values of group cohesion, interpersonal harmony, and social hierarchy. Where emotional restraint may be considered a sign of maturity in one culture, emotional expression is valued in another. The Eurocentric baseline that is widely supported once again excludes an entire population, further misunderstanding the immigrant and child-of-immigrant experience.

In her book *Between Us: How Cultures Create Emotions*, Dutch social psychologist Batja Mesquita presents two models for understanding emotions: MINE—or "Mental, INside the person, and Essentialist"—and OURS—or "OUtside the person, Relational, and Situated." The former espouses how feelings are important, positing that emotion seeks expression. Conversely, the latter posits that acts (not emotions) are important, and emotional acts seek to meet social norms. Mesquita explains that people who subscribe to the MINE model identify their emotions based on their internal and bodily changes, and this is the more common and conventional way of understanding emotion. However, those who subscribe to the OURS model identify their emotions based on what is happening in the relationship or social situation between people. Simply put, emotions may not live *within* us, as we are taught in the West; rather, they may live *between* people. Emotions are contextual.

Though most collectivist cultures subscribe to the OURS model, it's important to note that the experience of emotions and emotional expression varies even more between cultures. For instance, in contrast to people of Asian heritage, people of Latine heritage rate positive emotions as more appropriate to experience and express and negative emotions as more undesirable. We can't possibly extract culture from the way we experience mental health struggles or from the ways we express, or fail to express, our emotions. Children of immigrants tend to waver between different cultural norms, impacting the way they identify, express, and regulate their emotions.

Overall, many children of immigrants lack the skills for emotion regulation. Maybe we were never taught how. Maybe we experienced childhood trauma that impacted the parts of our brains responsible for identifying, expressing, and managing emotions. Regardless, these are important skills that help decrease emotional suffering. Instead of rejecting and ignoring our emotions, we should strive to accept them all as part of life—waves we must learn to surf, not try to control. When we cry, feel sad, laugh loudly, experience joy, seethe with anger, or are expressive in any way, it can seem like we are "too much." But emotions are not right or wrong. They just are.

You are not complaining when you are being honest about your experiences or feelings. You are being true to yourself and are inviting others to connect, show up, and respond.

Defense Mechanisms
Against "Feeling"

One of the main reasons why many of us children of immigrants struggle with emotion regulation is because *our* parents struggle with it. My mom was married and out of her parents' home by eighteen (and both of my grandmothers by sixteen). She then moved from Japan to India, leaving her entire family behind, including her parents and three younger brothers, to live with her new husband and *his* parents, grandmother, and two younger siblings. Within two years, she had my brother and then, after she and my dad moved to their own home, my sister. When my parents left India for the United Kingdom, they were twenty-four and twenty-nine—and had never experienced real independence, either as single people or as a married couple. They had never been without the input and presence of other family members. These circumstances changed their dynamics with their own families of origin and also, in some ways, stunted their emotional growth: they were preoccupied with survival. Many of my clients' parents married at a young age as well, and before twenty-five, the prefrontal cortex—the part of our brains used for logic and impulse control—isn't even fully developed. Knowing this, I often ask clients who come to see me for family-of-origin issues: "How old are your parents, emotionally?" Their emotional age is often much younger than their actual age. This can help reframe (*not* absolve) their lack of emotion regulation, healthy communication skills, or maturity. Our parents' lack of emotional maturity is often a sign that *they* were deprived of the knowledge and freedom to express their emotions—the very same things we so crave from them.

> Remember: There is a difference between your parent being intentionally harmful and your parent not having the emotional acuity to form a healthier relationship. Both are painful. The former may require you to consider what boundaries you need to establish in order to protect your well-being while preserving your child-parent relationship, if you so choose. The latter can be an invitation to provide support through modeling or sharing resources for a healthier relationship.

In her book *Adult Children of Emotionally Immature Parents*, Dr. Lindsay C. Gibson shares that emotionally immature parents are often self-centered, a theme I have seen consistently in my work and conversations with other children of immigrants, as this self-preoccupation can lead to a reliance on someone else—in our case, us, their children—to intuit and soothe their emotions. This, in turn, reinforces our beliefs that our feelings are unimportant, disrupting our own development of emotional awareness.

It makes sense, then, that as adults, many of us also struggle with some version of emotional immaturity, something that requires self-awareness and accountability to outgrow. We are uncomfortable with emotions—like our parents—and even use defense mechanisms to avoid them.

Examples of defense mechanisms include redirecting our feelings onto others, refusing to accept our feelings, and regressing to child-ish behaviors when dealing with uncomfortable feelings. These are coping skills, and like all skills, they're not *always* negative or wrong. Avoiding our feelings may be a measure of self-preservation or sur-vival in relationships or situations from which we may not yet be able to extricate ourselves—like living at home as an adolescent or not having the privilege to leave a toxic work environment. It can be easier to cope with emotional distress, conflict, or threats in a be-numbed state. However, many defense mechanisms are associated in the long run with lower psychosocial functioning—or a decreased ability to perform the activities of everyday living and engage in re-lationships.

Two of the most common defense mechanisms I have observed in many immigrant communities and families are intellectualization and rationalization. Where the former is about shifting focus from the emotional to the intellectual, the latter involves explaining or justifying a situation. Either through my own work or through sto-ries in my community work, I come across children of immigrants who will say: *Tell me what I need to do to be okay. Give me the homework. Tell me which books and articles I should read to intel-lectually understand my situation. Teach me the clinical words and language for what I'm feeling.* Often, what's really happening is that we are just giving our brains something to do—thinking we are *pro-ductively* tackling an issue when, in reality, we are merely working *around* the issue or the thing we are actually avoiding, like having that difficult conversation, setting that boundary, or accepting the reality of a relationship. Intellectualization can be a way to buy time, but when used compulsively, it can create long-term problems. Even if you cognitively recognize that you are dealing with something, you can't simply think your way out of feeling. At some point, you have to address the emotional impact and ramifications of your ex-periences.

Rationalization, a sibling of intellectualization, also uses logic and rationale to avoid feelings. I have worked with and talked to children of immigrants who often rationalized their parents' behav-iors: *If I hadn't been a difficult kid, my parents would have been kinder.* Or: *My parents lived through war, so it's okay that they used physical discipline and ignored me when they were upset with me.* This goes back to the self-rejection I named earlier. We might use this mechanism to get through our childhoods or traumatic experiences, but by trying to be objective and justify our experiences, we distance ourselves from recognizing the emotional impact. Explaining something doesn't excuse it, and the reality is that rationalization maintains the harmful status quo. It allows us to continue to do what is expected of us and fulfill our duties—at a cost.

I see this happen in our parent-child relationships in more insidious ways. Many immigrant parents don't say "I love you" or "I'm proud of you." When I ask my parents if they love me and request that they explicitly say the words, they will confirm that they do and speak the phrase, but they will usually also add a qualifier: *I did XYZ for you; of course I love you.* Emotionally immature parents who utilize rationalization tend to get angry and refuse to take responsibility for their actions. For example, when a child points out something that is hurtful to a parent, the parent might respond, "Fine! I'm a bad parent even though I gave you everything!" This is a way to rationalize their love rather than accept that even though they did *some* things well, there are *other* things they did (or didn't do) that were hurtful and harmful. This ties in with how a lack of verbal affection—and how emotional neglect—can impact the development of our brains and our well-being as kids. Actions and behaviors are often rationalized to signify what so many of our parents are scared to express. Stoicism, a black-and-white mindset, and a need for control not only stunt emotional awareness but also contribute to a lack of vulnerability within our relationships.

During the years I lived at home after my assault, my own parents rationalized my depression and migraines by focusing on—and essentially blaming—my tumor rather than addressing the trauma I had experienced. It was a way for them to be comfortable confronting emotions they could not make sense of. The truth is: intellectualization and rationalization allow us to maintain our core beliefs. *See! I care. I'm a good mom!* Or: *I'm a bad daughter, so it's my fault that my parents were mean to me.*

Emotions are often telling us important messages, but when we refuse to listen, we can fail to make changes or pursue growth in ways that can be difficult yet beneficial. So how do we learn to regulate our emotions if we aren't taught the tools at home?

Learning to Identify and Name Your Feelings

One really common theme that comes up in my work with immigrants and children of immigrants is the desire to acquire language for our lived experiences and emotions. We co-construct our realities with those around us, so if we grew up in a household where there was limited emotional expression, or where feelings were labeled either "right/good" or "wrong/bad," then it makes sense that being in tune with *all* of our emotions may feel uncomfortable for us. Comfortable numbness reinforces our inclination toward emotional suppression.

Cultural layers compound this experience. As Mesquita points out in *Between Us*, culture and language shape the way we express ourselves. Words don't always translate between languages; some are untranslatable. This can impact the ways we communicate our feelings to our loved ones. Community members across different races and ethnicities have told me that they don't even have proficiency in the language of their own parents. Even if there is a shared language, research suggests that there may be a cultural mismatch between immigrant parents and kids when it comes to their patterns of emotional experience and/or expression. This is known as emotional acculturation, and it highlights how exposure and socialization in a different culture inform not only the way we live our lives but also the way we communicate and express ourselves. For instance, in one culture it may be considered appropriate to talk directly about your anger, sadness, or pain with a peer versus an elder, as you may feel more inclined to defer to the elder and therefore suppress your own emotions. In another culture, however, you may be expected to explicitly and directly advocate for your needs with your elders/ superiors. The cultural conflict persists.

According to a study done in 2007 by UCLA psychologists—a study often referred to throughout research today—verbalizing or naming feelings actually decreases activation in the part of the brain that contributes to intense and negative feelings.

But what if you struggle to even identify your feelings? Here are ten tips and tools for identifying your feelings:

1. Challenge your narratives around emotions. First, remember that having emotions doesn't make you "too emotional." Second, keep in mind that learning how to identify and embrace your emotions builds self-trust, which in turn gives you more confidence to own—and determine—your narratives.

2. Explore the mind-body connection in two ways:
   a. If you struggle to name an emotion, tune in to your body. Is your heart rate speeding up? Are you clenching your fists? These may indicate that you're feeling anger or rage.
   b. Once you're comfortable naming an emotion, focus on talking/writing about it in other ways. What does it feel like in your body? What is its intensity?

3. When you find yourself intellectualizing or rationalizing a situation, ask yourself: What am I trying to avoid here? Be specific.

4. Try to stop using concept words, and use feeling words instead. For example, some clients use the word *interesting* or *weird* to describe something. These are not feelings! Feeling wheels can be found online that can help you expand your emotion vocabulary.

5. If a certain emotion makes you feel uncomfortable, take a second to accept it and welcome it. Remember that emotions are messengers. They are not facts; they are not permanent. The more you judge yourself for having various emotions, the harder it can be to manage them.

6. My go-to question: What emotion word best describes what you are feeling, and what does the word mean in *this* situation? This will help you explore how feelings are tied to situations and cultural context.

7. If you speak more than one language, practice thinking of synonyms in different languages, or make it a group activity with friends/family. Reflect on how/why certain emotion words don't translate and what that means from a cultural standpoint.

8. When you are watching your favorite TV shows or movies, take a minute here and there to pause and name the emotion you see a character express. This will help you build emotional intelligence. Consider the following questions:
   a. What emotion are they feeling?
   b. Why are they feeling this way?
   c. How do they express it (verbally and nonverbally)?
   d. How does it impact the character's behavior, or how are they handling the emotion? (For example, if they are

angry, are they punching a wall, or are they going for a walk to calm down?) This will encourage you to identify helpful and harmful ways to manage emotions.

9. Take some time to consider how you respond to *other* people showing emotions. Are there emotions that make you feel uncomfortable? Why is that? How can you respond differently?

10. It's easy to treat feelings as fact, but remember, while they are telling you something, it doesn't mean that thing is *factual*. When you feel strong emotions—like shame, or self-disgust, or frustration—consider asking yourself: What is this feeling telling me? What's the evidence *for* this conclusion?

Facing Our Demons: Anger and Shame

As my depression persisted, my relationship with my parents grew fraught. I was often irritable, snapping at them or shutting them out, which only confused them. They categorized me as distant and uncommunicative when, in reality, I was just angry. I was angry that I wasn't getting the support I needed. I was angry that I had been assaulted. I was angry that I felt so alone. Reeling in the aftermath of my trauma and living in my parents' house, I felt myself regressing into a younger version of myself—one who was trying to carry her big feelings in silence, only to detonate at random in an unsustainable system of suppression.

Every day, moving around the house felt like tiptoeing through a minefield. My dad was struggling to manage his disappointment and fear; his anger scared me at first and then riled me up, too. Meanwhile, my mom would play middleman, trying to calm my dad while protecting me from his unfiltered rage, which, on occasion, had me literally running away from him, around and out of the house. Years later, when I was interning at a family clinic, I began to see how a parallel process can silently unfold between family members, with both parties blinded to it. Often, a mother and a young daughter *both* feel unheard, or a husband and wife *both* feel unappreciated. Both parties dig their heels in, unable to see how the other is mirroring their feelings and needs. This realization has deeply resonated with me and helped me better understand what was happening all those years ago in my own home. While my dad and I were each navigating our own hurt, we were taking it out on ourselves and each other instead of building a bridge and connecting over these shared feelings.

I didn't know then what I know now: anger protects us from feeling our shame and fear. We may feel internally motivated to choose it over the discomfort of disappointment and disconnection. When we are feeling shame, whether internally or externally imposed, there are different ways we may learn to cope with it. Developed by psychiatrist Donald Nathanson in 1992, the Compass of Shame suggests that the four shame-coping styles are withdrawal, attacking self, avoidance, and attacking others. In my work with second-generation immigrant clients, I have observed attacking of self to be a primary method of coping with shame. *If I can just become prettier, thinner, smarter, less difficult, etc., then maybe I won't feel like such a failure, or feel unlovable, or feel poorly about myself.* I theorize that this impulse for navigating shame is linked to our tendency to learn self-oriented perfectionism—both due to growing up in critical and demanding environments.

I lacked agency during the years before and after my assault, so anger became my resistance to a reality I felt like I couldn't control. My dad lacked control in our relationship, and it scared him, so anger became his mechanism to exert his authority. The explosive nature of anger, directed inward or outward, is a result of an inability to manage our emotions in a healthy way—first, an inability to identify what we are feeling, and second, an inability to learn how to manage *that* feeling before it turns into anger. Anger is often a secondary emotion, which means it's alerting us to something else that is happening and has been ignored. Anger gives us a false sense of control over our emotions, but it's usually not productive. With that said, anger is *not* a "bad" emotion. It's healthy and can alert us to feeling betrayed, frustrated, sad, disappointed, and so on. It has only been categorized as "bad" socially and culturally. The reality is that anger management is emotion management/regulation.

One client started seeing me for anger management because those close to her had told her that she needed it for lashing out suddenly and unexpectedly. In fact, after months together, we were able to identify that her anger was the result of relationship trauma that had started in childhood when a parent abandoned her and later resurfaced with a partner who often made her feel similar feelings of betrayal. By pinpointing the roots of her anger, she was able to work toward communicating her feelings healthily and approaching her current relationships from a place of curiosity and connection rather than defensiveness.

Anger manifests and impacts us all differently—especially because of sociocultural and gender narratives. Even today, my mom often tells me that I am "scary" when I am outspoken or advocating for myself. I don't yell. I don't use harsh language. I am just clear and direct. Often, she is joking, and I know that, culturally, my way of communicating is strange to her; I am going against the norms of what an "Indian woman" should or shouldn't sound like. But by labeling me scary rather than showing curiosity about or compassion for where I am coming from, she burdens me with the shame of feeling too much. In this vein, one community member shared that there were double standards in his home when it came to expressing anger.

Though emotional expression was generally discouraged, he was, as a man, more entitled to expressing anger than his sisters. These narratives we learn about emotions and emotional expression are ones we may have to practice unlearning over and over again—collectively and individually.

For many of us second-generation immigrants, anger at others feels like it's not ours to claim. This may be because of the hierarchical nature of our family systems and communities, which makes it feel like those with more power (men, elders/superiors, and so on) are more entitled to anger than we are. This is a phenomenon called anger privilege, and it begs the question: *Who* is entitled to emotional expression? One study found that Japanese people with higher social statuses expressed more anger than their lower-social-status counterparts, while lower-social-status Americans expressed more anger than their higher-social-status counterparts. In this study, anger for higher-status Japanese individuals was a display of authority and power, highlighting their freedom from cultural restrictions around emotional expression. These findings corroborated those of other studies that have suggested that because Asian cultures prioritize interdependence, objective social status reached by social/cultural criteria of social standing matters more than an individual's subjective appraisal of their own social status. Conversely, anger for lower-status Americans was a display of personal frustration in a culture that prioritizes independence and subjective social status and thus individualized personal goals, which may be blocked due to limited resources. Race, class, and gender play unavoidable roles in anger and rage. Asian Americans may feel a need to seem outwardly polite, and because of racism and socio-narratives about race, Black people may elicit fear or discomfort in others simply by speaking up or showing anger.

Even more, anger may be used by those in power as a tool of

authoritative communication and dominance, while everyone else maintains the cultural norm of emotional suppression to retain interpersonal relationships. In my family, anger expression was maintained at the top—with my dad—and characterized by one-way dissemination. I theorize that this anger expression is similar across most immigrant families—regardless of ethnicity, race, and culture.

> The next time you are feeling anger, which may turn to shame for having this feeling, reframe your language use. Instead of *I am angry*, try *I feel anger*. This will help you externalize the emotion, separate it from your core identity, and learn how to embrace it as one of many that come and go.

AS I PROCESSED my assault in the tumultuous years after I left college, I was continually trying to figure out what it meant to be in community with others while recognizing my own needs. I felt estranged from my relationships because of the shame I harbored and the secrets I was keeping. So I withdrew. Seth, my boyfriend, who wanted me to pursue therapy, encouraged me to consider writing, nudging me to find some way to externalize what I was feeling and struggling with. While I think he meant for it to be a private endeavor, I jumped in very publicly.

Despite all the ways I co-constructed my reality with the language my parents gave me—or didn't give me—I never knew that it would become essential for me to have access to more words so that I could fully express myself. In turning to writing, I discovered these words. Words to describe emotions I couldn't articulate because I had been made to feel that they were wrong or unimportant. I also learned to give myself permission to express these words.

My first blog was called *Ultimate Love Affair*, and a lot of the initial posts were just streams of consciousness, but even that was more than I had allowed myself in the previous couple of years. This was right when Instagram was starting, and blogs were still all the rage. My third post was an ode to Brené Brown's new (at that time) TED Talk on vulnerability and how much it spoke to me. I wrote: "I will never trade any of the feelings I have felt, bad or good. Everything is a lesson, and I truly believe I come out working to be a better version of me from every experience I endure." I read this now and have no idea who that person is or where her fortitude to keep pressing on came from. I struggle to reconcile her with the experiences and memories I—and other family members—have from those years, the ones that position me as weak and helpless.

Looking back now, I suppose that writing, in some way, became my version of letting my inner child come alive and a way for me to give her the things she needed but hadn't yet received from others. I also recognize my constant proclivity for writing, especially as a mode of processing, whether it was the letters I penned to my parents in my teenage years, apologizing "for being a bad kid," or the journals passed back and forth between school friends, logs of our days and unfiltered thoughts. During one of my semesters in college, I even wrote a song for the friend of mine who was struggling with severe depression as a way to remind him that he was not alone.

I also kept personal diaries for much of my life—most of which serve as relics of my past and validation of what I experienced so that the future me couldn't try to disregard the emotional impact. One of my first journals is from middle school. Each line only has about two or three words on it because my handwriting is so comically big and bubbly. My first journal entry reads: "I've realized my dad hardly hangs out with me. I mean, we do yard work or occasionally play checkers together, but I feel that I have to impress him. I love him so much though." And then later on: "My mom likes to compare me with Chandani and Ajay. I feel like I was a mistake, but I love my mom." I ramble about a crush and wonder whether my siblings have ever told their crushes that they like them. Suddenly, it takes a turn again: "My siblings are perfect, and I am not. I really do wonder if I was a mistake." The rest of the journal is about finishing school, angst over starting a new one, and friendship drama. I see a stark difference between how I wrote about school and extracurriculars on the weekdays and how I wrote about being at home for the summer or the weekends; the latter entries contain repeatedly gloomy notes—things like "miserable" and "What's wrong with me?" and "hate"—in response to my family dynamics. Even the handwriting gets smaller and less bubbly, perhaps, I imagine, to give the things I didn't know how to articulate more room to breathe in the white space—a visual representation of my conditioned emotional suppression.

My dad has always told me that actions speak louder than words, but the truth is: writing saved me. It gave me purpose and a reason to continue living through the days at home, despite the crushing weight of my depression and trauma. Writing gave me an outlet to explore my mental and emotional pain, where previously my frustration had turned to rage, my sadness had led to isolation, and my anxiety had caused me to distrust myself. I even have a bucket list that I wrote in the throes of my depression and taped on my wall next to a vision board and the Tsalagi tale of two wolves and which one you feed. It has different goals on it, such as "Swim with dolphins," "Finish my bachelor's degree," "Do a TED Talk," and "Write a book—your story might help others." I'm overcome with emotion reflecting on this, because I have since done all these things.

Though it sometimes felt like my emotional pain was drowning me, I wonder, looking back, if that pain was just trying to get me to swim deeper into myself.

Living at home, I was eagerly searching for encouragement. I was reading Cheryl Strayed's *Wild* during this time, and I was completely enamored and inspired by her courage to take off on her own and choose to get to know herself, broken pieces and all. If I wasn't reading books, I was searching for internet advice on how to manage my depression, how to deal with the tension and disconnect between me and my parents, and how to figure out what to do next. I found random articles that helped me feel less alone but nothing that completely encapsulated my own cultural and social experiences as a first-generation American and daughter of Sikh immigrants who was living at home after essentially failing out of college and still healing from recent trauma. A bit nuanced, I'd say.

So I tried to create it myself, starting a second blog called *A Quarter Life Crisis* (QLC). QLC became a mental health and inspirational space for me to share how I was feeling—really—and give advice the way I needed it. Blogging still felt abstract and anonymous enough that it didn't seem to matter; *no one was really going to read it anyway.* When I confided in Ajay about the blog, he asked me why I was being so public with my feelings, and I remember pangs of shame mixed with a staunch defiance waiting to burst out, to defend me, to not let him make me doubt the words I was putting out into the world. To own the authority of my voice over the voice others imposed on me. I was discovering a safe way to manage—and defiantly stake a claim in—my feelings. Even more, writing was a validation of what happened. A reminder that my feelings and experiences were real and a counter to anyone who would try to convince me they weren't.

. . .

I WAS STARTING to see more clearly that I had long been living in a state of shame and fear. Like a Russian nesting doll, I was shrinking into myself, and my innermost authenticity was hidden inside shame, inside a false facade, inside survival mechanisms. I had developed a learned helplessness that I couldn't shake. Nothing I did seemed to matter. I felt like a victim, and I felt apathetic toward everything and everyone. Research even suggests that depression, anxiety, and PTSD can contribute to learned helplessness. In an environment where I wasn't getting the external support I needed, my shame blossomed. I want to take a moment to distinguish between shame and guilt. Whereas guilt is based on internal values and expectations (more on this later), shame is based on external values and expectations. Whereas guilt may tell you, "I feel bad," shame may tell you, "I am bad." They are not the same.

Mesquita shares how shame is cultivated and experienced within different cultures. Shame can strengthen bonds between parents and children in some cultures, especially when it is cultivated to remind kids that their behaviors and actions are a reflection on their parents. Though it can be harmful, it's usually the result of a parent's effort to meet external demands *with* their kid. In essence, in some cultures, shame is a virtue, a tool to promote social cohesion; it is motivated by a desire not to burden others, and as previously mentioned, it is tied directly to cultures rooted in saving face and preserving honor.

Shame can cause us to internalize a sense of unworthiness, which can contribute to low self-esteem. But, of course, self-esteem and shame look different in different cultures, something that isn't overtly addressed in present-day conversations. In collectivist cultures, we may measure our self-esteem based on the groups (family, community, and so on) we participate within. Often, our personal self-esteem is tied to our collective self-esteem. And to further complicate the matter, many of us are then socialized in an environment that encourages us to build our self-esteem around our ability to be individuals by Western standards.

If I had understood that my shame was stemming from the values of my culture, thus imposing certain expectations on me, I don't believe this would have changed the fact that I felt it. But I do think that understanding how I got there in different ways would have been meaningful to the younger me. Under an individualistic lens, I may have felt like I was not smart enough or good enough, leading me to feel personally worthless and therefore inducing shame. But under a collectivist lens, I may have thought I was exposing my family to scrutiny by failing school and thus felt shame for that. Generally, this may not sound that significant; after all, the outcome was the same: I internalized shame. However, as a mental health professional, I know that it's important to recognize the nuances in how and why shame manifests in order to better serve clients who struggle with it. The relational aspect of shame, not just the individual aspect, is worth exploring. This goes back to the way we learn to construct our identities as people—through both the individual and relational roles we play.

Due to the various factors that interplayed with my shame, I learned to say sorry instead of being honest. *I'm sorry I'm depressed. I'm sorry I'm irritable. I'm sorry I talked back. I'm sorry I don't want to hang out. I'm sorry I can't seem to focus or concentrate. I'm sorry I let you down. I'm sorry you feel like this is your fault. I'm sorry I'm so difficult to love.* Saying sorry became a filler—and a plea. *Please don't give up on me. I don't know what's wrong with me.* I felt so terrible that my struggles were affecting my parents. Shame can feed our tendency to fawn, or people-please, causing us to revert to safety behaviors like apologizing, even when we don't quite understand or believe in what we're apologizing for. We learn to say sorry to gain permission to stop feeling bad; we look to other people to validate or heal us. I needed my parents to help me and love me, and I thought that apologizing would get me there. I didn't feel enough emotional safety within those relationships to explore the unknown or uncomfortable. So I ingratiated myself with others and assumed they must know better. I was happy to be in the wrong if it meant keeping myself safe.

As a child of immigrants, you may struggle with creating a strong sense of self because you may not fully align with all of the values and norms you're expected to uphold in either of the cultures you're raised within. Ultimately, you may feel shame, or be shamed, for not belonging. As you reflect on this, you may start to realize that your sense of self is determined and shaped by the role shame plays in your life and in your relationships. Shame's function within our different systems is to hold us accountable to values, morals, and societal and cultural norms. It can be used as a preventive or corrective means for learning, justice, and growth. However, it can also be used as a tool for regulation and control that is defined by expectations others have placed on you (and you have placed on yourself).

While shame is a feeling of humiliation or distress caused by acting outside the bounds of what is considered socially normal or acceptable, many of us children of immigrants have been shamed in ways that are harmful and problematic, as we have learned in adulthood. We may have been shamed for things like seeking comfort, expressing emotions, pursuing our own paths, setting boundaries or saying no, prioritizing nonfamilial relationships, doing something only when prodded, or simply making mistakes. As such, when we are shamed for these things, it reinforces learned behaviors that limit us in some capacity. Shame shuts us down. When it is utilized against us, it can further isolate us from ourselves and from people and beliefs within our systems and different cultures. It shores up a sense of self-betrayal by encouraging silence, sometimes out of fear and sometimes in hopes of acceptance. Here's how shame might have been utilized against you:

- If you were raised in a household that prioritized certain religious or spiritual beliefs, then shame might have been used to instill fear of being ostracized or receiving religious punishment as a way to control your behavior.
- In some collectivist environments, shame can be used to preserve group harmony and respect, maintain the peace, and encourage fitting in.
- In some individualistic environments, shame can be used to encourage taking risks, being different, and having assertive or aggressive behaviors.
- If you live, work, or love in environments or dynamics where a hierarchy is prioritized, then shame can be used to retain or weaponize power, position, obedience, and respect.
- In some households where service to others may supersede one's own needs, shame can be used to discourage boundaries, privacy, self-care, and the pursuit of individual happiness.
- Shame may arrive as a reaction to criticism and can serve as a motivator to "save face" and uphold the systems that prioritize social capital, honor, and reputation over healing, choice, or fairness.
- In different contexts, shame may be used to feed competition and remind us that our peers are doing better than us, we aren't where we're expected to be, or we must be the best/ perfect to be worthy.

Writing as a Tool for Connection

By writing my blogs, I challenged my shame-driven narratives. I was giving myself the validation I hadn't found from others. I was gifting myself self-expression and a space where I didn't feel the need to apologize. I *wasn't* sorry for who I was or where I was in life. I could re-create myself: the version of myself I *wanted* to be. I've realized over the years that I'm not alone. Now that I have a community of creatives and writers, I see that we are all drawn to a medium that allows us to reclaim our own agency. Many of my friends who are fellow children of immigrants are unabashedly sharing stories and work that is representative of their own experiences or cultures, even if only tangentially. Especially when it comes to folks who are story-telling, I think these stories—fiction or nonfiction in any format (video, writing, podcast)—offer a cathartic release and a safe way for some of us to explore subjects and experiences we aren't yet ready or willing to confront head-on. They are a balm for our own wounds—individual and collective. Writing may not be for every-one, but expression in any form is a reclamation of our voices and our senses of self. When I asked members of the Brown Girl Therapy community what outlets they use to express emotions, I was inun-dated with hundreds of replies that centered creative or physical stimulation, such as dancing, painting, martial arts, scream singing, stand-up comedy, and more.

Writing allowed me to learn cognitive reappraisal, a form of emo-tion regulation in which one reframes their thoughts about an event to change its emotional impact. Instead of solely focusing on the ways I felt not enough, I was able to acknowledge my tenacity and resilience. I never explicitly shared my stories of depression, trauma, and perceived failure on *QLC*, but I did write generally about mental health, life transition, and sociocultural expectations and pressure. I was able to redefine and reevaluate my narratives, especially as they relate to my perceived failure and the tying of my self-concept to it. I stopped giving meaning to "failure" and started considering my journey as a redirection. Expressing and externalizing allowed me to create space between myself and my emotions rather than internalizing them as part of my identity. Cognitive reappraisal also gave me room to expand. I claimed a little corner of the internet, and it was mine. It was space for me to take up.

After about a month of writing, I publicized my blog, sharing it on Facebook and emailing a few close friends to tell them that it might explain why I had been MIA and give them a glimpse into my head- and heartspace. I started to get messages from peers whom I'd either lost touch with or been disengaged from for months; they told me that they related to what I was writing. Some even sent paragraphs to me, sharing the comparable and current hardships that they felt lonely in. It was the first time that I learned the power of sharing oneself with the world—a reminder that we don't have to navigate our struggles alone and, even more, that when one person shares their story vulnerably, it can give others the courage to do the same. Suddenly, I was connected with others amid my isolation.

I would hear from a therapist much later in life that when something terrible happens to you, you have two choices: you can become bitter at the world and to other people because you have been hurt, or you can become deeply empathetic toward others and help them heal because you truly understand pain. I look back on Sahaj then, and I remember a twenty-two-year-old shell, overshadowed by despair and disappointment. I wanted someone I loved to help me, to hold my hand. Then I realized I had to hold my own hand. It wasn't a sudden shift for me; instead, gradually during those years at home, I stopped focusing on what I couldn't change—and how resentful and frustrated and angry it made me—and I started to focus on what I could. A lot of time went by where I was still waking up in the same house with the same problems and the same sense of demoralization. There was no doubt that I still needed professional help, but since I didn't have access to it the way I needed, I found other ways to forgive myself for my paralysis over the years and to explore the gray, challenging this tendency to overgeneralize.

I shifted from learned helplessness into learned optimism. Instead of continuing to see myself through a deficiency lens—all the things I could not do, all the things I believed I was too stupid or too broken to do—I explored what it meant to accept my limitations and honor my strengths. In one of my first posts, I wrote: "Embrace the breakdown. That's prime time for recreation. . . . One time, it really will all fall into place. Until then, let yourself fail, fall, and break apart—because that's when you are in the perfect position to piece yourself back together into a better and stronger person." I finally felt tethered to something with passion *and* purpose for the first time in my life. Though it can be difficult for me to see or feel connected to post–high school Sahaj, she's there, she persisted, and she came out the other side.

One of the pillars of my work as a narrative therapist is considering the landscape of identity. This involves exploring with my clients not only stories that are painful but also ones that provide exceptions to their current dominant narratives. When I was working with a client debilitated by low self-esteem, we discussed people, conversations, and times she felt *good* about herself. Though she was convinced these were few and far between, by challenging her story, we were able to list over one hundred instances in just the previous six months. It's important for us to indulge in alternative storylines, because they can plant seeds for new perspectives.

I recognize now that through writing, I was able to indulge in alternative storylines in my life narrative—the moments I helped others, even when I was struggling, or finally paying attention to the fact that writing has been a passion of mine since I was a young kid. I have always been enough, just a different type of enough. I have not been failing; I have been navigating setbacks. And in giving myself permission to give life to these alternate storylines, I started to disempower my dominant narrative. After all, it's the little shifts that lead to the breakthrough.

Though QLC was more informal than the kind of writing I would post publicly now, I can't ignore how closely tied it is to the work I do today. I interviewed other people struggling with their quarter-life crises. I also added a section where people could write in and get short pieces of advice from me on their dilemmas. Some of my first posts were about the stress of following your own path, how to self-care in a community, and trying and failing! I see now that these formed the early foundations for what I have built with Brown Girl Therapy, *Culturally Enough.*, and my advice column in *The Washington Post.*

The Domino Effect

A few months after I started my second blog, one of my posts got featured on Paulo Coelho's blog; coincidentally, it was about putting your own oxygen mask on first and, more importantly, learning to be a friend to yourself. This feature was a tangible success I could brag about and share with my parents, as I still ached for their validation. Though this turned my family's eyes onto my writing, it was still something I was doing for myself. Looking back, I presume this was probably the first seed that planted the idea that writing could *actually* be a career choice.

A few months later, I received an email about a contest to win an internship at an AOL company, including *HuffPost*, for the summer. I was certain that there was no way I could win something like this. *I'm not competent. I'm not qualified. I'm not worthy.* I've since learned that these thoughts don't necessarily go away, but we can choose to scoot them into the background and bring to the forefront a different voice—the one whispering that it wants to try anyway and all we have to do is take the first step.

That's what I had done: listened to the voice and entered anyway. Three weeks later, I was sitting in the parking lot of my community college, listening to "Titanium" by Sia and eating french fries, when I got the call that I had been chosen as one of the finalists for an internship at *HuffPost*. After a round of interviews, I was selected to spend the summer in New York interning at the company. This was my first formal foray into writing and the media world.

Because I was still finishing my associate's degree, my time in the city was short-lived and hectic. When I wasn't at work, I was at my sister's apartment, where I was living, finishing assignments for my online courses. I had no idea how this internship would build foundations for an entire career; it was just an eight-week commitment. But in retrospect, I think the experience allowed me, for the first time, to consider a different future for myself.

I can look back now with a magnifying glass and find the strengths I was blinded to then. I was smart, just not in the way that my family defined it. I was creative. I had grit. And I was resourceful like my parents had been when they were flung into a new situation. It wasn't a moral failing that I couldn't make it work in college right away. I didn't choose to struggle (though struggling is okay!), but my family treated me like it was a choice I had made. I can't change who I've been or what I've been through. But I can change what happens next.

My parents were taught that certain things are mandatory, but growing up in the West, I learned that I actually had options. This was an immense privilege that my parents didn't have access to. After moving back home to Virginia when my internship ended, I finished my associate's degree and, with this new door open to me, came to a crossroads in my educational journey. Did I attempt to go back to a four-year college in Virginia, or did I try something else?

Learning emotion regulation and exploring your shame-based behavior

Seven Useful Emotion Regulation Strategies

- Practice cognitive reappraisal skills, or thought replacement. This will allow you to make room for varied emotions and thoughts and invite a different perspective. For example, if you have a friend who hasn't responded to a text, you may think, *My friend hates me!* Replace that thought with a more balanced alternative, such as *My friend is busy at the moment. I am sure we will touch base soon.*

- Engage in an activity or a hobby that requires concentration and helps you feel grounded (e.g., playing a video game, reading a book, or doing a crossword puzzle). This will occupy your mind and disrupt a negative thought/emotional spiral.

- Practice mindfulness through deep breathing, counting to ten, or engaging in a sensory relaxation exercise or activity.

- Tune in to the needs of your physical body. Are you drinking enough water? Eating well? Moving enough? Getting restorative sleep?

- Explore situation selection and situation modification to help create situations that are more emotionally desirable. For instance, imagine you are going home for a weekend and have to see a sibling whom you don't enjoy being around because they are constantly berating you. Instead of doing it anyway, because it's expected of you, consider where you have agency that feels right. This may be choosing a different weekend so you don't overlap at all, or modifying the current situation—like shortening your trip—to decrease or alter your emotional experience.

- Practice emotional expression in safe relationships to help counteract any internalization of negative familial or cultural narratives about having and expressing feelings. This may be difficult at first, but it can be life-changing to find even just one relationship in which you feel safe being honest and vulnerable.

- Instead of seeing situations as challenges or attacks *on* you, view them as opportunities for you to grow, respond healthily and differently, or make a change. This builds emotional flexibility and adaptability. (This does not apply to systemic oppression, discrimination, or racism.)

Unpacking Your Shame-Based Behavior

In order to unpack our relationship with shame, we must be curious and honest about what we feel ashamed of and where we learned to feel that way.

Shame-Based Behavior Cycle

1. Action.
2. External responses that induce shame.
3. Internal shame-based belief.
4. Learned behavior to avoid shame.

Example #1

1. As a kid, you make a mistake.
2. A parent reacts: "You should have known better" or "Why did you do that?"
3. You believe that your worthiness is tied to your ability to be perfect.
4. You learn to develop perfectionist tendencies, and you start setting unrealistically high expectations in an effort to protect yourself from feeling shame.

Example #2

1. You set a boundary around a behavior you no longer wish to tolerate.
2. You're told that you are ungrateful or disrespectful.
3. You start to believe that speaking up for yourself is less important than other people's comfort.
4. You engage in unhealthy relationship dynamics for fear of seeming impolite, disrespectful, or ungrateful.

Example #3

1. You are the first in your family to pursue something different.
2. You're shamed for not being like the rest of your family/community.
3. You feel like you are betraying others if you pursue your own happiness.
4. You start to live a double life and hide parts of yourself for fear you'll be rejected.

Example #4

1. You don't act in a way that is expected or considered appropriate in your parents' origin culture.
2. You're shamed and scolded for being too "Western."
3. You feel like you don't belong and are not understood.
4. For approval and belonging, you develop performative behaviors that may be inauthentic.

Example #5

1. You struggle with your mental health.
2. You're shamed and told that you shouldn't be feeling this way.
3. You feel like your problems aren't valid.
4. You learn to struggle in silence.

Now I want you to reflect on your own shame-based experiences.

- What's something you've been shamed for?
- How did you know you were feeling a product of shame?
- What did it make you believe about yourself? Pay attention to your negative self-talk and the story it constructs.
- What other feelings are accompanying the shame?
- What is the social or cultural context that led to feeling shame?
- What behavior did you adopt to avoid feeling this shame again?
- Even though this learned behavior technically has a purpose, how does it *not* serve you?
- What can you do in similar moments to feel less shame? Is there something you can do or say to yourself that will help you get out of the shame web?

Journal Exercise on Shame

What is something that you wish everyone knew about you but find hard to share? Why is it hard? Where did you learn to be ashamed of this?

Chapter Six

Where Do My Parents End and I Begin?

---

often tell my clients that nothing will change until something is changed. I was struggling, and I was banging on the same door that seemingly everyone else had walked through, but I didn't have the code or key. My dad and I continued to get into explosive arguments, deteriorating our relationship and any opportunity to connect. He couldn't communicate his concerns, so instead they were conveyed as distrust, control, and anger; I couldn't communicate my needs, so I retreated, seeming disinterested and dismissive. Something needed to change.

And, at twenty-four, I was ready to be out in the world. Ajay had graduated with his third post-college degree—a master's, a juris doctor, and now a medical degree—and was living in Atlanta with his wife and three-year-old son. Chandani, who had gotten married to a family-approved Sikh man and moved out of New York, was venturing off on an extended honeymoon. I felt stuck in place. I wanted to put my family's dreams for me aside and bring my own needs and desires to the forefront. (If you're from an immigrant family, you probably shuddered at that sentence.)

So, two years after my assault, I decided to move to New York City. My boyfriend, Seth, had moved back after his Fulbright. My brother and sister had both lived there for several years, and I had witnessed their own love affairs with the city. And I had already dipped my toes in for two summers and loved it. I wanted to officially call it home.

I once had a client tell me that she craved moving to a new country, even if just for a year, to have the independence and experiences of living on her own. She had lived within a twenty-mile radius of her family for her whole life and was expected to go home often. In one session, she recalled how her aunt practically begged her not to move far away; her aunt was getting old and didn't know how much time they had left together. My client considered where her aunt was coming from as a Vietnamese refugee who had fled for fear of political persecution. Moving to a new country had been a scary experience for her. Why on earth would her niece *choose* that? My client wondered what fears and traumas she had inherited from her family members who were forced to flee their home country. For many immigrants and refugees, change signifies the possibility of risk and failure. My parents were driven by a similar fear-based mindset as a result of struggling during their early years in America.

Yes, many of us children of immigrants inherit the fears and traumas of our parents and ancestors, but we also inherit their dreams and resilience. Of course, there were risks involved in moving to New York City. I didn't have a bachelor's degree. I didn't have an apartment lined up and would be couch surfing with friends. At the time, I didn't know why my dad finally gave in, but recently, my mom told me that she had encouraged my dad to support me in leaving because things were so awful between the two of us. She thought it would be best for us to have space from each other. When my dad and I would get into explosive fights, she would physically place herself between us, begging my dad to stop. When we'd split to our designated rooms, my mom would come upstairs to check on me. I'd be pacing at the foot of my bed or sobbing into a pillow—wavering between rage and debilitating helplessness. "It'll be fine tomorrow," she would often say. "He'll cool down tomorrow."

This always infuriated me. *Tomorrow, tomorrow, tomorrow.* I mistook her inability to discuss what had happened *today* as an endorsement of my dad's temper and an assumption that, somehow, I deserved it. I couldn't see then that she was acting in the only way she knew how. She wanted to physically protect me, but she didn't understand the emotional impact or how to tend to my emotional wounds. I never knew she had these private conversations with my dad. Even though she may not have understood it herself, she knew something—anything—needed to change.

I had spent years so eager to please my parents that it eroded my sense of self. I was now desperate to figure things out for myself.

Filial Piety, Enmeshment, and Codependency

Moving to New York wasn't meant to hurt my parents; it was my way of running toward something different. It can sometimes feel like immigrant parents and grandparents have dibs on how many risks are allowed in a family. They took risks to pursue a different life; therefore, their kids should never have to take any. Much like my Vietnamese client, I was carrying the experiences of my grandparents and great-grandparents, who fled their homes during India's Partition of 1947. *How can I choose something for myself when so many in my family were forced to make difficult choices for their loved ones?* But this thinking isn't fair.

Our parents expect us to trust and respect them implicitly, but we may get very little trust and respect in return. The concept of filial piety—an expectation and reinforcement of duty, loyalty, deference, and service to one's parents/elders—is very common across varying immigrant cultures, particularly those originating in Asia. This often involves honoring and maintaining a certain social order within the family system. Filial piety may look like obeying your parents' expectations and requests, offering to care for your aging parents in your home, unconditionally loving and standing by your parents, or financially supporting your parents.

Recent psychological research suggests that many children who are in family systems that prioritize filial piety fall somewhere on the spectrum between reciprocal filial piety, or *wanting* to do good by their parents out of sincere affection, and authoritarian filial piety, or *needing* to do good by their parents out of obligation. This can vary based on how close a child really feels to their parents and whether, or to what degree, the relationship between child and parent is rooted in affection versus rigid demands.

Filial piety intersects with an implicit belief in many immigrant households that children are indebted to their parents because their parents brought them into this world and took care of them. Whereas Western narratives of parenting tend to discourage conditional reciprocity for simply being someone's kid, espousing raising children as independent and freethinking individuals, filial piety prioritizes interdependence and indebtedness. In fact, filial piety can compound the gratitude shame that many children of immigrants experience, reinforcing the notion that our choices are tied to how much we love or care about our parents. This goes back to the duty-versus-fulfillment narratives that many of us struggle with.

However, that's not to say that filial piety is *bad*; it's a beautiful value. It's also not unique to Asian or immigrant family systems;

however, it is recognized as more of a norm in these cultures. When I asked members of the Brown Girl Therapy community what aspects of their families and cultures felt misunderstood, or were even considered negative, by outsiders, the most common response was how normalized it is in non-Western cultures to live at home and be interdependent with family members and parents. The value of familism is a strong cultural value for many, emphasizing supportive family relationships. One study researching this value found that among Asians, Europeans, and Latines living in the U.S., Latines—most specifically Latinas—have the highest levels of familism.

Familism and filial piety look different for every child and sibling, though. Filial piety emphasizes the importance of the moral obligation of firstborns—especially sons—to take care of their parents and execute family duties. I see how my brother has internalized this pressure so deeply that it sometimes creates tension in his other relationships and with his ability to put himself first. I've heard from many community members who've shared how being the eldest created a pressure they haven't been able to escape, even in older age. One mentioned that she had to do everything her parents expected of her to set a good example for her younger siblings. Another shared how *he* had to deal with the consequences of his younger sibling's mistakes, hearing things like "Why didn't you guide him the right way?"

These dynamics trickle through the family system, impacting its functioning as a whole. In Western families, family members are given a bit more independence throughout, and siblings are viewed more as peers. By contrast, Eastern families (and some non-Eastern immigrant families) posit a vertical social hierarchy depending on sibling order and gender—men before women, oldest before youngest—and reverence is unidirectional. Even in Punjabi—and many other cultures/languages—there are proper terms that younger siblings use to address older siblings, and when I wouldn't use *didi* or *veerji* growing up, I was castigated for being disrespectful.

I stopped using *didi* and *veerji* earlier than my parents wanted. Even though my sister and I are now very close and have a strong sisterhood and friendship, I still sometimes feel pressured by this expectation of reverence and deference toward her, and I still struggle with a fear of questioning or correcting her. She herself doesn't expect this, but I've so internalized the emphasis on hierarchy that I'm unsure if I'll ever *really* unlearn it.

THERE CAN COME a point, though, where interdependence morphs into dependence within a family. This can lead to enmeshment. An enmeshed family is one in which there are permeable boundaries and a lack of autonomy between members; in fact, separateness can even be perceived as a betrayal of family. This can show up as having to account for every minute of our time or needing confirmation from others that we are making the right decisions; basically, a lack of autonomy equates to a lack of agency over our lives and choices. Just to be clear: if enmeshment is understood as closeness in a way that feels good to someone, it's not necessarily negative. But for most children of immigrants, enmeshment and the *idea* of family closeness come with stipulations: expected compliance, unconditional tolerance, lack of autonomy, unilateral control (usually top-down in family hierarchies), and a lack of privacy.

I once heard someone describe enmeshment as a loofah in which a bunch of fibers mesh together to make a single ball. Family ties and relationships are intertwined, and boundaries are created around that family system. In Western narratives of boundaries, everyone is their own person, and everyone has permission to create boundaries around their sense of self; they can choose to incorporate their relationships but are not necessarily mandated or obligated to do so.

In Western models of family functioning, high rigidity, or set rules and discipline, and family enmeshment are correlated with negative family functioning, but this is not the case when researchers study families in non-Western cultures. In fact, religion and culture can promote a sense of dependency between people, allowing members of a family or community to understand their roles and find purpose within them. Generally, these underlying differences serve as another example of how our study and understanding of families and family functioning further alienate entire populations and their cultural values. At work is the misleading assumption that "function" and "dysfunction" are the same for everyone, in the same way "normal" may be used as an umbrella term.

Enmeshment entails an overinvolvement that is normalized in many immigrant families. It's normal for my parents to open my mail without my consent, even though I'm an adult. It's normal in my Indian culture for married adults to live at home in joint families with their parents/in-laws and extended family members. For many children of immigrants, parents have a say in career or partner choices. Elders and community members talk freely about our bodies and our looks or ask intimate questions about our marriages or child-rearing plans. Parents may even have access to their adult children's finances. Several of my second-gen clients felt extreme pressure from their parents that went well beyond an expectation to financially care for them. In one case, my client's mom expected her to share detailed records of how she was spending the money that *she* earned in her day job. Her mom would often excuse this behavior as just wanting to prevent her from making the same financial mistakes that she made.

Enmeshed families also like to keep all discussions about anything difficult or negative inside the family. Sound familiar? My family has struggled with a sense of shame over things not being perfect, someone being mentally or physically unwell, and someone struggling in their career or relationship. We hoard family secrets, reaffirming the isolation and expectation of silence. And because only a handful of us are privy to these secrets, we start to rely on each other to degrees that may be unhealthy. Yet we do not get the care we need or deserve. This perpetuates the idea that no one else will be able to truly care for us or understand our pain and struggles. As such, we sink even deeper into our silence. Then add in parentification, and we build our entire identity around a narrative that we must be of service to others to be worthy. Like me, many children of immigrants I have worked with and talked to became confidants for at least one parent at a young age. In such a scenario, the parent will often share inappropriate personal information about their marriage or emotional state. Sometimes this dynamic even replaces the intimacy that parent has with the other parent/spouse. It's one thing to seek support and love from a family member but quite another to rely on them to help regulate difficult emotions or navigate *other* relationships. The latter can lead to a dependency or codependency—often a mark of enmeshment—in which the child feels responsible for the parent's well-being and happiness. My mom often tells me, "I don't know what I would do without you," inadvertently placing this pressure on me to ensure she is taken care of.

Often, emotional transference between family members skews downward in the hierarchy, and a younger family member absorbs an older family member's feelings and emotions. In some households with traditional gender norms and embedded patriarchal values, this can also happen between men and women unidirectionally. As the youngest, I was often expected to put my needs aside for my older siblings and my parents. And so I learned to align my own feelings with theirs: when they were upset, I usually began to feel similarly. There wasn't any barrier separating their emotional experience from mine.

For many of us children of immigrants, this enmeshment can further complicate our efforts to emotionally self-regulate. Because we are conditioned to prioritize our parents' or others' feelings over our own and absorb their tension and anxiety, we make a home for it inside ourselves. This prevents us from being able to set boundaries, let alone identify or understand our own feelings, thoughts, and opinions. When I took to Brown Girl Therapy to poll children of immigrants about the responsibility they feel for their parents' and other family members' feelings, 92 percent of 6,092 said they feel responsible for them. In *Adult Children of Emotionally Immature Parents*, Dr. Lindsay C. Gibson discusses internalizers versus externalizers, a concept that outlines how people fall into one of two different groups in the way they assess problems that they encounter in their relationships. According to this theory, externalizers—who are marked by emotional immaturity—tend to think of problems and solutions as someone else's fault and responsibility, while internalizers often assume it's their job to fix or take care of things when there's a problem. I've observed through stories and anecdotes that a lot of immigrant parents are externalizers raising internalizers. Repairing, reestablishing, and even maintaining connection should be the role of a parent or guardian, but many children of immigrants feel the need to step into a "rescuer" role and make things right or manage their parents' emotions. This is another clear sign of enmeshment and a lack of boundaries. Blurred roles due to unhealthy family dynamics can reinforce enmeshment, too.

I had a client who struggled to form a healthy relationship with her younger (adult) brother because she couldn't stop acting like a second mom to him. On the one hand, she had been conditioned to step in as a parental figure growing up, and on the other, she had absorbed her mom's feelings and thoughts when her mom complained about her brother. Much of our work revolved around her challenging her belief that providing support meant taking on *their* roles—as mom and son—and doing the work for them. This looked like encouraging her to not only listen to and validate her mom's and brother's feelings but also urge them to talk *to* each other rather than *through* her. By differentiating her roles—as daughter and sister rather than partner and mother—she was slowly learning to reinvest in healthier relationships and unlearning codependent tendencies.

Compliance and loyalty to our families or parents may come at the expense of everything else—our needs, passions, desires, and even basic functioning. So many children of immigrants I work with and talk to are constantly confronting the conditioned belief that in exchange for unwavering commitment to our parents, we can guarantee their love for us. There's a difference between being close and being in codependent relationships that may be hurting us.

This goes both ways. For most of our immigrant parents, our successes and milestones are considered to be a direct reflection of *their* parenting, which is classic enmeshment thinking, as it hinges their self-worth on our accomplishments. This blurs the lines between supporting/celebrating our goals or achievements and imposing their opinions and needs on them. Again, sound familiar? When I fail, they feel like failures, but when I am happy or celebratory, they feel like they can take credit. The enmeshment and emotional transference make it hard for individuals in a family system to separate themselves from the thoughts or feelings of their family members. Instead, they absorb and permeate into one another. Making choices for our own reasons is a form of emotional gymnastics that can often take Herculean mental strength.

In her book *Codependent No More*, Melody Beattie talks about how codependency is often a reaction to extreme and prolonged stress, and she says that families whose norms discourage open and vulnerable communication can have a higher risk of codependent relationships.

MOVING TO NEW YORK meant going out into the world, publicly, without a degree. In turn, and more importantly, it meant I was defying and disappointing my parents. After merely surviving through trauma, illness, and failure for years, I wanted to know what it could feel like to thrive.

It's clear to me now that I had developed a dynamic with my parents wherein we were so intensely focused on one another that I began to internalize their anxieties, worries, and feelings. As I felt more paralyzed and trapped, they became more anxious and concerned, and so on. It was a negative feedback loop. Through a family systems lens, and as someone who has worked with immigrant families, I have learned that—even though it was no one's intention—this entrapment made me feel completely enveloped by my identity as a daughter rather than as an individual human.

Differentiation of self, or individuation, can be considered a Westernized concept, so it's something I don't accept as an inherent good or automatic goal, the way it is so often presented in therapeutic contexts. It really does depend on the client and their own cultural and personal goals and needs. For many, complete detachment is not the goal. But neither is enmeshment. This is where I believe differentiation can offer a middle ground. Though differentiation can feel selfish, it's also a way to acknowledge your own emotions and needs while retaining the capacity to be emotionally connected with—not overwhelmed by—another person. It is effectively turning your relationships from a circle—where you feel trapped—into a Venn diagram—where there's room for you to exist with and alongside them. It is not being emotionally closed off but, rather, having awareness of what *you're* feeling and not automatically absorbing what *they're* feeling.

My personal goal has never been to detach from my family system; instead, it has been to lovingly detach from internalized narratives not of my authorship while also picking and choosing what aligned with my own values and beliefs. If my parents and I were ever going to have a real, honest shot at having a healthier relationship, I was going to need to separate myself from them for a period of time in order to truly tune in to my own voice and detangle myself from some of my codependent behaviors. (It's a privilege to even be able to conceptualize this—a product of growing up in the U.S., with access to choices and different gender norms. I also know that for some children of immigrants, the mere act of separating themselves from their parents can mean losing them altogether.)

At this point, I didn't know where my relationship with my parents would go. I just knew that it couldn't stay where it was.

Exploring Our Own Values

Moving to New York was exhilarating. It was every bit the experience you see in movies: young woman moves to New York with big dreams, struggles with big-city life, realizes she's not that important in a city with more than eight million others, and adapts. It was dynamic in all the ways my life at home had felt static.

After several weeks of couch surfing and feverishly looking for an apartment, I found a Craigslist ad from a similar-aged Californian woman who was also new to the city and looking for three roommates to join her in a four-bedroom, two-and-a-half-bath apartment on the ground floor in the East Village. She was specifically looking for roommates who had shared interests and wanted to be friends outside the apartment. We met; I saw the place. And then I was living in my first adult home with three like-minded women.

I learned how to live on a very tight budget, since I was burning through my minimal savings. I learned to listen to the voice in my head about what I liked when it came to design, or furniture, or artwork—without someone else telling me if it was the right aesthetic. These were small choices that allowed me to create and explore my own opinions. I reveled in having my own space, even if it was an eight-by-ten-foot makeshift room that was technically part of the kitchen but had French doors put in as a divider. I learned to discern between what I wanted and what I really needed. I learned accountability—to my roommates, to my workmates, and to myself. Even the smallest of choices can teach us how to really care for ourselves. And I wanted to make my own choices, even if they were sometimes the wrong ones.

I felt, to my surprise, a lifting of the layers of shame that had been building up over years and years of living inside survival mechanisms, of overwhelmingly feeling that *nothing matters*. The new pressure to make a life in New York challenged me to provide for myself an internal support system. For once, I didn't feel helpless. I saw I could find what I needed, and I could give it to myself.

Through my physical, and thus emotional, separation from my parents, I started learning what I value. I grew to be wildly compassionate and empathic, advocating for mental health any way I could. My first September in the city, on World Suicide Prevention Day, I printed one hundred flyers with suicide statistics to hand out in Union Square by myself. Somewhere inside me, I knew this was eventually going to be my life's work, but I couldn't fathom where I was in my journey. I told only two or three people. I remember feeling embarrassed for putting myself out there so vulnerably, stopping people before or after their commutes to spread information on a topic I was passionate about. Most of the time, I was ignored or waved off, but having that literal and figurative room to expand allowed me to give life to new parts of myself. Though I had previously been driven by my vulnerability in some ways (writing and showing up for loved ones who were suffering) and had been shamed out of being vulnerable (my failure and saving face), it became clear to me then just how much I value vulnerability. This is a value of mine that has not wavered since that day in Union Square. If anything, it has only strengthened.

I had grown up believing that my loyalty to my parents, to their dreams and desires for me, should supersede anything I ever wanted for myself. I didn't know what my values were apart from theirs, and it took my moving to New York to even begin asking myself those questions, let alone to begin figuring out the answers. And I know I'm not alone. In my work with children of immigrants, conflicting values come up time and time again. We have not done the requisite level of self-reflection and self-exploration—and likely have not been encouraged to pursue it—to truly know our own values.

Over the years, I have observed that the two values many children of immigrants struggle with the most are loyalty and fairness. And they go hand in hand. On the one hand, we must be loyal to our parents, usually at the expense of the loyalty we owe ourselves. We are expected to choose between them and ourselves, and also to implicitly understand that choosing loyalty to ourselves is immoral. On the other hand, when we choose them, we can end up feeling frustrated or cheated. It's unfair—that we can't express ourselves and that these expectations are unidirectional. That sense of injustice often then serves as a catalyst for the anger and/or chronic guilt many of us feel if we do choose ourselves. Then we struggle to even know or understand how to express these emotions.

Humans have a strong desire to maintain the status quo, and children of immigrants are no different. When you're feeling displaced between communities and cultures, it can be easier to convince yourself that the way to claim ownership over your experience is to adopt the values and norms of those around you (your parents, say, or your friends), even if those don't feel authentic to who you are. Fitting in can be a form of self-preservation.

For us children of immigrants, there's often a disconnect between how we engage and live our lives outside the home and how we engage and live our lives with our families/communities. This disconnect between immigrant parents (who likely uphold the values and norms of the countries they came from) and their children (who likely start to adopt those of the new country) has been called intergenerational cultural dissonance, which can lead to intergenerational conflict. And it can significantly impact our mental health. Even more, these handed-down values and norms can feel like relics of pasts that no longer even exist in our parents' countries of origin, yet they hold on tightly in the name of cultural preservation.

The solution isn't necessarily picking one or the other but, rather, gaining a personal understanding of what is important to you. Once you start to excavate your values, you can begin reorienting your life toward your own sense of security and happiness. Values-driven choices can be hard because they require understanding how your own values may overlap with or differ from those of the people you love. They also require getting clear, for yourself, on how living out your values may change certain relationships, and whether you are okay with that. These moments of self-discovery can be overwhelming, but be patient with yourself; change doesn't happen overnight.

The Dreaded B-Word: Boundaries

In learning our values, we can begin to learn boundaries. Living in New York, I could decide when and how often to be in contact with my parents, and I could decide when and how often I needed time to myself. Factoring in self-reflection time allowed me to get to know myself and what is important to me. Physical distance drew some lines that I was not able to put in place on my own. Because flights were expensive, I couldn't be expected to go home on a whim. I could come up with a valid excuse as to why I couldn't pick up the phone. I started to get a sense of myself by exploring my own limits. I finally had the space to become who I wanted to be rather than who I was told to be—and I was willing to respond to the pull I felt.

What I didn't learn until much later is that there are many different types of boundaries—intellectual, emotional, temporal, material, professional, financial, and physical—and there are different strengths of boundaries. You can have rigid or really tight boundaries about one thing and porous or really loose boundaries about another thing. Or your boundaries may change between different people and relationships. In my clinical work and through my many boundaries workshops, I have observed that the most common types of boundaries with which children of immigrants struggle are temporal and emotional. This means that many of us struggle to set boundaries around how often and for how long we see, talk to, or interact with people, leaving these decisions up to the whims of the other party. We also struggle with protecting our emotional energy and setting limits on our emotional capacity to listen to, manage, or be responsible for others' feelings.

DIFFERENT TYPES
OF BOUNDARIES

EMOTIONAL: Learning to identify and name your feelings. Paying attention to how people make you feel and advocating for yourself and your emotional needs.

TEMPORAL: Learning and recognizing who respects your time and who expects your time. Being mindful of where you spend your time and how much time you spend on different daily tasks.

MATERIAL: Being mindful of how you and others treat your possessions and your space, and learning what you are—and are not—comfortable sharing with others.

PROFESSIONAL: Learning to distinguish between work and nonwork priorities. Advocating for fair and appropriate compensation. Recognizing your comfort levels in how you engage with colleagues.

PHYSICAL: Learning what your physical body needs are (like sleeping, eating, and hydrating). Getting clear on your comfort levels around personal space and physical touch.

INTELLECTUAL: Allowing yourself to have your own thoughts and opinions. Paying attention to where and with whom you feel safe sharing them. Accepting a difference of opinions and learning how to have healthy dialogue.

FINANCIAL: Recognizing your own needs to maintain financial wellness, including advocating for and prioritizing your own budgetary needs and being mindful of what you spend daily.

The very first time I remember setting boundaries and saying no was when I was nineteen. NINETEEN! I was in my second year of college, and I had been seeing my college therapist, Mel. My parents often called me home on the weekends, especially if my older siblings were home. It was expected of me to always be at their beck and call, and there was no regard for whether I had plans or *wanted* to come home. Family was the priority. Plus, I was only one and a half hours away, so it wasn't a long trip. I remember one particular weekend when it was homecoming at my college, and I told my dad I didn't want to come home because there was a dance and I wanted to spend quality time with new friends. He wasn't having it. *Your whole family is together.* So I told him I'd come home later on Friday night, after dinner with my friends, sacrificing the rest of the weekend and the dance. As I drove home that night, I started feeling resentful and angry. I pulled up to the driveway, stopped the car, saw my parents and siblings in the kitchen through the windows, and then backed up the car and drove back to school. A three-hour round trip. I cried on the entire drive back to school, audibly talking to myself in the car, scared that I was doing something so wrong. I got into a terrible argument with my family that night when I called to tell them I wasn't coming home. They said I was being "selfish." There wasn't anything specific I missed; I'd just decided not to go home when I was told to do so. I know I didn't have the communication skills in my toolbox at that point to constructively explain how I needed to do some things for myself and that didn't mean I loved my family any less. I know I handled it poorly. I spent the rest of that weekend making memories with new people who would later become like family to me, and though I didn't regret my choice—and through a Western lens, I wasn't doing anything "wrong"—I felt like a bad daughter and sister for choosing to prioritize myself and a new community of friends.

It's small now. I doubt my family even remembers this or knows I actually made that drive in the first place. But for me this was the first time I chose myself, *despite* the incessant guilt. I didn't know it then, but this was the beginning of my work toward developing an emotional and mental muscle that didn't exist yet: learning what was important to me and how to balance this with what was expected of me.

IN NEW YORK, one of my Craigslist roommates was also bicultural, a child of Iranian immigrants. Though this was not a specific identifier that we clicked over, it was clear that we shared similar values, and a lot of that was rooted in our efforts to honor our multiple cultures and live meaningfully as bicultural women. We lived together for five years, and in those years we celebrated our cultural holidays together, shared stories about our families, and bonded over the sometimes painful experiences of being women of color at work, in dating, and in life. It was a completely different environment than the one I'd grown up in. I felt safe and nurtured, and the environment we built within our friendship helped me explore boundary setting without feeling like a bad person.

Values work is closely tied to boundary setting. After all, it is much easier to set boundaries with those who share our values than it is with those who don't, because people who share our values are more likely to understand the reasons behind the setting of these boundaries. This is why setting boundaries with immigrant parents is often the hardest for children of immigrants. In an Instagram poll, 83 percent of about 2,500 children of immigrants who responded said they don't feel like they share the same values as their parents. And when they were asked to clarify if they believed that was because of differences in cultural values, 86 percent said yes.

As with shame, we can't talk about boundaries and enmeshment without talking about cultural context. What might be considered normal boundaries in one family or culture may not be considered normal in another. What constitutes healthy boundaries is dependent on the person, the culture, the family, and ultimately the impacts of these boundaries (or lack thereof) on the people involved. In individualism, pride and energy may be a result of self-care; in collectivism, pride and energy may be a result of other-care. It's okay to honor and protect that.

While having permeable boundaries—viewed through a Western lens as more straightforwardly negative—certainly can be harmful, for many people who come from collectivist cultures, the interconnectivity of people, emotions, and thoughts is actually a source of love, pride, energy, strength, and, ultimately, self. Our ability to deeply care about our relational roles is a strength. It's important to remember that, generally, boundaries are not one-size-fits-all. The ways we engage in any relationship are not black and white. Boundaries are fluid and change often; what works in one relationship may not work in another. What works for someone else when it comes to setting boundaries may not work for us. We can even have different versions of boundaries with the same person (e.g., porous with time but rigid with emotions). Culture, family dynamics, and settings can impact the way we decide to set boundaries, and that's okay. Ultimately, we get to decide what we are okay with and what feels good to us, *and* we can change our minds. The key, however, is to focus on self-reported issues, struggles, and benefits: to consciously decide for ourselves what we want and, crucially, to recognize how these learned relational dynamics show up in our adult lives.

> **REMINDER:** Boundary setting is a skill. Many people who struggle with boundaries want to go from zero to one hundred right away. Unfortunately, setting boundaries is hard. They need to be practiced and self-affirmed, and it may take time to get comfortable with them. It's hard to learn how to do something you were never taught how to do. Be patient with yourself. Have self-compassion, and don't feel bad about where your boundaries are! Remember that you can love and be grateful for your family, and you can decide to make different choices than they'd make or expect from you.

After deciding your boundary, you have to figure out how to communicate it. For many, the word *boundary* can feel foreign or too aggressive and rejective of the other person. If I were to tell my parents, "This is my boundary," they would probably laugh at me. *Boundary* may not translate across cultures or across relationships, so consider other, more applicable words to express yourself accurately and in a way that can be understood and received by the other person. For example, instead of firmly declaring that I need something, I have told people I care about: "For me to show up more fully with you, I am realizing I need . . ." Highlighting the shared interest—the relationship—can help frame it contextually for others and demonstrate how a boundary will benefit it.

When I asked children of immigrants in an Instagram poll if boundaries are a struggle for them, 90 percent of 2,614 said yes, and 89 percent of about 2,600 said that boundaries were not modeled for them growing up. When a child of immigrants finds their desires and needs at odds with what their parents or other family members want, it's an exhausting and tough reality—especially for someone who also grapples with people-pleasing. A common struggle I hear about from second gens is giving an inch and having immigrant parents ask for or take a mile. While we are unlearning our tendency to want to rescue others or people-please in our families, our loved ones may push back. It's a tug-of-war.

For many of us, learning to set boundaries requires excavating to the root of our propensity to be self-neglecting, a result of our codependent and enmeshed behaviors. Self-neglect may look like ignoring our own needs, talking ourselves out of what we're feeling, distracting ourselves from unpleasant feelings, lacking self-compassion, getting easily frustrated with ourselves, and prioritizing other people's feelings and needs. It's connected to our need to people-please. Out of 3,755 children of immigrants who participated in an Instagram poll, 96 percent said they identify as (or are unlearning to be) people pleasers. Now, not all people-pleasing behaviors are harmful or negative; there's a difference between pleasing others to connect with them and needing to please others for fear of criticism, rejection, or not getting external validation. We have to decide what the parameters are and how much of ourselves we are going to cut off to try to make others happy. Here are five tips for working toward the unlearning of people pleasing:

- Practice disappointing people. Stay with me here.
  Disappointing someone and wronging someone are two very
  different things. So find a safe person to disappoint, and start
  small. This will help you build a tolerance for discomfort, as
  well as confidence that neither the relationship nor your sense
  of self will crumble if you don't get the external validation you
  have grown used to.
- Stall, and take time to respond to a request to assess if this is
  something you *want* to do, if you have the capacity to do it,
  and if you *should* do it.
- Remember that saying yes to something means saying
  no to something else. What will you gain? What will you
  lose?
- Start small. Instead of having that difficult conversation in
  person, try to start saying no over text or email to build
  confidence and self-efficacy. Baby steps still get you moving in
  the right direction!
- If saying no is too difficult, consider offering a compromise
  that works for you. This can look like setting a time limit,
  asking for an extension, or offering an alternative plan.

I often didn't have tolerance for disappointing my parents, and I
see this in the community. But I've had to learn myself—and teach
clients to accept—that the emotional energy and discomfort are
often the same no matter what decision we make: we can be uncomfortable in crossing our own values and making our parents happy,
or we can be uncomfortable in pursuing our values and potentially
disappointing our parents. Boundaries may feel unfamiliar, and we
often trick ourselves into believing that if something is unfamiliar, it
must be bad. But that's not true. It's unfamiliar because it's *new*.

Why you struggle with boundaries:

- You don't yet have the tools to communicate them efficiently and healthily.
- You're not ready to stand by them and potentially change a relationship dynamic.
- You don't believe that you deserve your own love and space, too.
- You grew up in an environment where you were always expected to be available, responsive, or accountable for your time.
- You have been taught that your worthiness is tied to your service to others.
- There's no consequence when your boundary is violated.
- You expect the other person to be a mind reader.
- You need your boundary to be validated by the other person before you can enforce it.
- You aren't clear on why the boundary is important to you.
- You don't practice setting boundaries.
- You don't have a support system to reinforce your new behavior.

Reimagining what a healthy relationship* looks like isn't about declaring a boundary and calling it a day. It's often about considering what practical boundaries look like; it's not saying yes all the time,

---

*Boundaries look different in households where abuse or neglect was or is still prevalent. In these cases, it may not be in your best interest to try to retain a relationship.

and it's not saying no all the time. So what's the middle ground? What does it look like for you to love yourself and your parents—or other loved ones—at the same time? A big misconception in the community is that boundary setting is about changing the other person, when it's really about protecting your own finite resources and energy. Boundaries are a limit around *your* capacity and what you can handle. Boundaries allow *you* to be a better version of *yourself*. They allow you to show up more fully without resentment or burnout. In short, boundary setting is an extension of emotion management.

For many children of immigrants, boundary work will also include interrogating some automatic thoughts that make it difficult. These can include the all-or-nothing mindset, in which we struggle to recognize there's a middle gray area where healthiness can exist; overgeneralization, such as assuming that one reaction will *always* be the reaction we get or that one family member's feelings represent those of the rest of the family; and catastrophizing, or assuming the worst will happen and therefore refusing to even try. In challenging these thoughts and reactions of ours, we also confront the ways in which we *show up* in our relationships. By disappointing others, we begin to unlearn a role we're used to playing. *If I don't help, then who am I? How does this relationship work now? How am I loved?*

Boundaries are relational work, and the reality is we can only stand firm in what we *want* from—and in—our relationships when we're able to be honest with and committed to ourselves. One client and I spent a significant amount of time narrowing down the types of boundaries she struggled with and in which relationships they felt the most difficult to set; ultimately, what we realized was that she consistently crossed boundaries with herself. She didn't value her own thoughts or opinions. She didn't respect her own time. She didn't believe she deserved to rest. If the setter of boundaries lacks a strong foundation of self-esteem and self-worth, boundaries with others will consistently fall through the cracks.

Affirmations
for boundary setting:

- Just because you can doesn't mean you should.
- Feeling bad doesn't mean you are doing something wrong.
- Someone else can feel bad about your boundary, and it can still be the right thing to do.
- Your worthiness is not tied to how boundaryless you can be.
- Boundaries allow you to show up more fully and presently.

Remember that boundaries are *invitations* to be loved in ways you need, not *barriers* to keep others out.

Embracing Growing Pains

I had lived a double life for so long—hiding things from my parents, existing in fragments across different parts of my life—and I was ready to bring all the parts of myself together and build a life for her. I knew that I had to make it work in New York. I didn't feel like I had an alternative plan. So I hustled. I worked odd jobs. When I had been living at home, I hadn't been deliberate about how I filled my time; instead, I had used busyness as a way to avoid the things I was struggling with and convince my parents that I would be okay. In New York, though, I was intentional about building a life in this city. I wanted to live a life, for myself, and I knew that meant I would have to find ways to survive while I figured out what my next, bigger professional move would be. I was giving myself permission to start over, as many times as it would take.

I randomly filled jobs as a TaskRabbit tasker, transcribing notes and sometimes education curricula for strangers. I reached out to a local neighborhood yoga studio to offer social media branding services. I worked a short stint as a creative director with the founding team of a mental health center for folks coming out of rehabilitation. I worked as an assistant to a life and recovery coach, helping her with editorial and administrative projects. I had my heart set on ending up in book publishing and used LinkedIn to network any chance I got. After making it through rounds of interviews at one of the top publishing houses only to be told that I didn't have enough experience, I was connected with someone at *HuffPost* who was looking for a short-term fellow to serve on her team as an editor. It felt serendipitous to see an opening at a company I had hated to leave two years prior. The fellowship was supposed to last nine months, but it turned into a full-time job. It was the first time in almost a decade that I felt like I was going to be okay.

Ultimately, moving to New York was when I realized that I needed to stop trying to fix, change, or fight my parents and instead be accountable to myself. I needed to shift the focus from what I wasn't getting from them to what I could provide—and create—for myself. I had to do the inner work to let go of the programming that had been done to my psyche. I had to let go of certain narratives that didn't allow me to show up authentically. I had to let go of who I thought I needed to be in order to make room for who I really am. New York is where I learned that, frankly, I'm not that special! There are so many of us who are facing hardships and struggles—to different extremes—every day. I gained perspective on what I needed to change and what I needed to accept. I did things I wanted to do for myself and not because I was told to. I learned to parent myself in ways that my ill-equipped parents couldn't. I experienced growing pains that are common to a lot of children of immigrants. These included:

- Needing space to figure out who I was without being told who I was supposed to be.
- Embracing my emotions as they came and learning to manage them rather than be managed by them.
- Appreciating everything that my parents had done for me and recognizing that they could have done some things differently.
- Learning how to give myself permission—rather than externally seeking it—to make choices that my family might not agree with.
- Learning that my worthiness of love is not tied to my ability to be of service to others or agreeable to others.
- Recognizing that I can have gratitude for a space, person, or culture and that I can speak up for myself or speak out against toxicity.
- Having self-compassion and recognizing that it's hard to do things you were never taught or encouraged to do.
- Differentiating between shame and guilt and knowing that some of my decisions did not make me an inherently bad daughter, even if I felt like I was doing something wrong.

I have joked with my parents that they never really taught me how to live without them, despite their having to learn how to live without their own parents at very young ages. I am grateful for the time that I have been able to spend exploring and building my own sense of self without it being tied to another human—a parent or a partner—knowing that my mom and many before me didn't have the same privilege or opportunity. And though I didn't want to know what it was like to live without my parents per se, I did want to learn what it was like to live on my own and be able to integrate them into my life rather than live my life *for* them.

Learning about boundaries

and your values

Boundaries 101

- Get clear on why setting this boundary is important. This is a practice of self-care, of understanding your needs, and of being able to recognize the transference of energy between you and others.
  - This will help you determine how strict of a boundary to set and how to communicate your needs.
- Get clear on the outcome you are hoping for. Are you looking to just express yourself and practice speaking your truth, or are you looking to get out of a situation/relationship?
  - Other people are not mind readers—what do you want to get across?
- Know your limits. Ultimately, you get to decide the purpose of your boundary and how you may want to assert it. There's usually a way out, and it's up to you to decide what you are okay with.
  - Knowing your limits, values, and priorities will help you figure out if these are being crossed, which can be

subsequently helpful in communicating your feelings and
needs in relationships.

- Reflect on *whom* you struggle to set boundaries with and *why*.
  Is there a difference in values? Reflect on times when you felt
  resentment or anger toward something/someone else.

General Boundary Reflections

- To uncover your beliefs around boundary setting, consider:
  What is the first thing that comes to mind when you think
  "boundary"? And how do you feel when others set boundaries
  with you?
- How were boundary-setting behaviors modeled / passed down
  to you?
- How has your parents' parenting style impacted your view of
  boundary setting?
- Are there noticeable intergenerational patterns of boundary
  setting in your family? What boundary behavior, if any, have
  you witnessed between your parents and their parents? What
  about between your parents and their siblings or your
  siblings?
- Is it easier or harder to set boundaries with certain family
  members?
- What boundary do you struggle with the most?
- What do you fear about boundary setting?
- A small and realistic boundary that will serve you right
  now is:
- One safe relationship where you can practice boundary
  setting is:

Before setting a boundary:

- Your intention for setting this boundary is:
- You feel guilty about:
- You fear it'll be perceived as:

After practicing setting the boundary (preferably in a safe relationship to get comfortable):

- What were your concerns before setting the boundary?
- How did it feel to set the boundary?
- How was the boundary perceived?
- How did you feel after? What did you learn?

General tips for setting boundaries:

- Use I-language when communicating your needs so as to minimize defensiveness in the other person.
- If you are setting a verbal boundary, be communicative and clear about the boundary; explicit communication helps prevent misunderstanding or manipulation by the other person.
- Don't try to start with the big boundaries right away! Lead up to them—remember, this is skill learning; take your time.
- You will set boundaries that aren't respected, and that can be discouraging. You have to be consistent. Use trial and error to practice different ways of setting the same boundary, and see what works. If you don't stick with your ask/boundary, it's less likely to be respected.

- If your boundaries are ultimately not respected, you may have to explore what will need to change and whether you can tolerate the relationship as it is.
- Ask about and respect other people's boundaries; model the behavior you are hoping to see in return.
- Build a community to get support in the forms of professional care, friendships, and family relationships.

Culturally sensitive tips for children of immigrants (informed by my work):

- While boundaries usually need to come with consequences for there to be real change, setting immovable boundaries isn't necessarily a healthy endeavor for children of immigrants, no matter what is espoused in Western media about boundary setting. So, instead, consider where you can stand firm and where you're willing to compromise.
- Boundaries don't always need to be communicated. They can be about what you don't say/share. They can also be behavioral boundaries—calling less or walking away when you observe a family conflict that doesn't involve you to ensure you don't get roped in.
- Give to get. For example, set a boundary around one thing, but give in return something that feels right for you so the other person doesn't feel like you are solely taking from them. Maybe it's telling your mom that you are not coming home for dinner tomorrow but offering to meet her for lunch next week. Or maybe it's setting parameters around how long your sister vents by saying, "I'm happy to listen for the next fifteen minutes, but then I have to go finish my homework."

- Like talking about mental health, have conversations about other people and things, such as movies, that showcase the boundary as a positive thing.
- You are likely the first person in your family learning how to navigate emotional security and health; keep learning, and share the wealth with your loved ones.
- Find the agency you do have within the system in which you live. You always have some agency. Maybe that takes the shape of a microchange or microboundary.

Values

To successfully set boundaries, it's important to have clarity on your values. We all have cultural, familial, professional, and personal values, but these vary depending on the systems and environments in which we exist.

Exercise #1:

Write down the three most important values in your ethnic-cultural community. Then write down three important values in your host culture. Finally, write down the three values that are most important to your mom, dad, sibling(s), best friend, and partner, too. (If you feel comfortable doing so, you can even ask them.) Now, spend some time reflecting on how similar or different these values are to or from one another; also consider whether you find yourself adopting certain values because of the people with whom you surround yourself. What's coming up for you?

Exercise #2:

Consider which ideal values you'd want to live by, and make a list. Who are some people you admire or look up to? What values do they live by? What would it look like for you to adopt these values into your life?

Now write down three of the values you live by today. How do they compare or contrast with your ideal values?

Exercise #3:

Reflect on questions like: What is important to you? When are you the happiest? What values are being honored during these times? Conversely, when are you the unhappiest, what values are being suppressed or crossed?

Exercise #4:

Even if you aren't intentionally or consciously rooted in any values right now, you are still living by values. Ask people close to you how they would describe you. Ask them what values they think you live by. Consider how you handle failure, setbacks, or conflict.

Chapter Seven

Investing in Community
Care and Self-Care

———————

Six months after I moved to the city, I was celebrating my twenty-fifth birthday with dinner at a Thai restaurant in Union Square. I had invited a handful of my friends—old and new, a collection of people I had met along the way on my tumultuous journey. My best friend from high school lived in New York, so he was there, along with two newer girlfriends, a visiting college friend, my brother's best friend (who was like an older brother to me), and a mentor-like friend whom I had worked with at the mental health start-up that didn't pan out. They all represented a different part of my journey and a different part of myself.

At the beginning of dinner, I handed each friend a postcard, and I asked them to write down something they thought I could do better. I was asking for constructive criticism about who I was as a person and as a friend. My friends were taken a bit off guard. Some refused to do the exercise, but many felt safe being honest with me about how they perceived me.

At the time, this felt like an important thing for me to do. I was away from what had always been my center of gravity: my parents, who were always pulling me back to where they were. Without that center, I was free-falling, trying to find solid ground.

I did genuinely want to learn more about myself and grow as a human, and even now, I believe that in building intimacy with others, we must be willing to confront the versions of ourselves that *they* see—regardless of whether we agree—because intent does not always lead to the hoped-for impact. However, as a mental health professional, I can now see that I was feeding the belief that others' opinions and validation of me were more important than my own. In this case, I was just trading my parents' approval for that of my friends. I had been trying to unsubscribe from the narrative that my identity was "failure," but I was still ascribing to the idea that I was worthy only insofar as I could be of service to others. I saw feedback as a gift that allowed me to better myself; the way I viewed it, I was always a project to be worked on, with the goal of making myself more likable to others. My fawning tendencies made me chameleon-like among my friends, and I know I'm not alone. Several clients and folks I have talked to in the community have shared that they, too, feel pressure to be *everything* to their friends in order to maintain the friendships and feel worthy. This may reflect codependency traits from family dynamics trickling into friendships.

I now know that we all replicate dynamics that exist elsewhere in our lives. I have seen my own clients experience transference, where they redirect their feelings about someone else onto me. Even more, I have had clients who caused me to experience countertransference because they reminded me of someone in my personal life (present or past), and I have to be very aware of the assumptions I make or the dynamics that I might be succumbing to as a result. While these concepts have been studied specifically in therapist-client relationships, I would argue that we entangle our emotions and parts of ourselves with others—in all relationships—because of our own personal blueprints for what it means to be in relationships. We are continuously learning how to integrate these different parts of ourselves, but they compound on top of our previous definitions and experiences of relationships, too.

My mentor friend filled out the postcard and told me that I am too hard on myself and that she would love to see me have more self-compassion. My roommate told me I have a tendency to make things about myself when she's sharing something with me. I cried when I read this. *How can she possibly think my relationships, her included, aren't the center of my world?* But she wasn't wrong. I had always been convinced that to feel like I could connect or relate with others, I needed to share my opinion or tell a story about myself—a tendency many people share. Now, I understand better how to just listen, and I have learned that you don't have to relate to connect; you just have to care, be curious, and listen.

Over the years leading up to this point in my life, I had swayed between being entirely dependent on others for love and validation and not trusting anyone to make me feel safe. This lack of trust had been exacerbated by my sexual assault, after which I put up walls and became hypervigilant of how others were treating or mistreating me in order to protect myself. This combination manifested in my relationships as insecurity, anxious anticipation of betrayal, and quiet hypersensitivity. I pretended I was always fine, even when things didn't feel good. I saw the world around me as a threatening place.

Building a Community of Friends

Chosen family, for many children of immigrants, can be the refuge we need to feel safe and loved. However, many of my clients struggle with communicating, being honest, and understanding mutual accountability in friendships. Some of this is rooted in growing up in households where love was expected to be unconditional (at least toward elders and parents), so it was okay for anyone to hurt anyone else. And some of it is pinned to a lack of skills in knowing *how* to have hard conversations and resolve conflict.

Many of us from immigrant families were taught that family is more important than friendships, and when I polled members of the Brown Girl Therapy community to see if this was the case for them, 94 percent of 822 respondents said yes. I subsequently received many messages about this experience. Several community members said they had an obligation to spend time with family whom they didn't even like or feel safe around rather than with friends they loved. Others said they were never even taught how to be in friendships, because family and community were the priority. This, too, made me an unreliable friend growing up. I would get into lots of tiffs with my childhood best friend over how unreliable I was, as I would often commit to things only to cancel at the last minute because my parents expected me to be home for dinner or at some community event or another.

We learn how to be in relationships with other people from our relationships within our own family systems. Research even suggests that the relationships we have with our caregivers impact how we develop relationships with friends as we get older. Individualism and collectivism can play a role, too, in how important friendships are to us when it comes to considering relational satisfaction or loneliness. For example, in individualistic cultures, people list their lack of friendships, or their lack of interactions with friends, as the main source of their loneliness, whereas in collectivist cultures, people list poor family relationships and communication as the main source of their loneliness. As children of immigrants, we struggle with both.

. . .

COLLEGE HAD GIVEN me a first taste of freedom to explore without judgment parts of myself that I'd had to hide at home, to be a version of myself that I didn't get to embrace with my own family. Through the bhangra team, the South Asian Student Association, and other like clubs, I instantly flocked toward a group of folks whose parents were from all over the world. I didn't know it then the way I know it now to be true: having friends who shared in my identity and cultural struggles was such a saving grace. While certainly not necessary, this shared background allowed me to explore all facets of my multicultural identity without feeling weird, or bad, or observed. Even though many of my memories from those days are suppressed or negative, it was the first time I saw flickers of the notion that everything that made me, me—even the things I'd previously hidden—could be loved. Unfortunately, my college relationships were strained by my academic suspension and subsequent deepening depression. Though I maintain relationships today with some of my friends from back then, I always wonder how these relationships would have developed—and thus contributed to my own growth—if my life trajectory had been different.

In New York, I was at last experiencing this freedom again. It was the start of a chapter in which I would set down my own roots, and this meant finally creating and nurturing my own community. I was hungry for relational care—that is, forming bonds with people who would support my growth as a person, and vice versa. I had autonomy to find this community and engage with it on my own terms. My friendships in New York became relationships in which I could explore my own needs and desires and test the waters to see what kind of person I could be. I was learning how to recalibrate my own self within the context of my relationships. It wasn't about unlearning interdependence; it was about having roles in others' lives *while* not losing myself within these roles. This required facing many parts of myself that I once would have called ugly or embarrassing, like being "too sensitive" or expressive or excitable. Owning these traits was essential to becoming an interdependent person who could exist as an entity within the relationships I chose. Finding true community allowed my walls to come down.

At any point where I felt some semblance of a connection with another person, I nurtured it. I sought out friendships with coworkers who seemed cool. I also asked friends who had friends in the city to connect me if they felt comfortable doing so. I pursued hobbies and went to meetups, all leading me to find my people. In building and investing in this community, I was literally restoring my own sense of self, and the more I found people who accepted me, the more whole I became.

It wasn't easy, and it took time for me to feel okay showing up more authentically with friends. As with the postcard activity, I would often try to find ways to be more likable to others. I was still trying to protect myself from rejection, which ultimately held me back from being truly present and honest in friendships. Validation from others was a tangible sign of worth to me. As such, I found myself sometimes investing in the wrong people, which led to painful friendship breakups. Understanding my own needs remained a struggle. I would often feel privileged when someone wanted to be my friend, never questioning if their intentions were good or if it was a healthy dynamic for me. I still didn't know how to love myself, and I didn't think I was lovable. What's more, my codependency tendencies would still surface.

I feared abandonment, and I deeply internalized this narrative that "no one will love you like your family." My own mom would often say, "There's nothing like blood," which was always frustrating to me. Why is family so important when it can be so volatile? Where are the standards for how we *should* treat people, regardless of how much we love them or they love us? This has led to so many of us not being able to maintain friendships or struggling with extreme guilt for prioritizing friendships. This, coupled with the narrative of "keeping everything in the family," can make it feel difficult to have true intimacy and vulnerability in friendships.

Over time in New York, I learned to cast off the hierarchy of relationships that so many children of immigrants have been taught, in which friendships are near the bottom (but more important than "self" because they're still "others"). I invested in friendships that were patient, gentle, and reassuring, and I learned to receive love given to the parts of myself that had felt unlovable for so long. In return, I started to experience a level of relational safety that allowed me to look inward without fear and with the knowledge that I would have soft places to land when I needed them. Within these safe relationships—the ones where I could change my mind, be insecure, and show up as an imperfect human—I realized that I do not have to know it all. I finally had people close enough to me to engage in difficult, honest conversations. I felt that I had space to grow and work on myself and also that it was okay if I wasn't perfect. During this time, I learned that I could continue to be a work in progress, but I was not a project in constant need of work. I was lovable regardless of where I was in my personal journey toward healing and growth. Even more, I learned how to be accountable to others in ways that did not always mean sacrificing myself. Instead of apologizing for having needs, I was able to exercise my newly developed muscles: boundary setting, values exploration, and self-care.

Redefining Self-Care for Ourselves

Many of us children of immigrants grew up in households where we weren't modeled or taught "self-care." Self-care narratives in the West, of course, have a major theme of individualization, focusing solely on the self, and like differentiation of self, this can be a foreign concept in immigrant households. When I host Redefining Self-Care workshops for children of immigrants, most attendees share that self-care was modeled as self-sacrifice. In fact, out of 2,376 children of immigrants who responded to a poll, 77 percent said that they struggle with self-care because it feels selfish. Even when encouraged by their friends, partners, or colleagues to pursue self-care, and even when they themselves know that they need to have better self-care practices, they still have difficulty setting time aside. For some, self-care practices were encouraged in the family only if they served a greater purpose, like taking care of body image and sleeping well before a big workday or exam. Such self-care narratives are centered around other people and family perceptions: *Will others think you are more marriageable or more attractive? Will our family attain social status if you do this?*

For many children of immigrants, self-discovery and self-care are acts of rebellion and means of survival. So many of us have had to find what little agency we can within the systems in which we live, and often the very things we do out of self-preservation are things that would seem embarrassing or childish/inauthentic in Western narratives of self-care. These can be things like choosing between what is actually good for us and what looks good to others, such as deciding to spend the weekend with friends instead of family, even when we know our parents will be upset. It can be loving where we come from but hating the archaic norms that we're still held to. It can be taking baby steps in introducing our immigrant parents to a creative skill before making it a career or to a "friend" before admitting they're a romantic partner. Sometimes self-care is keeping quiet when we really want to speak up, because we know we must pick which battles to fight, and they're not all worth it. Sometimes it's giving a domineering family member control over something specific so that we can focus *our* control on what matters to us. Sometimes self-care is pursuing our dreams and forgoing the support of our families—an experience that is all too common for immigrant kids who marry a partner of their choosing, select an "unconventional career," or otherwise make a decision that their parents don't agree with. Self-care can be telling little white lies out of survival and self-preservation, like pretending our phones died or saying we have a work dinner so that we can be there for a friend who needs us. Self-care might be lying about going to therapy to learn how to communicate with our parents about our mental health, or it might be teaching ourselves about our sexual health and making our own doctor's appointments to avoid our parents' or family's intrusion.

In New York, I started to learn more about self-care. I began to cultivate joy and to relish little, seemingly inconsequential things, like being able to wear what I wanted without feeling judgment or criticism and not having to account for my whereabouts at all times of the day.

Even more, I learned how to differentiate between self-care and self-soothing (though the latter isn't something I actually had language for until recently). The simplest difference between the two, I've learned, is that self-care is proactive and self-soothing is reactive. Of course, it's important to note that some self-care and self-soothing practices require a certain level of privilege and wealth, as the wellness industry has become more commodified and monetized. Both are important, but some folks are stuck in cycles of self-soothing because that is *all* they have access to. At the end of the day, we can't self-care our way out of oppression or oppressive systems.

Self-soothing practices are often coping skills in moments of acute crisis, helping people feel more immediately grounded. I always thought I was practicing real self-care when I cried, performed deep breathing, or distracted myself; in reality, these are reactive, self-soothing behaviors that helped me manage the stress and overwhelm I was feeling in the moment. While these are useful in managing internal experiences and emotion regulation, it's important to consider what real self-care is. Real self-care practices support an individual's growth in the long term and help people feel rooted in their lives and values. Often, self-care requires a level of safety and means to plan for your life rather than react to situations. When I was avoiding my plummeting grades or sleeping in instead of going to class, I was self-soothing to such an extreme that it became detrimental to my own well-being. Learning to manage the discomfort of having to do the hard thing—and regulating your emotions while doing so—is real self-care. It takes a level of discipline and emotional maturity—traits I didn't have back then. Through building a life with stability in New York, I was finally able to get out of survival mode and engage in real self-care. This looked like learning how to budget and gaining an understanding of financial wellness, as I started to live financially independently from my family. This looked like prioritizing my physical health, carving out time to find medical professionals I trusted, and making sure I was hydrating, nourishing my body, and sleeping well. Self-care doesn't always feel good in the moment. Self-care also looked like returning to my roots in ways that felt authentic to me (even if it felt uncomfortable to try as an adult without a set community in place). I attended Sikh conferences and invested in extended familial relationships, which allowed me to continue discovering my place in my world.

Another way that I began to invest in a relationship with myself was through solo traveling. I was working with a small salary, but I had studied ways to travel on the cheap, subscribing to newsletters and learning about different airline credit cards and points systems. I opted for budget over comfort in travel and lodging, as my goal was always to see parts of the world, learn about other cultures, and spend time with myself. Like self-care, self-love has always felt effusive to me, a concept that has been tagged with a bright red "Selfish" sign. But self-love isn't about loving yourself more than you love others; it's about tending to yourself in the same way you feel compelled to tend to others. My self-love journey has been about unlearning that my worthiness is tied to what I can achieve and instead learning to love myself—and the values I try to live by—as a human.

Pursuing Play to Heal

During my second year in New York, I saved up enough money to take a solo trip to Croatia and Iceland. It was timed after my college boyfriend and I had broken up and as I waited for my *HuffPost* fellowship to potentially turn into a full-time position. In Croatia, I was forced to pay attention to how I handled things on a day-to-day basis. I pushed myself to talk to strangers. I made mistakes in planning my itinerary that only I was responsible for. I could choose to do things, or not do things, at my own whim. On my first day in Croatia, I was walking the wall around Old Town in Dubrovnik when I found myself alongside a group of three Spaniards; we ended up joking around and taking photos for each other throughout the walk. I worked up the courage to ask them if they wanted to grab dinner together after. I had never dined alone at a restaurant before, and frankly, I was too scared to. They essentially said no, though they stammered through the turndown and clearly felt really bad doing so—they were having a boys' weekend. It was only the beginning of a two-week trip in which I learned to be brave and to be alone (including at restaurants), which felt like a direct challenge to the narrative I had been taught as an Indian woman that being alone or independent was the saddest or worst thing in the world. At another point, I rented a bike and attempted to navigate a narrow uphill mountain road to get to the lavender fields. It was strenuous and scary, but at the end was something beautiful and rewarding. I'll never forget how proud I felt and how much I relished finally getting to the top of the old road on the island of Hvar. Funnily enough, I forgot to check if the lavender fields were even in season. They were not, but the breathtaking views overlooking the Adriatic Sea were still worth it. In Iceland, I met other solo travelers in a shared hostel and made myself vulnerable to them while we caught glimpses of the aurora borealis or ate Icelandic hot dogs in Reykjavík after a night of dancing. I created bonds—and a best friendship—that still exist today. I later wrote essays about these travels and how much they changed me.

I continued to travel solo, regardless of whether I was in a relationship, and have since made it to eleven countries by myself. I sometimes wondered if this was a way of running away, but I have come to learn that the more I pushed myself out of my comfort zone, the more I was able to increase my self-efficacy, or this belief that I could, in fact, exert control over my life and that I did have the capacity to do things, even hard things. Solo travel is not accessible to everyone, of course, and it's not the only way to build self-efficacy. Self-efficacy can be built in various ways, such as through vicarious learning—reading articles and books or watching movies about people who are enduring and overcoming the same kinds of challenges you face—or through mentorship, encouragement, and visualization (in which you visualize yourself successfully completing the task or challenge at hand).

I also increased my cognitive flexibility. I realized that I do like learning and growing, that my insatiable curiosity had been a constant through the years. In college, I had vehemently believed that I should know everything and that if I failed, I could never try again. But this was not true at all. I failed my classes for several reasons, some internal and others external, but failing out of school did not make me a failure in life, and it did not mean that I wasn't curious or enthusiastic about learning. And through my first couple of years in New York and my solo travels, I got to discover the ways in which I was successful and capable and creative and disciplined, all while learning to have compassion for the times when I was not as strong as I wanted to be.

I found that I could, in fact, learn things on my own time. I finally started shifting from a fixed mindset to a growth mindset. Given a chance, instead of seeing myself through a deficiency lens, or as always lacking, I started to accept my personal areas of improvement and find ways to strengthen them. Instead of assuming that my intelligence was static, I learned that discipline and training are part of growth. Instead of feeling threatened by others' success, I learned how to be driven and inspired by it. I surrounded myself with people who were also learning things as adults. I cultivated joy through play, something that feels so deeply counterintuitive to many children of immigrants, since we are taught to pursue things that are deemed worthwhile by our parents and that we will excel at. I wanted to lean into this, so I took classes in American Sign Language, travel writing, and poetry. I signed up for a club field hockey team. I learned how to play chess and then wouldn't stop playing it in Union Square, or at brunch, or on benches in Astoria overlooking the East River. Embracing nonevaluative play allowed me to learn things simply because I wanted to rather than because I felt pressure to prove myself in them. I decoupled my sense of self from what I could *do* and started learning to just *be*.

> When we tie our worthiness to what we can produce, we forget to cultivate joy and play in ways that have nothing to do with how good we are at something. What are some ways in which you can incorporate more play into your life? This will increase your flexibility in life and strengthen creative thinking.

Investing in My Mental Health

As I spent my day-to-day in New York exploring what it meant to exist as a young professional, living paycheck to paycheck, I continued to be drawn to investing my money in experiences over things. I recognize that in a capitalistic world where currency is required, money provides access to comforts, services, resources, and opportunities that are otherwise unavailable to many. With self-care and consumerism so often intertwined in mainstream conversations, it can be difficult to understand what is considered an investment when it comes to mental health and self-care and what isn't—especially given today's social media and influencer landscape. For us children of immigrants, this can be exacerbated: we may struggle with spending money on things that seem frivolous to our parents, even if they're no longer active participants in our monetary decisions. Many of us inherit financial fears and trauma from our parents. Out of 5,041 children of immigrants who responded to a poll on Instagram, 83 percent agreed that spending money on self-care feels wasteful. Our personal self-care narratives are informed by the self-care narratives we were taught in our families and cultural communities. When thinking about the *self* feels selfish in a collectivist community, then pursuing mental health care or doing things for the sake of our own enjoyment may feel countercultural and immoral. I continued to struggle with unlearning this narrative in New York City, but I had more energy, a steady paycheck, and time to consider it for myself.

Around this time, I was also reeling from the end of my relationship with Seth, who had been a lifeline for me through my assault and the years after. I had relied heavily and solely on him as I navigated my own survival, which reinforced my codependent tendencies. When we started living in the same city after his Fulbright concluded, the dynamics within our relationship permanently shifted. I was encroaching on *his* life, and I didn't know how to build my own life and be a stronger, more capable version of myself because I believed I needed him to protect and help me, especially in regard to my triggers. Further, though he wanted me to be more confident and independent, he would also act in ways that held me back. We were unable to break the cycle; my insecurity would provoke his avoidant tendencies, which would intensify my insecurities. There was no denying that we truly cared for each other, but we both struggled with healthy communication and emotion management, and as such, we learned to operate our relationship under a need for control, weaponizing guilt and shame whenever we lacked the language to express ourselves.

Our breakup was a catalyst for my recognition that I needed to seek professional care. I could no longer be dependent on someone else. I finally realized—after breaking out in hives at an airport baggage claim and falling to my knees, unable to catch my breath; after feeling trapped in crowded Coney Island; after having to avoid certain areas in New York because of my triggers—that no trip or hobby would help me process my assault like therapy could, so I decided to pursue it again. This time, I didn't have to convince my parents of anything. This meant that I could center my own growth and worry about telling them when I was ready.

My therapist—Dr. T, as I started to call her—was referred to me by my ex-boyfriend's therapist at the time—a parting gift—and that seemed good enough to me. I didn't know then how to question the services I would get or ask what kind of therapist she was. This is an issue that crops up time and time again in direct messages from children of immigrants: *What do I need to ask a therapist? Is there anything I should consider before deciding to work with someone? How do I know if it's a fit?* (These are valid questions and worth getting clarity on before jumping into a relationship with a therapist. I expand on this topic more in the guided reflections on page 236.)

Dr. T was an older white woman who saw clients in her Upper West Side apartment, and she offered a sliding scale that was doable with my budget and salary. I felt lucky because this allowed me to commit to weekly sessions. Though I was excited to have a confidential space where I could talk about my daily struggles, my relationship issues, my trauma, and my thoughts and feelings, I was hesitant to fully dive in at first. Many people don't realize that going to therapy is hard work. It requires being proactive in your own healing and treatment in ways that can make many people feel wildly uncomfortable and vulnerable. I found myself longing to be liked by her, just as I had with my college counselor, Mel. Despite this—or perhaps because of it—I canceled a few of my first appointments with Dr. T before realizing that her cancellation policy would either make her stop agreeing to work with me or cost me, without the possibility of a refund. I couldn't afford that, nor could I justify wasting my money like that, so I gritted my teeth and started showing up. Though therapy shouldn't have the financial barrier that it does, in this case, investing in my mental health encouraged me to hold myself accountable.

In pushing myself to commit to therapy—something that can be incredibly daunting for many people—I strengthened my discipline. It became apparent to me that if we want to do something, we often have to set ourselves up for success, even when this means doing things we don't want to do.

At the beginning of therapy with Dr. T, I finally took the time to grieve my unconventional career and life paths, which allowed me to make room for possibility. I had been digging myself deeper and deeper into feeling stuck, fighting against the reality that maybe I needed help, or a break, or a change of course. I was trapped in suffering, without realizing that I could reach a new destination if I chose instead to move through pain. Dr. T helped me pull myself up out of that quicksand.

THROUGH OUR WORK together, I learned that I could forgive myself for the mistakes I had made. When you grew up in an environment where needing to be told twice came with consequences, it made sense that you would grow into an adult who was fearful of making mistakes and sought perfectionism. Kids need safe spaces to make mistakes and learn to build self-efficacy, self-compassion, and tolerance for the discomfort of growing pains. From a young age, I remember feeling humiliated and at fault whenever something went wrong. Common responses I would hear cast blame on me: *Why weren't you more careful? Why didn't you think of that? Why weren't you paying attention?*

Research suggests that this kind of linguistic framing can influence our levels of shame, blame, and punishment. Think about it.

When we go from "I am upset" or "This situation is upsetting to me" to "You made me upset" or "You are at fault," we start to assign blame, which can increase levels of shame—and punishment—for those who are blamed. It's an insidious cycle. Many of the second gens I work with feel like they are at fault for anything—or everything—that goes wrong in their relationships. If you grew up in a household where someone always needed to be blamed for anything that went wrong, you may struggle with black-and-white thinking. Parents' tendency to blame each other or their children is often rooted in an inability to manage their own anger or emotional dysregulation. It can also be a defense mechanism, protecting them from having to confront truths that are uncomfortable to face or that they don't have the skills to handle.

Overall, blame-riddled responses can encourage the belief that mistakes (even honest ones!) take away from our worthiness as people. Of 5,147 children of immigrants who responded to an Instagram poll, 92 percent agreed that they struggle with self-compassion after making a mistake. Many of us are made to feel inherently careless, so we learn to be vigilant and extra careful as adults.

In working with my clients and with immigrant families, one question I often ask is: "Did you do something wrong, *or* did you make a mistake?" For example, one client of mine was extremely self-deprecating for missing a meeting that she forgot to put on her calendar. She was being so negative about her worthiness and even admitted to having to text a bunch of her friends to get validation that she was not a bad person. It can be easy to get carried away in a tsunami of negative thoughts, and once they take over, it can be really difficult to stop them. When I asked my client the aforementioned question, she paused and wasn't sure she understood the difference. These can feel like the same thing to many of us children of immigrants who were never encouraged to build autonomy or self-reliance for fear it threatened the family/cultural system. As such, we often have a hard time finding personal agency because our immigrant parents, while trying to protect us and lead us down the right paths, actually disempowered us from learning to make our own choices and mistakes. We are not our mistakes. Doing something wrong does not make us inherently wrong.

Making mistakes is how we learn, and it should not feel like the worst thing in the world. We are allowed to struggle and not have it all figured out. We can't learn if we aren't given grace or extra room to slip up and find out how to correct our own behavior. Along with the various classes and skills I pursued during my first few years in New York City, I also took up flying trapeze lessons. I am terrified of heights, but for some reason, I really wanted to conquer this fear through trapeze. Something about it seemed liberating. In one of my early lessons, I learned how to hang upside down from my knees and was then modeled a "catch," where another flyer and I would catch hands, and I would flip and hang from their hands before releasing onto the net. When it was my turn, I missed the flyer's hands but had already released myself from my bar, so I fell with my hands up— reaching for him. Sure, I was upset that I hadn't "made it" as some of my classmates had, but I remember that, more so, I was exhilarated by this attempt to try something so wildly new. There had been a shift in how I responded to slipping up. I wanted to try again.

Making mistakes means being able to try new things. To make corrections. And while we are told that we should know what we want and go after it, there is something to be said for learning about who we are *not* and what we do *not* want. Giving myself the gift of exploration and curiosity has helped me release some of the weight of the unrealistic standards to which I hold myself, and I have continued to surprise myself along the way with the things I can do and/ or feel passionate about.

Practice self-compassion

1. Write a kind and encouraging letter to yourself to read and reread as needed. (If this is hard, consider writing it as if you are writing to someone you love.)

2. Honor your humanity. One way to do this when you are navigating shame or negative self-talk is to add "just like everyone" at the end of the thought. For example: *I made a mistake just like everyone does.*

3. Combat inner negativity by focusing on solutions rather than on problems (e.g., *What will help me right now?*)

4. Challenge your negative self-talk:

   a. Is this thought true? How do I know it's true?

   b. What is the evidence? What is the evidence against it?

   c. Was there a time when this thought wasn't true?

   d. What narrative does it uphold?

   e. Is this thought helping me or hurting me?

I remember that in one of my sessions with Dr. T, I was crying and telling her that I was a bad person and a mean person, that I had done and said things I was ashamed of when I was depressed, especially in the context of my relationship with Seth. I blamed my depression for our breakup, trapped in this belief that if I hadn't been depressed, I would have been a better version of myself, and we would have been fine. She looked at me and said that there's a difference between being a deliberately mean person and being someone who is acting in survival mode. It was the first time I learned that I didn't have to hold myself hostage to everything I had ever done or said.

I would end up seeing Dr. T on and off over the course of four years, and my sessions with her were transformative and life-changing in helping me grow and self-actualize as a human being, as well as heal from past traumatic experiences.

I STARTED TO see signs of my healing when I noticed the effects of my work in therapy manifesting in my day-to-day life—small changes became big improvements. I could make connections between why something triggered me and what relational blueprint I may have been replicating in present-day dynamics. I became less reactive to my emotions and feelings, taking pauses to process and digest before responding to something or someone. I learned to self-advocate at work and in relationships, communicating and identifying my needs and desires—even when it was difficult. I stopped expecting others to absolve me of my pain or to manage my emotions for me, and I started to learn how to do these for myself.

Doing the work to drudge through my past experiences was heavy and difficult. My Iranian roommate at the time, who also became one of my best friends, would know not to bother me on Monday evenings because I would often come home from therapy emotional, and I would get in bed and cry until I couldn't anymore. Therapy is hard work, but it can be really rewarding, too. I was moving the dial slowly; it may be static for a while, but eventually, the more you turn it, the more likely it is that you will get to clarity.

I often think about what version of myself I would be today, and how that would have changed my life choices and my career trajectory, had I not gone to therapy. I even wonder how my relationship with my dad would have been stunted.

After all, it was through these moments of self-awareness and growth that I was able, a year after starting therapy, to go on the trip to Maine with him and begin the process of building a bridge between our generational, cultural, and gender differences. I had to be honest with myself about what I could expect from him. When we have expectations of the people we love beyond their capacity to meet them, we will always be disappointed in them. I knew that I could never actually do the work for my dad, but—thanks to therapy—I could continue to drop bread crumbs leading him to a place he'd never been before. I accepted that I would have to advocate for myself and teach my parents how I needed to be loved. I opened myself to different possibilities when it came to what our relationship could look like, and thankfully he met me there. I approached our time together with this reframe: It wasn't that I didn't want his love and approval; it was that I didn't *need* them anymore to believe I was worthy as a human being. I could love my dad, and want to get to know and have intimacy with him, *and* I could love myself, and want to get to know and have intimacy with myself, too.

I credit therapy, and my willingness to be open and commit to it, as a fundamental reason why I was able to return to my relationship with my dad with an open heart. I recognize that I was lucky to be functional enough and financially able to seek professional help in the first place. Not everyone is as privileged as I was—and barriers to accessing quality mental services are amplified in minority communities. Unlike many, I had minimal limitations obstructing my care. And not everyone knows exactly how to do therapy or is ready to do so when they start accessing care.

While therapy is certainly not the only path toward healing and self-exploration, many children of immigrants ask me how therapy can be beneficial to them. After all, many of us were never even taught what mental health *is*. This lack of psychoeducation and emotional expression, as well as a learned inability to communicate our needs, holds us back from even considering therapy as an option.

Instead, we are taught that something has to be extremely wrong or bad—as it was for me—to seek help, or that seeking help is counter-cultural or a betrayal of one's community. We feel as though our struggles or pursuits of emotional and mental well-being are unwor-thy because of our parents' experiences.

What if we unlearn these core beliefs? What if going to therapy can also be about breaking cycles, becoming empowered, and work-ing toward personal development? What if it's about learning more regarding our attachment struggles, unlearning productivity as worthiness, navigating our bicultural identities, practicing effective communication strategies, learning boundary setting, healing from racial or generational trauma, distinguishing between shame and guilt, and learning how to self-regulate our emotions? What if the therapeutic relationship is the *one* relationship in which we can safely and effectively talk about ourselves and what we want in a confidential, productive space without fear of our communities find-ing out? What if therapy can empower us to write new narratives? What if seeking therapy is our way of healing those before and after us?

How to find a therapist and how to be in therapy

Mental health care is not one-size-fits-all, and there are very real barriers to seeking care or receiving the care you deserve. I hope this can serve as a resource.*

Five Common Therapy Myths to Unlearn

- "My therapist needs to share an identity with me in order to help me."
  - While this may be conducive to your own comfort and levels of safety in the room, don't assume that your therapist will be more effective because they come from the same background as you. *Every* therapist should be unassuming, nonjudgmental, and curious about how your identities affect you—regardless of whether they're shared.
- "I have a healthy network of loved ones, so I don't need therapy."

---

*For up-to-date resources, please check out my website (www.sahajkaurkohli.com).

- Therapy is not the same as friendship. It's a one-way relationship that focuses solely on you and your growth.
- "Going to therapy means I am admitting that I am broken or weak."
  - Going to therapy is courageous, and it is an indication that you are taking care of yourself.
- "If I seek therapy, it means I am selfish and ungrateful for what I have."
  - Exploring your own needs does not mean that you are selfish. You can be grateful, *and* you can know that this is what is best for your mental health.
- "Therapy is focused only on childhood and relationships with parents."
  - There are different approaches to therapy and different aspects of your life and well-being that you can focus on.

Where to Look for a Therapist

- Databases such as Psychology Today, Open Path Psychotherapy Collective, Inclusive Therapists, Latinx Therapy, South Asian Therapists, National Queer and Trans Therapists of Color Network (NQTTCN), and Therapy for Black Girls.
- Ask friends for referrals—or ask them to ask their therapists for referrals.
- Graduate and training clinics nearby often offer low-cost services.
- Private group practices with interns/graduate externs often offer cheaper rates.
- Community mental health clinics may offer free or low-cost services in your area.

- Insurance, employee benefits, and company well-being partners (if applicable).
- Group therapy options to subsidize costs and connect with other folks who have similar issues.

What to Look for and Consider

- Get clear on *your* why! Why do you want to go to therapy? What are you hoping to gain from it? What current struggles are you hoping to manage through, say, weekly therapy for six months? What is the goal?
    - Remember that goals can change and therapy is dynamic. You're not expected to have complete clarity on what your goals are, but it makes sense to start with the thing that led you to seek out therapy in the first place. Sometimes, in delving into one struggle or issue, your therapeutic work may lead to an excavation of something deeper.
- You need to be comfortable to be vulnerable. Therapy won't be successful if you can't build rapport or trust with your therapist.
- Be honest with yourself about any other criteria that are important to you (e.g., gender, race, degree, experience).
- Therapy *is* a transaction. You are paying someone for a service. It's okay to be as picky as you can afford to be.

Questions to Ask during a Consultation, a Service Most Therapists Offer for Free!

- Can you tell me more about your professional background? What are your specializations?
- What does a typical therapy session look like with you? What role do you believe you should play?
- I don't understand what X therapy is. Can you explain it to me?
- How are you supplementing your practice with trainings?
- How does multiculturalism inform your practice?
- How do you incorporate your client's culture into therapy or treatment planning?
- Do you have experience working with individuals of color? With someone struggling with X? With someone who is Y?
- In what ways have you done your own identity work?
- I am nervous that we both share X identity / don't share X identity. How will this inform your work with me?
- In the past, I have had X experience with a therapist, and I feel Y about it. What are your thoughts on this?
- Do you offer a sliding scale? Do you offer your services virtually or only in person?

What to Expect and Know

- You might have to try a few out—like dating or finding the perfect pair of shoes—and it might feel weird at first.
- Be honest with yourself about your comfort and trust levels! One of the top indicators of success in therapy is the strength of

the relationship a client feels that they have with their therapist. If you don't feel comfortable with someone, you may end up being too preoccupied with managing the lack of comfort or safety you feel in the room to put in the important work.

- Remember that you deserve quality care.

Tips for Doing Therapy

- Show up early, and consider a pretherapy ritual to separate therapy from the rest of your day and to avoid starting sessions feeling stressed.
- Write things down throughout the week that you may want to share in sessions.
- Show up even when you don't have anything to talk about.
- Remember: Therapy is not just the therapist doing the work. It won't be as effective if you're not engaged in the work, too.
- Reevaluate often. Make sure you're comfortable with your therapist, and if you're not, speak up. They can't read your mind.
- Remember: Progress and healing are not linear. You may feel worse (or feel nothing) before having light-bulb moments.
- Give yourself time to process or decompress after the session, if possible. Create a grounding post-therapy ritual.
- Use journalysis. Journal after, and between, sessions so that you can keep track of how things are going.
- Provide your therapist with resources or readings to minimize explaining versus sharing.
- You're allowed to say no to homework, correct your therapist, disagree with your therapist, or set boundaries around what you're ready to talk about.
- If your therapist doesn't check in with you, check in every now

and then to ask them how they think you are doing and to
reevaluate your therapy goals collaboratively.

• Remember that it's okay to take a break, end therapy, or
change therapists.

• You deserve quality care. Ultimately, you're doing yourself a
disservice if you invest in a therapeutic relationship that isn't
working.

> • I know that confronting or breaking up with a therapist
> may be incredibly hard for a people pleaser; you can
> always write an email or practice the conversation with a
> friend. Remember that therapists are *meant* to be
> working themselves out of a job, and they should want
> what is best for *you*!

Therapist Red Flags	Therapist Green Flags
• They are disclosing too much or centering themselves in the sessions. • They have inappropriate boundaries. • You experience microaggressions in the room with them. • They are combative or aggressive. • They assert that they know best. • They make assumptions and judgments about you and your culture/family. • They consistently forget things that you share.	• They are collaborative. • They are honest about their trainings and education. • They respect your boundaries, and they model healthy boundaries. • They give you undivided attention in sessions. • They are open to feedback. • They remember things you say. • They respectfully challenge you. • They treat you like an expert of your own life.

Chapter Eight

When You're the Only One

After my trip to Croatia and Iceland, and after my six-month fellowship at *HuffPost* ended, I was in limbo for a few weeks, waiting to see if I would be chosen for one of the few full-time transitions available. At this point, a few manager-level colleagues and my boss were supporting and advocating for my professional growth. So when I was offered a full-time job as an editor, I was ecstatic.

I'd always been taught to take my work seriously. When I was a teenager, I'd really wanted to get my own job. I'd only ever worked for my dad's office and had spent the rest of my time pursuing volunteer opportunities, academics, or extracurricular activities. I'd had the privilege of not having to worry about money, but there came a point when I really wanted to make my own. So, to my parents' dismay, I got a waitressing job at Buffalo Wild Wings one summer. My parents were embarrassed and felt like it reflected their inability to provide for me, but I was adamant. And I loved it. I thrived during rush hour, keeping track of big tables, multiple orders, and rude customers who were too busy watching sports on the TV screens to acknowledge me as a person. Regardless of how grueling it could be, it gave me the freedom to be myself, untethered to my identity within my family. At work, I wasn't a daughter or a sister; I was simply a teenager who took busing tables a little more seriously than my co-workers.

When that summer ended, I typed up, printed out, and hand-delivered my two weeks' notice to my manager. I'll never forget how funny and formal he thought it was. "You know you can just leave whenever you want, right? This is just a summer job for most of you," he'd said. My parents had always told me to take pride in what I did and to do it with all my heart, regardless of what it was. I'm sure they weren't specifically referring to my summer job, but I'd internalized that mindset, as well as the importance of being part of a system and goal that was greater than my individual self while simultaneously respecting and appreciating other people's individual work, no matter what they did.

Extreme dedication to one's work is an embedded value in many cultures. What I would eventually have to learn on my own, though, was that workplaces have their own cultures with values and norms that are (or aren't) upheld. I genuinely enjoyed my work at *HuffPost*; I felt like I was coming into my own. I was stimulated almost every day, and I worked with incredibly smart people. And yet the newsroom was a product of the larger system within which it existed (as are most Western workplaces)—one rooted in the historical context of capitalism and white-supremacist ideology. These systems can reinforce and contribute to several learned ideals, including unhealthy productivity measures (such as progress being equated with *more*), a sense of urgency, a scarcity mindset, and impostor syndrome.

The Immigrant Mentality

From my first day as an editor, I flung myself into work; I believed it to be the most important aspect of my identity, and I couldn't yet shake the belief that I was "less than" because of my school experiences. I felt indebted to *HuffPost* for having shown me a glimpse of light with an internship when I was in my darkest years and then again for hiring me. Instead of giving myself credit for working hard, I wrapped my entire sense of self around the belief that *HuffPost* had saved me. While people knew I attended college, no one except HR employees knew that I had only an associate's degree, and I was consumed by self-doubting thoughts: *Did I take someone else's spot who was more worthy? Did I deserve to be there?* It was hard for me to discern between impostor syndrome and internalized shame. I was preoccupied with the story that was holding me back: I went to college, but I didn't graduate from college. Therefore, something must be wrong with me.

In my editorial role, I had a lot of freedom to explore stories and ideas about which I was passionate. I wrote articles on mental health and served as a liaison between my team and the Lifestyle team. Over the years, I happily offered to do more work than was expected, with no additional pay. I drummed up stories about mental health and therapy, ran a Facebook page on solo travel, and attended brainstorming meetings with other teams to help launch initiatives around men's mental health, grief, and Asian American voices. In the early days, one family member told me I was "drinking the Kool-Aid." I scoffed, but the truth was that I was guzzling it down and jonesing for more when it ran out. *HuffPost* and my work in the media became my entire personality. I loved that my job raised eyebrows on dates and even satisfied my parents' appetite for my success. I checked my email at all hours, said yes to everything sent my way, and believed that my boundaryless can-do attitude was a strength. If nothing else, it would at least give me distance from the version of myself who dropped out of four-year college.

The "hustle" mindset is renowned as an immigrant mentality—the idea that we can achieve the things we want through hard, persistent, tireless work. It's admirable, but it ignores the real systems at play. I can't pretend that my parents got here out of sheer luck. They were allowed in because of a value placed on the service they were expected to provide to this country. Capitalism took a beautiful immigrant mentality and exploited it. Our immigrant parents succumbed to it—often in order to survive—and we, as children of immigrants, were taught the same. Take what we can get. Keep our heads down. Be one of them. In the "Exploring the Intersection of Identity, Culture, and Work" workshops I host in corporate environments, I pose anonymous questions to attendees through an interactive app. Attendees are mostly immigrants or children of immigrants and generally BIPOC. One of my questions is about what "immigrant mentality" means to them. Here are some of the most common responses out of nearly one thousand: *Don't complain. Survive. Be risk averse. Hustle. Go from rags to riches. Work harder than others to prove your worth. Be agreeable and willing.* Phew. Even if we aren't consciously aware of how our parents modeled hard work and passed down the narratives they internalized, these still manifest for many of us.

Our struggle with this inherited mentality is compounded by white-supremacist values that are still upheld in Western workplaces. These include power hoarding, transactional relationships, and narrow valuation of intelligence, among others. In 1999, Tema Okun wrote a groundbreaking article on white supremacy culture, and she has recently updated it with the help of her colleagues. They have done extensive research on how workplaces can instill in their employees the aforementioned values, along with urgency, fear, perfectionism, and paternalism. Under white-supremacist ideology, assumptions are made about people's intelligence based on their "otherness"—anything that's different about them, from their clothes, to the food they bring to work, to their accents. Many an immigrant parent or loved one has experienced workplace discrimination and racism, or has been mistreated and misjudged as "dumb" or "incompetent" because of their accent or language barriers. And these assumptions occur, too, at the system level, where accreditations that someone earned in a different nation are not given any credence in their host country. I have friends and acquaintances whose parents lost years' or even decades' worth of degrees and credentials by moving to the West and had to start over in service jobs. Because of these realities, many children of immigrants are encouraged to work the system to move up and "make it." I, too, deeply internalized this idea of meritocracy, and I'm not alone. In my corporate workshops, I hear time and time again from children of immigrants about how they struggle with the belief that they just need to work hard; when hard work alone doesn't make things go as expected, they are left feeling defeated and like they have experienced personal failures. The reality is that individual merit, privilege, and power are often allocated based on where someone is from. Research has found that when workplaces try to be meritocracies, they can actually perpetuate the very inequalities they are trying to eliminate. Among racial groups, Asian Americans are the least likely to be promoted into management roles, and overall, women of color are the least represented group in leadership. So how do we establish ourselves within systems that are stacked against us?

My dad has always said that working hard is the most important thing and that I can rest when I'm older. This mentality has always made me feel guilty for resting, or prioritizing self-care, or saying no because I don't have the energy or bandwidth, or because I just don't want to. The reality is that this sense of urgency as a value has historically been weaponized against BIPOC, increasing the standards by which we can feel "successful" or good enough. It's important to note that Western countries are not the only ones that nurture cultures of overwork. In some Asian countries, a heavy value is placed on work and overwork. Capitalism is everywhere.

I witness so many children of immigrants caught in a productivity paradox: a cycle of needing to be more and more productive, which leads to anxiety, burnout, or unhappiness, which then makes it harder to be productive, which then leads to anxiety, and so on. At *HuffPost*, I started to hold myself to an impossible standard. I was trying to make up for "lost time" and prove my worth, but I felt like nothing I could do would be good enough.

I even oriented any attempts to take breaks around how they could help me be yet more productive. In the same way, we often reframe boundaries and self-care around how they serve our relational roles; we reframe rest around how it serves our productivity. These are "gateway" reframes, often essential to helping clients who are starting with minimal self-compassion. But it's important to establish that we deserve to be restful, nurtured, cared-for individuals— no matter what.

A large part of the work I do with clients is showing them how to slow down and separate themselves from their problem narratives— or how to externalize certain problems rooted in systems or circumstances that should not be tied to their identities. Our narratives are just as much about who and what we are not as they are about who and what we are. Marginalized folks in the West spend enough time being told—in some way or another—that they are not enough. *If you're not perfect or the best, you will become obsolete. If you're not demonstrating your intelligence in a very specific way, you won't be considered smart. If you exhibit behaviors or norms outside those of the white-supremacist culture, you are wrong or bad. You must act quickly to ensure success or hold on to your sense of worthiness.* Many of us internalize these in even subtler ways. By separating our senses of self from our problems, we can make room to explore where we can reclaim agency. This also allows us to question the metrics and definitions we have been using to measure and define "enough"—changing our narrative from one that revolves around needing to always *be* or *do* more to one that centers contentment. If the system that is judging you is deeply flawed, it's not about whether you are "enough."

One South Asian woman wrote in to my *Washington Post* column because she was experiencing guilt for feeling content with her career rather than being ambitious and working toward *more*. If you've been sold a story about how your life is *supposed* to look, you're likely going to feel a disconnect if you don't act within that dominant storyline. This reinforces beliefs: *Others are chasing things, so I should, too. If I'm not doing that, I am lazy. Career achievement should be prioritized.* Challenging years of social, cultural, and familial conditioning and redefining what career success means for us is difficult, and it's even more difficult when different systems are reinforcing who—and how—we should be.

Taking care in a hustle culture

Think back to self-care versus self-soothing, and consider what parts of your life and self you are neglecting (physical, mental, financial, emotional, social, etc.). Remember that the more time that goes by between the filling of these buckets, the longer it may take to fill them back up.

Instead of seeing self-care as a big burdensome beast that you have to tackle and carve out time for, consider how you can more seamlessly integrate self-care behaviors into your routine. There is no such thing as a small self-care behavior; each one adds up in your bucket. Integrating smaller ways to care for yourself will help you feel more in control of your time and allow you to build a firm foundation.

Final reminder: Your self-care and mental health practices may seem like attempts to make yourself more productive. You don't have to earn your self-care or rest. You deserve to enjoy your days, to feel rested and calm, and to be intentional with where your time goes. Full stop.

Culture and Identity in the Workplace

A couple of years into my job, I was promoted to senior editor, and I helped manage the daily output and operations of a team. The following year, I transferred to a team that focused solely on writing, acquiring, and editing personal essays and stories. I worked closely with a large, diverse network of freelancers and continued to specialize in mental health and identity-driven content. The longer I worked at *HuffPost*, the stronger and more efficient I became as an editor and a writer. I started to find ways to incorporate not just my passion but my *own* identity into my work. This coincided with Trump running and getting elected into office, and with the rise of hate crimes, generally but also specifically in the South Asian and Sikh communities. I worked with the Sikh Coalition to raise awareness and discuss media and representation, and I started to write my own essays. Once again, writing became the conduit that catapulted me into a deeper exploration of my relationship with my race, my identity, and my culture(s). Even more, in seeking out and publishing essays by marginalized writers, I encouraged others to do the same. But writing and editing these essays became a double-edged sword. On the one hand, I wanted to express myself and use my access to a major platform for uplifting marginalized voices and sharing my stories. On the other hand, it frustrated me that some of my colleagues weren't held to the same standard. My need to hold two opposite feelings at the same time was constant: the immense responsibility and privilege of bringing in historically marginalized and underrepresented writers *and* the pressure to publish pieces that would resonate with "mainstream" audiences. I loved some of my coworkers and genuinely appreciated and enjoyed what I was doing, *and* I wanted to hold my colleagues accountable to being more inclusive.

I quickly observed that I was among the few representing my community, even when I didn't particularly want to do so and didn't feel like I should have to do so. Writers of color would often seek me out because of our shared identity or because they preferred to work with an editor of color. I was honored, and I took my position as a gatekeeper seriously, wanting to unlock the gates altogether, yet I was restrained by other barriers when I was told that certain stories I wanted to commission weren't mainstream enough. It also wasn't lost on me that the pieces I wrote on solo travel never performed as well as the pieces I wrote about navigating tensions of identity or about the negative, and traumatic, things that were happening to me and my community out in the world. Don't get me wrong; I was happy that my work was garnering views, but I felt like only parts of my story mattered. In my writing communities, other writers of color have shared similar stories about feeling pressured to expose themselves—and their trauma—in ways that were not required or asked of white writers. This started to become more and more apparent in my own day-to-day work. I felt responsible for the representation I wanted to see in our content. When you work in media, where everything is fast-paced—especially with the rise of social channels—and you are up against the ever-decreasing attention span of readers, you learn that the more sensationalized or shocking the content, the longer the lifespan it will likely have on the internet.

During those years in that newsroom, the diversity of the teams I worked on varied, but I was often the only woman of color (or one of two), and sometimes the only person of color at all. Many of us people of color feel like we have to leave parts of ourselves at the door in order to fit in, or we feel that we must highlight our heritage in every way possible to combat the feeling of otherness with pride. Regardless of how we try to contort ourselves, we are left with a similar fallout. Compartmentalizing parts of ourselves is a survival mechanism, but it will still chip away at our own self-esteem and self-concepts. This causes many of us to subscribe to narratives that tell us our wholeness is not worthy, and we may struggle to speak up for fear of being othered even further.

Over the years, I survived several rounds of layoffs, always questioning whether I was kept on because I was brown or because I was good at my job. And every time it seemed like a mistake that I had been spared. I felt like I was always slipping through the cracks, and I was convinced that other people thought so, too. I always worried about seeming "difficult" in the workplace, a narrative I had learned at a young age and one that had followed me through life. I thought it was a me problem—until I talked to more people of color in legacy media and realized that we all felt, to some degree, like we were supposed to hold back or keep quiet in order to preserve our jobs and continue to get opportunities. I can't help but wonder how much of my being "difficult" was a product of my temperament and personality and how much of it was because I never fit the mold expected of me as a daughter or a woman or a South Asian woman. I internalized all of this, and at *HuffPost*, I unknowingly made myself small. I strived to be as agreeable, nice, and hardworking as I could, not realizing that I was internalizing the model minority myth, or the flattening stereotype that not only lumps Asian Americans together as one homogeneous group* but also pits us against other people of color because we are categorized as "the model minority" or the "right" kind of minority. This drives behaviors related to saving face, stoicism, and people pleasing.

When it feels like you don't necessarily belong in any community—or within one or both of your cultures—performative (and inauthentic) identity behaviors may feel like the only lever you have to create a sense of belonging and connection. This need for belonging can drive affiliation behaviors: curating parts of your image and how you act or what you say for fear your wholeness will be rejected. So many children of immigrants have not been encouraged to express their individuality, so they conform or adopt chameleonlike tendencies in different environments to "fit in."

---

*Asian Americans are not a homogeneous or monolithic group. More than twenty-two million people in the U.S. are of Asian descent. In addition to vast differences in historical contexts and the diasporic experience, there are significant economic disparities among this group.

. . .

WHEN YOU ARE CONFINED to a set of values and expectations that don't encompass *all* of who you are, you will inevitably feel like you don't belong or like you're a fraud. Instead of considering this a *you* problem, consider the ways in which the systems are failing you. While anyone and everyone can experience impostor syndrome, those who identify as Black, Indigenous, Latino, or people of color may experience it more frequently and intensely. Gender and family dynamics also play a role in the experience of impostor syndrome. In a 2020 *Harvard Business Review* article that went viral, Ruchika Tulshyan and Jodi-Ann Burey reframed impostor syndrome for women of color, placing an emphasis on the reality that being excluded in white- and/or male-dominated workplaces can exacerbate self-doubt. It's not a flawed mentality on our part but, rather, a logical reaction to our environments.

I have also found research suggesting that if you grew up in a highly demanding family system, where you were expected to be a high achiever, or with dynamics that led to perfectionist behaviors, you are more likely to struggle with impostor syndrome. Even parentification can lead to impostor syndrome as an adult. The culture of silence we may have been raised with is experienced out in the real world, too, further isolating us from the community and connection for which we so deeply ache—all these different pieces creating an insurmountable wall.

I never really fully felt like I fit in with many of my coworkers, especially toward the end of my time at *HuffPost*. I could never pinpoint why, but the tension and discomfort were omnipresent. Sure, in some cases, it could be chalked up to differences in personality, but in others, I felt like I had to make myself small to be likable. For many of us, the reality is that systems pit us against one another, and then our families learn to do the same, reinforcing behaviors rooted in the immigrant mentality or the model minority myth.

In past "Impostor Syndrome" workshops, several Black attendees and other people of color have reported the same experience, often tying it to having to operate within a broken system. In the same way we seek validation from our parents at home because we don't feel good enough, many of us have learned how to work a professional system stacked against us by constantly seeking reassurance that we're on track or "fitting in." We are once again encased in feelings of not being enough, and we become preoccupied by how others perceive us.

DURING MY SIX and a half years at *HuffPost*, I received only two raises (not including the annual cost of living increase given to all employees): the first was tied to moving into a salaried position after my fellowship, and the second was a union-mandated raise to reach the floor salary of a senior editor position. For three years after that, I asked every six months, and every time, I'd be told that I was doing great work, with zero critical feedback and no tangible way to achieve fairer pay. I even found out that a white colleague of mine who did the same work as me but had been given a higher title made more than one and a half times what I did. If that's not bad enough, most of the time I would be told in casual peer-like conversation with my superiors to be grateful for being part of a company that offered a lot of flexibility and allowed me to travel or work remotely (before this was normalized). This is a common message that so many people of color and children of immigrants hear in professional settings. As if our gratitude should outweigh what we believe we are worth.

When I would vent about it to my dad, he would often laugh.

How trivial this problem seemed to him. I was living in New York City and working at a well-known media company with good benefits, flexibility, and decent pay (albeit much lower than it should have been in comparison with salaries paid to colleagues, to which I was made privy during my tenure at *HuffPost*). He told me to be thankful and to put my head down. *Don't disturb the peace. Don't make trouble.* I heard: *Just be grateful that you have been accepted in some way.* This mentality is so typical for us children of immigrants who have heard about or observed the struggles of our parents and grandparents. It can feel stupid to ask for more, to admit that we've had enough. To put our foot down. Even now, my dad will often tell me not to be greedy as I try to navigate self-employment and set my rates for speaking engagements. The gratitude shame creeps back in. Here's the thing, though: when we are made to feel *ungrateful*, the focus is on what we are *not* feeling rather than on what we *are* feeling. For many of us, this may be feeling frustrated, overworked, invalidated, overlooked, and so on. At *HuffPost*, I *was* grateful and I felt discouraged by my lack of compensation and, frankly, appreciation. To continue to do work I genuinely loved, I had to brace myself to manage all of the other feelings that were also involved.

Cross-Cultural Communication

For many children of immigrants, because of the emphasis on hierarchy and respect for superiors or elders, it feels next to impossible to assert oneself in the workplace or have an informal, blurred-boundaries relationship with superiors. However, in Western workplaces, assertion and sometimes aggression are actually rewarded and encouraged—though not necessarily when exhibited by people of color. White Americans may view quiet communication as passive and guarded, while in Asian and other cultures, it may signify wisdom and maturity. Not to mention the gender and racial-ethnic factors at play. I asked community members if they had ever been labeled with stereotypical descriptors at work for speaking up, and they responded with a range of racial pejoratives, such as "angry Black woman," "tiger mom," and "spicy." Naturally, none of their issues were properly addressed—and they were left feeling even more unheard.

For many of us who grew up in households where we were discouraged from asking for what we needed, the barrier is very high for reaching out or speaking up in predominantly white institutions that have continuously relegated us to the background. It makes such a difference to clearly recognize and address what is happening (in the world, in the community, and in your employees' and students' lives).

After working in a majority-white newsroom for more than six years and then being in graduate school during a pandemic, I am *still* surprised at how little explicit compassion or modeling of healthy behaviors is provided to employees and students by those in positions of authority. Ideally, it's those in positions of power who should be modeling mental health care and giving explicit permission to their subordinates to do the same. Instead, in capitalist systems, the onus is often on employees to self-advocate, which is especially difficult when so many of us have not been taught how to do so because it's countercultural. This may not be as extreme as requesting a sudden mental health day; it could be as simple as asking for clarification on an assignment, correcting someone when they overlook an item on the agenda, or saying no to an extra task because of an already full plate.

Not everyone communicates in the same way, and not everyone understands implicit communication in the same way. There are differences between what we call high-context cultures (e.g., Asian, Russian, Arab, and African cultures) and low-context cultures (e.g., American, Swiss, English, and French cultures). These differences in communication styles can seem unimportant to people who only exist in low-context cultures, but miscommunications and misunderstandings can put a lot of important things at stake—not only job security but also friendships, promotions, acceptance, and belonging.

In a high-context culture, communication is heavily dependent on contextual cues. For instance, many immigrant parents don't say "I love you." Instead, they show it with actions—like preparing a favorite meal or cut fruit—and behaviors—like when my dad clips mental health articles from newspapers and saves them for me. It's assumed rather than stated explicitly. In high-context communication, a lot of things may be left unsaid. People may expect what feels like mind reading to those who don't pick up on nonverbal or tonal cues. For many of us children of immigrants, this learned mind reading leads us to tie our worthiness to how well we can anticipate the needs of our elders or superiors—at home and at work. Conversely, in low-context cultures, communication is more explicit. We see detailed emails and paper trails; there is shared knowledge and openness in relaying information. In one communication style, we are guessing and stumbling our way through interactions, and in another, we are asking and being told directly. Explicit and verbal communication is not better; it's just different.

A lot of children of immigrants feel trapped between implicit and explicit expectations. We're just expected to *know* how to communicate, and this can cause stress and anxiety until we become better equipped at picking up on cultural cues. In one environment we may be too direct, and in another we may not be direct enough. Growing up, I was told I would make a good lawyer because I wasn't always agreeable or willing to conform—a trait that has led me to be called confident or proactive in professional settings. When I would try to assert my feelings or opinions, I was often mistaken for being in debate with my parents rather than in dialogue or communication.

Gender roles compound these communication expectations, too. Though I like to believe myself liberal and open-minded, I am a product of my own socialization—rooted in patriarchal norms—and to this day still struggle to speak up or disagree with an elder or, worse, an elder man. Many children of immigrants, like me, grow up with a very specific understanding of gender roles, and children of immigrants in the West are often the ones in their families to question and rebel against them. We are exposed to gendered socialization that impacts the way we feel we *have* to show up in order to fit the norms of how a traditional man or woman should behave, dress, and sound. I hear about this dynamic in every corporate workshop that I host.

When I polled my Instagram community, 96 percent of almost 2,400 participants said that respect for elders was expected, not earned, in their family systems. This value shows up at work and makes it that much more difficult for someone to correct or say no to another person who is older or in a superior position. The dynamics and hierarchy we learned at home replicate themselves at work. Deference to a parent becomes deference to a manager. Devotion to our family becomes devotion to our work. Intensifying this transference is the reflexive nature of the impression management strategies we have learned to ensure that we appear okay, competent, capable, and grateful. In the workplace, multi- and bicultural folks adapt to a differing cultural environment by changing their behaviors and mannerisms, especially if the environment conflicts with their values—a concept called cultural code-switching—and it's symptomatic of a larger systemic issue due to an exclusionary or homogeneous workplace culture. This has a significant impact on our mental health and self-concepts. Who are we when we remove others' expectations? Many of us don't know, are scared to find out, or anticipate real and negative repercussions. After all, for many folks, code-switching is a survival tactic used to avoid racism, discrimination, and unconscious bias by managing how other people—primarily white people but also just people, generally, who have internalized white supremacy—feel about their races, identities, or cultures. This directly impacts the sense of belonging that someone will feel in a largely white workplace.

Even though I worked in the same newsroom for six and a half years, colleagues still pronounced my name wrong. Once, years into the job, I corrected a white colleague (repeatedly!), who said that she had heard another white colleague say it the wrong way, so she had assumed that was the right pronunciation. Ultimately, this reinforced my belief that what I say and think aren't as important as what my white colleagues or peers say and think—even when it comes to the pronunciation of my own name. I questioned whether these colleagues could value my work and my contributions if they weren't even able to value or respect me enough to ask me how to say my name. These microexperiences build up, and like all microaggressions, they take a toll on one's self-esteem.

These experiences and cultural differences can also prevent anyone from a marginalized group, let alone children of immigrants, from feeling a sense of psychological safety at work. Psychological safety is "being able to show and employ one's self without fear of negative consequences of self-image, status or career," and contrary to what many people believe, safety is determined by the person experiencing/seeking it. If a person does not feel comfortable speaking to you about their struggles, then you may not be a safe person with whom to do so. Transparency in decision-making; having norms for how mistakes are handled; explicitly expressing value and appreciation; inviting participation in neutral, nonthreatening ways; offering different formats for feedback and reviews; and, as mentioned, making decisions that prioritize the well-being of employees (without assuming they will take advantage of them) can all help create a sense of psychological safety. Regardless of cultural background, there is always a power deferential at play in workplaces. Though everyone was around my age at *HuffPost*, this didn't change the fact that some people were in positions of power, while others were not. It's important for us to constantly challenge and question the dominant culture and *whom* it actually serves.

Only after leaving my job at *HuffPost*—which I didn't do until several years later—was I able to process how little psychological safety I had felt there in the end. I hadn't even been able to be completely honest with my boss about some of the factors that contributed to my departure, which had to do with the fact that almost none of the women of color I knew in the company were getting raises, and I felt like I had been tokenized in ways that made me feel uneasy and unappreciated. It was one of many instances in which I invalidated my own experience to make others more comfortable.

At the time, I talked myself out of thinking that my discomfort had been about race, but after some weeks outside that environment, I realized how much it *had* been about race—even if only subconsciously. Later, I would learn that the HuffPost Union had reported that twenty-eight people of color (including me) had left *HuffPost* in the previous two years, and twenty-five of those were women of color. A month after my last day at the job, a white manager wrote to me after seeing a tweet in which I expressed solidarity with the union and shared that many POC, including myself, felt unsupported in the newsroom. He told me that he knew I'd had some issues but he didn't know that I hadn't felt supported. He said he wished that I had talked to him. I didn't reply, and for a long time, I couldn't pinpoint why his texts enraged me. Now I know: allyship and support as reactive behaviors are not the same as allyship and support as proactive measures. *He* didn't open the door as a higher-up at a company that people of color were leaving in droves. *He* didn't broach the conversation with me until after I said something, even though he admits to knowing I had some issues. Even in writing this, I am overwhelmed by the same narratives within my family: *Don't talk about it! Just be grateful!* As though mentioning anything negative eliminates everything positive.

I've worked with clients who navigate experiences ranging from microaggressions to ongoing racial trauma at work. In most cases, there is a lack of representation—or simply active care—in management, and there is a historical culture that wasn't intentionally created to be inclusive. When I asked Brown Girl Therapy community members what gave them a semblance of belonging at work, the two most common responses were employee resource groups and BIPOC or diverse supervisors/management. These enabled people to feel safe and comfortable in sharing salary information and working together to develop communication strategies and career advancement opportunities. It also allowed folks to see themselves represented in positions—making it feel that much more attainable to them, too. They're not a perfect solution, but they're a step in the right direction.

DURING THE YEARS I spent navigating my career and all the milestones and issues I experienced along the way, I continued to see Dr. T. She helped me build language around my own experiences and feelings. I practiced and brainstormed with her about how I wanted to communicate my feelings, expanding into a gray area of assertiveness and strength that I had been scared to venture into for fear of being unlikable or difficult. I released my frustration about work, and I started to explore leaving media altogether. It was clear that I was reaching my threshold, and I knew something needed to change.

Like a houseplant leaning toward the sun, I had always gravitated to wellness and mental health content. I started to think about what it might look like to pursue a mental health career in a more direct way. As soon as I started talking to people about it, I learned that a lot of folks weren't surprised—whether it was because they had been in my life since my early blogging days or because they had witnessed my advocacy and passion in New York. One college friend even sent me a screenshot from a conversation we'd had on Facebook Messenger in 2010—around the same time I was seeing my college counselor, Mel. Though I didn't have any recollection of it, I had talked about wanting to help people and be a therapist. Ultimately, I knew that if I wanted to leave media at all, I would likely need my bachelor's degree to do so. And if I wanted to work in mental health, I would likely need a graduate degree.

Writing is a form of therapy for many people, and as an editor, I had the privilege of being a trusted companion who assisted writers in diving deep into, and sharing, their own stories. I've even received two traditionally published novels by South Asian women who said that I gave them *their* start as writers while I was at *HuffPost*. A lot of personal experiences worth telling can bring up heavy emotions, especially when the goal is to share these experiences in such a public way. The work of a good editor requires invisibility and helpfulness, and I had time to master the art of putting in my own emotional and mental energy so that I could ask the right questions and, from behind the scenes, guide someone else toward peace with their stories.

These skills, I realized, were parallel to those needed to be a sensitive and effective mental health therapist. I had worked with writers through their guilt, shame, anger, sadness, and reconciliations. This specific angle of my job pushed me into a place where I discovered that I wanted to help people with their relationships and their struggles in a more focused and traditional manner. I had often found myself harboring questions for writers that would never make it into the pieces they were working on, and I felt drawn beyond one-off stories. Everything I had learned at *HuffPost* prepared me to finally pursue my bachelor's degree—and this time, not because it was expected of me. I wanted to do it for myself.

Reflections on being "the only" or "one of few" in the workplace

Unpacking Your Feelings of Impostor Syndrome

- As "the only" in a room, you may feel like you have to represent an entire group/population, and this can feed your core belief that you are not allowed to make any mistakes. You may feel the need to constantly overprepare and overachieve in order to uphold or maintain the reputation of your community.

- You may have been taught that your parents and elders know what's best, and this may have nurtured a sense of insecurity in self-advocating, speaking up, or taking up space.

- You may not have been taught how to "fail" or make mistakes, or that these are a normal part of success and pursuing achievement and growth. So when things don't go according to plan or as well as you hoped, you feel like a fraud or a failure.

- You were taught what "success" looks like, and you weren't encouraged to hone your natural skills or pursue the learning of new skills outside this box. So you berate yourself and feel like a failure if you can't "meet the expectations" that have been placed on you.

- You talk yourself out of feeling like you experienced a microaggression or an act of discrimination because no one else really witnessed it, or it was just micro enough that you don't want to make it about race. This kind of denial nurtures your negative self-talk.

- You may feel like a "fraud" because you've been made to believe that you slipped through the cracks into positions and institutions that weren't meant for you (because they likely weren't created *for* you).

- You may feel that if you don't share your progress or success with others, then it's not meaningful or worthy or real.

Tips for Managing Impostor Syndrome

- **Normalize and reframe failure.** Consider how you can reframe failure as something that is not tied to your self-concept but, rather, a part of the journey.

- **Keep an accomplishments journal.** This can help remind you of your strengths and what you have previously achieved. Normalize celebrating your accomplishments (along with your efforts!). This can also benefit you when it comes time to advocate for yourself in the workplace.

- **Become friends with your self-doubt.** Instead of letting your self-doubt own you and dictate your life, let it be a motivator rather than an inhibitor. Remind yourself: I can learn; I can grow.

- **Set realistic goals.** If you don't deepen your self-awareness about your limitations or incapabilities, you will continue to measure yourself against an impossible version of yourself, fueling your impostorism. You are not expected to know everything. You can outsource, ask for help, or learn things in your own time/way.

- **Instead of "faking it till you make it," embrace that you don't know what you don't know—yet.** This means that when you are in new roles, new environments, new cultural systems, new teams, and new careers, you adapt and grow—there's a learning curve. You are not meant to know everything; you are meant to learn. By adopting this learning mindset, you forgo harsh expectations and instead give yourself grace to be, well, human. You can learn through research, reading, skill development, allies, and mentorship. Remember that being unsure about something doesn't make you an impostor!

- **Have trusted allies and mentors to turn to.** They can help normalize setbacks as part of the journey, and they can give you trusted feedback on how you are doing and what you are capable of.

- **Delegate and ask for support where you can.** Part of struggling with impostor syndrome is believing that you should know everything. You can learn things, but you are not required to know *everything*. Where can you potentially outsource?

- **Remind yourself of your reality and whom you are comparing yourself to.** You may work in environments where values fail to be culturally inclusive or sensitive, or you may be evaluated by measures that are likewise lacking. This may make you feel like you are not good enough.

- **Build a life outside work.** Research suggests that if you are feeling unsupported or exploited at work, this can contribute to lower morale and even burnout if you overcompensate by taking on more work. You may experience self-doubt and feelings of underperformance. Dig deeper into *other* hobbies and relationships that bring you joy, help you feel safe, and nurture you.

Reflections on Impostor Syndrome

- What performative behaviors have you adopted that perpetuate your feelings of impostorism because they aren't authentic to you?
- What systemic narratives and experiences have affected your levels of impostorism? How do you manage this today?
- What values are represented in your different environments? Which ones reinforce your feelings of impostor syndrome, and why?

Chapter Nine

Love or Loyalty

———————————

In October 2016, three years after I had moved to New York and a year after my first father-daughter trip, my parents and I were in Albuquerque for the International Balloon Fiesta. It was supposed to be my second annual father-daughter trip, but my mom had really wanted to join us, so there we three were, sitting together at a restaurant in the majestic Sandia Mountains and talking about some of my upcoming life and travel plans. Unbeknownst to my parents, I was in a very new relationship. Usually, I prepared and analyzed what I was going to say to them and how I was going to deliver it, striking only when I could get them in their best moods. Conversations with them often required strategy. But in that moment, after my mom had shared her concern over the fact that I was unwed, I just blurted it out: "I'm dating someone. He's white American."

In the view of most traditional immigrant parents, dating is not *really* a thing, especially when it involves a non-family-approved partner. At one time or another, children of immigrants will likely find themselves stuck loving people, pursuits, hobbies, and other things in private because these things don't align with what's expected of them, what they were taught, or what they'll be supported in. This learned behavior has detrimental effects on our relationships with "love." We second-guess what we want or what we think is good for us. We make choices simply to avoid shame and rejection. We lead double lives, never fully happy for fear we'll be found out. Finding full agency as children of immigrants can look like navigating full relationships and heartbreaks (romantic or not) without the knowledge of our families—a million different lives being lived in secret.

In high school, I dated my first boyfriend behind my parents' backs and even had a second phone for talking to him. It didn't feel unusual to become such an expert deceiver; even then it felt like a survival mechanism. I wasn't given space or encouragement to explore, with the safety of a parental relationship to fall back on. It felt like my parents' love and approval were on the line every time I tried to do something "normal."

Because it always seemed like I had more at stake in my secret relationships, I had much higher expectations for them. I never knew how to be in a relationship for its own sake—how to be young and in love, just having fun getting to know someone. I desperately wanted every relationship I was in to work out, because I couldn't fathom having to start over. To my mind, if someone had deigned to love me in spite of the hoops I had to jump through, and in spite of never having my parents on board, they were already going above and beyond for me. I convinced myself that I couldn't ask for more from the relationship.

Just like with friendships, I was never taught how to be an active participant in romantic love. I wasn't taught to understand my own needs, to advocate for myself, or to communicate and engage in conflict resolution in healthy ways. I lived most of my life under the cultural assumption that when I got to a certain age, I would meet a partner my parents approved of (or introduced me to), and we would get married and figure everything out later; all would be fine. I didn't know that love required effort and a certain compatibility. And so I covertly explored my romantic needs, my attachment behaviors, and my ideas about what constitutes a healthy relationship.

I recently asked my mom if she really didn't know about my high school boyfriend, and she laughed the question off. *I guess I just didn't think you or your siblings would date.* I know that my brother and sister had secret relationships, too, but they were closer in age and got into their mischief together. I also think that my brother was given more freedom to push the boundaries of what was accepted because he was a boy (though he disagrees). I have heard stories from both my parents about some of the ways in which they, too, had lived their lives in secret. Maybe this was a survival trait passed down from one generation to another. Or maybe it stemmed from a fear of parents and was rooted in gendered norms around maintaining reputation and honor. Or maybe it was both. My dad hid his alcohol use from my grandparents, and my mom told me about how she would shorten the skirt of her school uniform and lower her neckline when she left the house. These moments of rebellion are seen as rites of passage rather than as things that might have brought my parents closer to me. I have never understood why they didn't want it to be different for us, knowing that their own secret-keeping led to fractured relationships with their parents. Back then, my parents—like most of their peers—were not friends with their kids, and they didn't know that they could be.

Of 5,910 children of immigrants who responded to one of my polls on Instagram, 74 percent said that they date/dated in secret from their parents, too. The lack of disclosure not only cements emotional distance but also reinforces secrecy, including for those who are in abusive relationship dynamics. I personally know many children of immigrants, all women, who went by the book and did what was expected of them—married family- and community-approved partners—only to end up in relationships with men who were abusive, manipulative, or controlling. It took months, if not years, for these women to speak up about their abuse—even with their own parents—for fear that it reflected poorly on *them* or their families. Some women never do. And it's not just a lack of communication around romantic love in families; it's also the expectation of stoicism, the learned rationalizations of abuse, the feelings of humiliation, and the fear about future prospects. It breaks my heart that social perception is upheld over safety, happiness, and health. And even more, for those who choose to be with partners their parents aren't wholly supportive of—whether it's because of race, sexuality, religion, or something else—there is paralyzing fear. I've talked to many children of immigrants who've been in long-term relationships behind their parents' backs because they are scared to tell them until they are 100 percent certain. Once again, we're left having to prove our choices. The looming prospect of "I told you so" creates an irreparable chasm in many relationships. And so we develop these chameleonlike tendencies to fit in and to receive the love we are so desperate for. They become the glue that holds our personal, generational, and cultural bonds together.

When I met Sam on a dating site in 2016, I wasn't making a conscious decision to be with someone who wasn't Indian or Sikh. After years of heartbreak and a series of terrible dating experiences, I just wanted to meet a kind, respectful, generous person. Sam's emotional intelligence immediately blew me away, and I learned quickly that he was very different from the men I had dated before. I was going into my third year of therapy, and as we fell in love, therapy became the place for me to unpack my insecurities. In previous relationships, I had gotten used to acting out for attention and people-pleasing to validate my worthiness. I was completely incapable of naming or communicating my feelings or needs. Dr. T countered my fears of everything falling apart with alternative scenarios: What if it didn't? She helped me learn how to show up vulnerably and honestly with Sam.

Early on in our relationship, Sam had made plans to hang out with one of his female friends. Usually, we would text at night before bed, but I hadn't heard from him again and knew this was unlike him. My brain started spiraling. I convinced myself that he was cheating on me or going to leave me. Thankfully, I had therapy the next day. Dr. T asked me why I was so fearful of telling him the truth about what I was feeling. Jealousy was unbecoming; I was convinced he would no longer want me if he saw my insecurity—one of the scars that my previous relationships had left behind. She reminded me that it's a feeling that doesn't define me but is telling me something, and by having a conversation, I had the chance to increase intimacy with someone I cared about.

That night, Sam and I were at a Party City buying a last-minute accessory for a Halloween costume. In front of the wigs and capes, I asked him to turn around so that he couldn't look at me when I was talking. I told him that I felt jealous and that because I had never heard from him again that evening, I had created stories in my head about what he was doing or thinking. I cried and apologized for being too needy. He turned around and hugged me. The first thing he said was: "You're not needy. I want to help make you feel more secure in these situations."

I didn't know then that my behaviors reflected a textbook anxious attachment style. I didn't know that since I was a kid, I had held on to a deep fear of abandonment. Slowly, though, I realized I was unlearning some of my preoccupied and anxious behaviors; in this moment, for example, I had been direct and forthcoming rather than passive-aggressive or reactive. I was learning, with Dr. T, to discern between my thoughts and reality. After all, attachment styles are not fixed; they are learned and reinforced. I had been in different relationships where my anxious attachment was weaponized against me rather than engaged with love and acceptance. My ex, Seth, had been more of an avoidant type, reinforcing my anxiety through his tendency to stonewall and refuse to communicate. He made me believe that my insecurities were mine to deal with alone, while Dr. T and Sam made me realize that needs are not a bad thing.

All children generally learn to behave in ways that get them what they need. They grow into adults who behave in parallel ways to fulfill those same needs. As I've discussed, children of immigrants from families with collectivist values may experience emotional insecurity, act as compulsive caregivers, or engage in extreme people-pleasing. These learned behaviors may culminate in an anxious-avoidant attachment style, found often in children of immigrants. When I asked members of the Brown Girl Therapy community to identify themselves with an attachment style, 65 percent of 4,191 said they identify with an anxious attachment style, while only 7 percent identified with a secure attachment style. Many of my second-gen clients also struggle with anxious attachment styles, highlighted by approval seeking, excessive worry about the status of relationships, and fear of rejection. In many instances, I am able to do for them what Dr. T did for me—explore their fears of abandonment in terms of their own childhoods and encourage them to own these feelings with their current partners. Unlike what I was taught growing up, we aren't born *knowing* how to be in relationships; we have to be willing to show up honestly and learn alongside someone else who wants to do the same with us. Relationships are dynamic entities that require active and evolving effort.

As a mental health professional, I view clients and humans holistically within the systems in which they exist. This includes exploring families of origin, cultures, relationships, and privilege and oppression. I strongly believe that we grow in connection with others and that our relationships bring out different aspects of ourselves. Often, our understanding of what makes us worthy discourages us from being able to speak up or even imagine the possibility of different, healthier types of relationships.

Sam wasn't anything like the man I imagined I would be with. I thought I would end up with someone who was more analytic, perhaps kind but with a demanding presence. Someone who would be questioning. Someone who would (intentionally or not) make me feel small as a woman. This says a lot, I know. Most of the men in my life until then had been emotionally distant, albeit loyal and reliable in other ways. They were confident, sometimes to a degree of self-importance. They were generous yet often motivated by their own needs. Instead, Sam is kind and sensitive, unafraid to express his full range of emotions. He's a professional drummer, film editor, and creative. He sees the world differently from me; he's generous without expectation, and he trusts people at face value. He is white and American and from Massachusetts. I felt safe with him, and it was a new experience for me.

No matter how secure I was beginning to feel in my relationship with Sam, I knew my parents weren't going to be happy. Since my college boyfriend and I had broken up a few years prior, they had been holding out hope that I'd finally choose someone Sikh. After all, marriage is the ultimate success for South Asian daughters, and my parents had been worried about me on that front for years. "We just want you to meet someone" had been my parents' long-standing mantra for me, repeated all through my midtwenties, through the times when I started therapy, lived independently in New York, and changed and expanded and contracted in ways I had never thought possible. I had been building my own community and chosen family. I had proven that there were many things I could do if I just put my mind to them. Still, no matter how I was growing or discovering my agency, my parents insisted that I needed to meet someone. They worried I was becoming *too* independent.

Intercultural Dating

I've always identified as a Sikh, but it's been hard to reconcile my identity in my dating life. Before I met Sam, I dated both Sikh and non-Sikh men, Indian and non-Indian men, knowing that, ultimately, my parents expected me to marry a Sikh. But, honestly, I often struggled when I went on dates with Sikh men, especially during the years when I lived in New York City, between dating Seth and meeting Sam. Sometimes, it was just a matter of timing or unreciprocated feelings, but in some cases, I felt either too American—like I couldn't relate with or match their cultural experiences—or like I was forcing myself to overlook a lack of chemistry or connection to make it work just because they were Sikh. In other cases, conversations about relational and marital expectations laid bare an underlying double standard—it was okay for men to grow up in this country and become liberal, opinionated, career-driven people, but the same did not apply to women, who were still expected to be more submissive, subservient, and motivated by domestic duties. Just because someone looks good on paper does not mean that a relationship with them will be unproblematic and healthy.

My parents struggled to understand this, often telling me that my standards were too high when I would report back after dates. To them, it was normal for parents to have a majority vote in who their kids were going to marry. Though my brother, Ajay, and my sister, Chandani, had their own experiences with dating and loving in secret, they both went the more traditional route. My brother gave my parents permission to introduce him to a Sikh woman they knew through family and friends abroad. After dating long-distance, my brother and this woman together made the decision to get married, even though they had met only a couple of times in person. And though my sister had a love marriage, it was to a Sikh man.

That day in Albuquerque, my mom was visibly taken aback when I told her that I'd met someone. "You have?" She immediately looked at my dad to see how he felt about this unexpected news.

"Yes, and it's still really early, but I really, really like him," I responded.

Before I could share anything else, my parents bombarded me with their pressing questions: What's his name? How old is he? What does he do? Where is his family from? What do his parents do? Does he have siblings? What do *they* do? To South Asian—and many other—immigrant parents, a person is not just who they are as an individual but also who they surround themselves with, what family they were born into, and what life they've built together. I could tell that my dad was processing quietly. My mom usually allows my dad to have the first reaction so that she can gauge how she should react. And so there was a lot of silence. It was a very brief but informative ten- to fifteen-minute conversation, and then we carried on with dinner.

It wasn't until the next day, when we had woken up and were about to start our morning trip to Santa Fe, that my dad finally exclaimed, "No, this isn't going to work!" My parents just couldn't wrap their heads around me seriously dating a non-Sikh man. They couldn't understand why I would make a relationship and potential marriage even harder by choosing someone so different from me. They pretty much banked on it being something that would pass. As with most things—my depression, my feelings, my need to move out of the house, my pursuit of writing as a career—I knew I would have to prove that this was not a whim. For many children of immigrants, this constant questioning about what we choose for ourselves and our happiness can lead to family fallouts and further deepen our self-doubts. It also leaves us unable to investigate our choices for ourselves, because any ounce of hesitancy on our end provides our parents with an inroad to try to pull us out of these decisions altogether. Once again, I found myself stuck in a negative feedback loop that I have since observed in many of us: if we were confident in our paths or choices, then our parents might not interject or question them, but their lack of trust strips us of our confidence.

A month after the trip to Albuquerque, I was invited to Sam's brother's wedding, where I met his family for the first time. My parents were on board; I think they knew I would go either way, so they saw this as an opportunity for me to gain more information and report back. I also think I was pretty clear on wanting to be honest with them about this relationship. Sam and I had been dating for only three months when Donald Trump got elected president in 2016, and though Sam and his immediate family are liberal, a lot of things just started hitting me in the face. It was the moment I knew that Sam and I would either be able to see this relationship through or have to break up. We had to talk about the elephant in the room: his privilege as a white man. Sam listened intently as I talked through my own identity crisis and my fears for the turban-wearing men in my family who live in the South. He also owned his place in these ongoing issues, learning to be an ally who knew when to stand back and listen and when to stand up and speak out. Of course, this was only one of many ongoing conversations in our interracial relationship, but the honesty and vulnerability we both shared set our relationship apart from many of the ones I have witnessed in my life, regardless of whether race and ethnicity are shared.

His brother's wedding was beautiful. His family was incredibly kind and generous and down to earth, and this broke a lot of stereotypes for me. I realized that I had been quite fearful of what his family was going to be like. In fact, they were the opposite of what I'd feared; they were so welcoming to me. They were curious about where I came from; his dad was researching Sikhism, and his mom had practiced my name (as well as my family members' names) many times to ensure that she would get it right in front of me.

I recognize there's a level of intimacy I may never know with Sam, since we don't share the same culture or background. I also know that if I were with a Sikh man, I wouldn't necessarily need to have emotionally laborious conversations with him about race, religion, and politics. Then again, it's not that emotionally laborious conversations would disappear; they would likely just be different ones. Differences are part of what make my relationship with Sam beautiful. All relationships require effort, patience and respect, and healthy communication. But because Sam and I were forced to address our differences very early on, we've also been able to address other big needs and desires in a partnership—from money and family involvement, to future religious involvement, to cultural traditions and potential children. I also know that I am not alone. I hear from many a community member about navigating an intercultural relationship—whether it's one with someone from the dominant culture or one with someone from another marginalized or immigrant background.

Much of what made me fall for Sam were his values: ones that are coincidentally foundational in the Sikh religion and of great importance to my family. They include his kindness, his generosity, his commitment to serving others, his respect and desire for community building, and his nonjudgmental nature and ability to treat everyone as equals. I know that by choosing each other, Sam and I may have chosen a tougher path to go down, but we have also been able to grow together, and so have our families. There's been a steep learning curve for all of us. Sam and his loving, open-minded, open-hearted family have been able to break down the stereotypes that my family had of white Americans. And I've been able to reconnect with who I am and where I come from by teaching my husband and in-laws about Sikhism and being South Asian in this country.

When Grief Meets Guilt

The handful of months after I told my parents about Sam were marked by stillness. My parents had accepted that I had nothing "negative" to report following the wedding and that Sam and I were still seeing each other. I knew they weren't totally supportive, but they were also four hundred miles away and unable to shake things up. Or so I thought. For many of us children of immigrants, the first factor we consider when making choices is what our parents will say or how they will feel. Regardless of distance, there's always a dull ache in the back of our minds. *Will they be upset? Hurt? Angry?*

It was a chilly Saturday afternoon in early December, and Sam and I were running errands at CVS in preparation for my friend's birthday celebration that evening when my phone rang. I was kneeling down in the bodywash aisle when I thoughtlessly picked up. "Hey, Mom!"

"Dadi died," my mom said, so matter-of-factly that I was convinced I had misheard. "We're making plans to head to India in the next couple of days."

Stunned, I asked, "How's Pop?" This was followed by a rambling of logistical questions: *Should I come home? How do I get home? When's the next bus? I need to go and pack. I'm in Midtown and need to get uptown to my apartment. I need to text my friend whose party is tonight.*

My relationship with my dadima, my paternal grandmother, had often consisted of a phone call every few months that covered the basic pleasantries and when we'd see each other again. Though I understand conversational Punjabi, I'd found it hard to always understand her, and her English was practically nonexistent. Most of the time, our calls would be short and sweet, expressing our love and care for each other and usually ending with Dadi asking me to tell her kaka—her small boy, my dad—that he needed to come home. I can still hear her laugh, more of a chuckle, and my fondest memory of her is when she sat next to me in her home in Patiala while I, then a young child, meticulously colored in a velvet banner that read "LOVE," which she framed and hung in her dining room to always remember me.

"Don't worry about coming home—we're going to make plans to leave soon, and it's far," my mom solemnly informed me.

I cried as soon as I got off the phone, not realizing that I was fully sitting in the middle of the aisle until strangers brushed past me, loudly uttering their excuse-mes. I cried because my grandmother had died. I cried because my dad had just lost his last parent. I would learn years later (because it's happened several times every year) that I was also crying because my body and brain were feeling the pain of another major limb being severed from my family tree, which was quickly getting smaller and smaller. I cried because I hadn't known her all that well. I cried because she would never meet my future husband or my future kids. I cried because she would have been so disappointed, I perceived, to know where I had ended up—questioning God and religion and being in a serious relationship with a white man.

My parents traveled to India for the funeral and to deal with the logistics of finances and property. The day they traveled back was a Sunday, and Sam and I were hanging out one last time before we went our separate ways for the winter holidays. I checked my phone to see what time it was and saw that my dad had sent me a text. It was a screenshot of a Sikh man's LinkedIn photo, followed by his educational history and a short résumé: "Worked in Amazon A9 division for 3 years, now at hedge fund. In California. Spends 40 percent of time in NY." The last piece of information was his full name.

"Okay," I replied. I didn't know if I should be upset or impressed that my dad had just cremated his mother and was somehow still determined to find me a man who wasn't the man I told him I wanted. I responded casually, even though the texts pierced the bubble of comfort and happiness wrapped around Sam and me in Central Park.

At this point, Sam still hadn't met my parents, and it was important to me that he see their best qualities, their protectiveness and generosity. Among all of the difficulties I encountered after telling my parents about Sam, the hardest thing to figure out was what I should tell Sam and what I should keep to myself so as not to sway his opinion about them. It was also impossible for me to pretend like I wasn't being affected by having to manage my parents' feelings about my choice of a partner who wasn't Sikh, or in a traditionally "accepted" career, or from a reputable or well-known family. My parents placed so much importance on qualities deemed brag-worthy that they were shortchanging what was more important to a sustainable and healthy partnership or merging of families.

I know that those first couple of years were not easy on Sam. He was frustrated to feel that his reputation had been tarnished before my parents even got to know him. He comes from a family in which people are taken at face value: no one plays games to get another's attention, adult children are trusted to make decisions for themselves, everyone is given the benefit of the doubt, and happiness—in whatever form it comes—is prioritized. It was a crash course in how different the norms and values of my culture and family are.

Though I often found myself caught between my parents and the man I loved, it was through my work with Dr. T and my pursuit of healing and self-examination that I learned to root into my own values and needs. I strove to be frank with Sam about what we were in for and what I needed from him through this, but I also made sure to show him the love and validation he needed to feel secure. In discussions with my parents, this enabled me to stay firm in my choices while also being respectful and engaging with my parents' fears and worries. No matter what, Sam's endless patience made room for me to navigate the situation without feeling like I had to choose a side or like I was trapped in the middle.

WHEN I WENT home for the holidays, I was unprepared for how to console my father, a private man who always wanted to protect his loved ones from seeing his feelings, while also compartmentalizing my own guilt and hurt over falling in love with a man my parents didn't want me to be with. I could see that my dad was going through his own identity crisis. His grief manifested itself as incessant questioning. *Did I do the right thing by leaving India and bringing my family to this country? Am I a bad son because I have always lived so far away from her? Am I a bad son because I didn't call her all the time and didn't visit as much as maybe I should have? Did I do enough?* Hearing him voice concerns like this pulled me away from my own peace and happiness, particularly since these feelings were at odds with those of my parents. In that moment, I saw my dad not as my papa but as the oldest son of my grandmother, a woman who had been widowed for the last twenty-five years of her life.

All the archaic beliefs and norms my dad might uphold had been passed down from the generations before him like family heirlooms. The eldest child, usually male, in immigrant families often carries a primary responsibility for their parents and their younger siblings. My dad had been the only one in his family to leave India and move West. He'd made choices for himself and for his pregnant wife and two kids. In the beginning, he didn't have the means to go back and visit as frequently as he wanted, often getting news of his family alone in the random phone booths he used to call home. And now, decades later, his mother and second parent was gone.

Even though my dad wasn't sharing all of this out loud, I'd been through enough of my own identity crises that I could see the questioning and regret playing out in his eyes and mind. He needed to exert control where he could in order to feel like he had a handle on his life. He was so scared that none of his life choices would matter. I had spent so much of my life wrapped up in my own struggles of belonging and identity that I tended to forget what my parents had gone through and what they had left behind. And maybe my dad's physical distance from his family was the reason why he was so overprotective and insistent on keeping his kids close. I was doing my utmost to focus on his happiness, and I was still shaken by his sending me potential matches despite knowing that I was dating someone. But when I finally sat with it, I could see: we had lived very different lives. He wasn't raised in this country, where dating is the way it is. He didn't understand having the agency I did. For my dad, creating the life that he thought *he* wanted—even by just reaching out and exploring if there was something better or different—had required leaving everything he'd known *behind*. To do more than that, he risked cutting off his roots entirely. Naturally, he would hold fast to whatever traditions or worldviews he had inherited; they were, to him, what was left of where he came from.

In some of the therapy work I have done with immigrant families, I have witnessed the cognitive inflexibility firsthand: many immigrant parents exert and maintain control through solving new problems with old solutions. I worked with an immigrant dad who dismissed his daughter's social anxiety because he didn't believe it was real. He kept forcing his daughter to engage in situations that were traumatizing to her because he believed that this was how she'd learn—the same way he had when his parents forced him to do things he didn't want to do. Instead of being willing to input new information or tools, he relied on outdated strategies. Often, the work involves unlearning what you have been taught to fear and what you think you know about how things "should" be in order to learn new ways for relationships and solutions to exist. Most of the time, children of immigrants are the ones who must learn this while simultaneously trying to teach it to their parents.

One evening over the holidays, I stopped at my dad's bedroom door to say goodnight, and I just started bawling. Though I never expressed these feelings out loud, I internally kept cycling through projected thoughts on how I believed my dad was feeling. I couldn't help but feel like my relationship with a white man was playing a part in my dad's regrets. I, too, grappled to make sense of our loss. If he hadn't moved here, I probably would have known my grand-mother better, and even ended up with a family-approved Sikh man. I felt at fault. I felt helpless. I felt in that moment like I would have given up everything to take my dad's pain away. I didn't act on this impulse, because I felt strongly confident about being with Sam; however, I know now that my inclination to try to solve my dad's pain was rooted in my tendency to intellectualize, as well as in a deep-seated conditioned belief that I *owed* my parents whatever they wanted. I was still battling people-pleasing and codependent narra-tives and the urge to rescue my dad from his own grief. The guilt I felt made me *want* to throw away my happiness, but I reminded myself—as well as processed all of this with Dr. T—that I was living out my own values, and I wasn't actually doing anything *wrong*. Choosing my happiness didn't mean rejecting my family.

I know I was desperately trying to find connection in a discon-nected relationship. My dad never explicitly told me to break things off with Sam, and he consoled me the best he could, telling me that he wasn't sure if he had done enough, but he didn't regret moving here and still loved me. I pocketed these affirmations away, but even in writing this more than five years later, I still feel the weight of the fact that the choices my parents made gave me different ones.

Unpacking Immigrant Guilt

In my work, I have observed how immigrant parents utilize their sacrifices in moving to this country to guilt their U.S.-born children into obeying them, thus increasing emotional distress in their children. I hear from many children of immigrants who are so riddled with guilt that they develop a baseline anxiety around big and small decision-making in their lives. After all, their parents won the green-card lottery, or their parents fled persecution, or their parents chose to leave *their* security behind.

It's not uncommon for many children of immigrants to experience guilt trips at the hands of their parents or families. This often looks like indirect (or direct) implications that they should have done, or said, something differently: *I guess everyone is too busy to come home. I would have done it for you, but it's fine. I didn't think it was too much to ask. I guess I'll just spend the day alone. I taught you better.* When the guilt trip is mixed with the black-and-white mindset, it may look like exaggerated conclusions: *You don't love me. No one cares about me anymore. I'm a terrible parent!*

Though guilt can be manipulative, the intention behind it isn't always malicious. Guilt-tripping is a poor form of communication, and it indicates a lack of emotion regulation and conflict-resolution skills. Our parents may guilt-trip us because they believe they know what is best, leaning into the idea of morality to plant seeds of guilt within us that lead to chronic guilt—or always feeling like we are doing something wrong if it's not *their* way. They may weaponize guilt for sympathy. Or they may be more overtly passive-aggressive and manipulative, utilizing the silent treatment, trying to one-up us, or bringing up past mistakes to continue to exert control over our behavior. One common kind of guilt-tripping I observe in immigrant households involves a parent/elder weaponizing their mortality or death: *Are you trying to kill me? I hope I die before that happens.* At its worst, this type of guilt trip can be a form of emotional blackmail and abuse.

Even when I do things for myself—like make travel plans with friends or buy something deemed frivolous by my parents—my anxiety is heightened. This anxiety often and suddenly manifests as thoughts about my parents dying, because I am convinced that I am letting them down or hurting them and that they are going to die before we can resolve it. I am deeply emotionally attached to my parents and have even gone so far as to feel like my life, my successes, and my experiences mean nothing if they are not there to witness them. This, in essence, is a result of codependency and enmeshment—the very qualities that inhibit my parents from seeing me as something separate from them, which only reinforces their tendency to guilt-trip me.

Regardless of the intention, guilt trips can be extremely painful for those on the receiving end. They can lead to shame and low self-esteem. Here are five tips for dealing with guilt trips:

- Get clarity on whether the guilt you feel is justified. (See the end of this chapter for more.)
- Invite your loved ones to consider their feelings by reflecting and reframing their guilt-riddled statements. For example, when they say, "Why can't you come home earlier?" it can be

easy to feel like they are not respecting your time or the energy it takes to travel home. Instead of channeling the irritation, consider responding with something along these lines: "I know you miss me. I miss you, too, but this is the easiest/best/cheapest thing for me to do." Reflecting the emotion allows you to feel connected with your loved one while modeling the appropriate or desired language.

- Directly ask about what they are feeling to withdraw from the guilt trip and redirect them to the root of their emotions. This may sound something like: "I want to hear what is really bothering you so that we can talk about it."

- Decide if you need to consider how to change the relationship dynamic, put a boundary in place, or engage in another communication strategy from page 52. This may be necessary if there's no intention of responsibility, communication, or accountability.

- Practice self-care to avoid rumination and negative self-talk as you explore how to handle the guilt.

If you grew up in an environment where you were guilt-tripped, or if you have long-lasting relationships with people who guilt-trip you, then it makes sense that you grapple with this emotion. One of my clients who was struggling to manage interpersonal and communication issues with his mom specifically sought me out as his therapist because of the TED talk I had done a year prior on how children of immigrants experience guilt and can learn to manage it. In my TED talk, I mentioned that guilt manifests in a couple of ways. Many children of immigrants feel a chronic sense of guilt for letting their parents down: for not being enough, for being too American, for seeming ungrateful. Because many children of immigrants are parentified, they also serve as mediators—of conflict or culture, or both. It is known that immigrating to a new country can increase intergenerational conflict, as everyone is navigating their own acculturation and sense of belonging within the host country. The second-generation immigrant's sense of responsibility for the well-being of their parents—whether explicitly or implicitly stated—can get reinforced over the years as an obligation. And this obligation can make a child of immigrants feel guilty for having divergent emotions or needs, for wanting something different. Internalizing such high expectations and standards—and constantly feeling like you're falling short—is exhausting. And many children of immigrants are not taught how to question, examine, or parse this guilt. Is it telling you that you need to amend or change something about your behavior? Or is it rooted in obligation, people-pleasing, and concerns about doing right by your parents out of a very real, big love for them? I see many children of immigrants falling prey to this line of thinking: *Either I'm wrong or they're wrong.* But it's often so much messier than that.

As I've seen in my work, two of the most common sources of guilt for us children of immigrants are feeling like we're not doing enough for our families or parents and feeling like we have more access or privilege than our parents or families. These can lead us to categorize choices that are unfamiliar to our parents—but that actually make us happy—as "ungrateful." Instead of being asked by our parents if we are happy, we often feel like our parents are asking us if we are happy in the way that they understand happiness. For so many second gens, this can be an uphill battle, but it's not impossible.

Helpful versus Unhelpful Guilt

Guilt isn't always a bad thing. Helpful guilt—the feeling of discomfort we typically have when we do something wrong—is productive.

It helps alert us to our morality, to the pain and hurt that we may have caused others, and to the social and cultural standards that we may have crossed. And it helps us redirect our moral or behavioral compass so that we can figure out how to change the offending behavior or make amends. Unfortunately, though, many children of immigrants struggle with defining "wrong" and are therefore riddled with unhelpful guilt, which is the discomfort we feel when we have done something that does not meet the exceptionally high standards we have internalized. Persistent and unhelpful guilt can be associated with depression, anxiety, obsessive-compulsive disorder, and insomnia.

> It's important to note here that we may actually internalize *external* expectations as our own road map for what is acceptable. This is where values work, self-awareness, and differentiation (not detachment) can be really useful in helping us decipher *our* understanding of social and cultural standards. Sometimes we feel guilt because we cross social or cultural norms in our communities, but we have yet to interrogate if they're norms to which we also subscribe.

Guilt is learned. It is constructed around social and cultural parameters and family expectations. And sometimes we do not align with these values. Many Western children of immigrants grow up in households that are run according to different sets of standards, values, and norms than those they are socialized in outside the home. It's okay to pause and reflect and ask yourself what is *wrong* with what you're doing. Why does it feel wrong? What standards or values or morals are being crossed? How does that feel to you?

What I frequently see happening is how children of immigrants have developed beliefs that set unrealistic standards for themselves— for instance, the belief that saying no is selfish or disrespectful, or the belief that other people's happiness is our responsibility and that if our parents aren't happy, we can't be happy. These beliefs become tied to our self-concepts and senses of self-worth. Almost all of my second-gen clients have conflated feeling guilty with doing something wrong, taking the experience of guilt as definitive. To them, the presence of guilt feels like a neon sign screaming "TURN AROUND!" A lot of children of immigrants will do anything to avoid that feeling, never having been taught how to examine it or what to do with it. The discomfort alone is enough for us to revert to a previous path, back to the comfort of social and parental expectations. Unfortunately, this reinforces those beliefs we've internalized and thereby perpetuates the cycle. It ultimately supports the people-pleasing and overfunctioning tendencies we've developed in a continuous effort "to make things right." In learning to mitigate unhelpful guilt, we not only must reflect on the motivations behind the ways we manage our guilt, but we must also unlearn feeling responsible for *everything* and *everyone*. This type of guilt can really only be addressed by first addressing the core beliefs of perfectionism, productivity, and exceptionalism. We must be able to build self-compassion as flawed humans who are doing our best in order to eradicate this unhelpful guilt. Guilt is a warning sign, a reminder to pause and reflect, but it is not absolute.

When reviewing research, I discovered that people from collectivist cultures may be more motivated than those from individualistic cultures to engage in reparative behaviors after a transgression in order to maintain group harmony. This may complicate a child of immigrants' reality that *they* are responsible for keeping the peace and maintaining their role within a larger group or family. This affirms the idea that we may be driven by guilt.

In her book *Codependent No More*, Melody Beattie talks about how to differentiate between the two: helpful guilt propels change, and unhelpful guilt causes pain and often anxiety. Even more, unhelpful guilt can turn into shame and self-punishment. You start to embody guilt as part of your self-concept, and you go from *feeling* bad to believing that you *are* bad. It's important to catch this cycle as it's happening and disrupt it. One way to do this is to reflect on what you are feeling, especially if you are overwhelmed with guilt. Instead of chalking everything up to guilt, go deeper and try to identify any other feelings that may be brewing underneath it. This will help you discern between feeling helpful guilt for something you have done, or want to do, and feeling guilty for having a primary emotional response. For example, are you feeling guilty for missing or ignoring your mom's call during work, or are you feeling guilty for feeling angry that she called you when she knows you're at work and can't be available to her?

Guilt is sometimes like anger in that it can serve as a secondary emotion instigated by a primary emotion that we tend to overlook. And as with anger management, we have to build skills to manage our guilt. I talk about a few techniques for managing guilt in the forthcoming guided reflections on page 303, but it's important to understand first and foremost that our feelings are not facts. Emotional reasoning, as it's called, refers to feeling something so strongly that we equate that feeling with objective truth. Just because we feel guilty does not mean we did something bad. Our feelings are impermanent, and as such, taking time to sit with them, reflect on them, and process them can allow us to get clarity on what is *actually* happening in our realities.

There's a difference between guilt that is handed to us and guilt that is ours to own. Many of us children of immigrants adopt our loved ones' guilt as our own. When we start to recognize that we may automatically feel guilt and monitor and track the circumstances in which this happens, we can start to reframe our thoughts around unhelpful guilt to allow ourselves to feel more competent and confident in our choices and behaviors. Being aware of whether our guilt is in line with *our* values also makes it more possible to set boundaries with others. By stepping into our own values-driven truth, we can start to gain assurance about where the guilt is coming from and how to manage it.

Next time you set a boundary that is rooted in your values, instead of focusing on unhelpful guilt, I invite you to consider that you made an adjustment to a dynamic so you can engage from a healthier and more present place. What's really happening is that you're deciding not to extend yourself beyond your own emotional and mental capacities.

Love and Loyalty

In May 2017, six months after I told my parents about Sam and four months after my grandmother passed away, I asked them to meet him. I knew we were getting serious pretty quickly, and I could tell they were getting more anxious the longer we stayed together. I wanted them to see for themselves how good of a conversationalist he is, to experience his disarming kindness and playful sense of humor. I thought that if they met him, they would change their minds. Because my parents, like a lot of immigrant parents, are inclined toward fear-based thinking, I worried about the version of Sam they held in their imaginations. I told them candidly that if they didn't approve, I would hear them out and consider ending it, as long as they perceived issues beyond his being white. This is something I would have considered with any potential partner. Even though I wouldn't be able to pursue a partnership with someone my family didn't approve of, I knew in my heart that my parents wanted the best for me and truly wanted me to be happy. I also knew that Sam was genuinely a good guy and that after they met him, they'd eventually come around.

Before Sam met my parents, I warned him that they were going to be judging him. I had told him that my dad is a man of few words, that it may seem like he's not interested in what someone has to say, but that's because he's trying to process things in his head. I had even asked my brother to come serve as the buffer, a role he had played many times over the years as a mediator of the generational and cultural conflict between me and my parents. It ended up being a lovely evening, and everyone was on their best behavior. But the next day there was a lot of questioning: *How much money does he actually make as a video editor? How will he support you? Is he well read? We couldn't tell last night.* I was frustrated. He's very different from my family, and for them, different equates to change equates to bad. At one point, my mom even said, "Thank goodness your dadi died before witnessing this." That was devastating.

I think my parents worried that Sam would take me away from my roots. Objectively, these fears make sense to me, especially since I have observed this struggle in people with whom I have worked. I knew that I would always be growing, sometimes in directions my parents couldn't fathom, yet I was confident that I'd always remain rooted. But my parents didn't trust the foundation they had instilled in me.

One child of immigrants wrote in to my *Washington Post* advice column to say that their parents were obsessing over their career, their age, and the acceptability of their potential marriage partner. In this case, for this person's parents, being a doctor or being married to a doctor was understood as the only way of gaining financial security. Being married by thirty was the only way of guaranteeing an acceptable partner. Marrying within the race, culture, and faith was the only way of maintaining a connection to cultural roots.

For many of us, it's important to confront and address these fears in order to move the conversation in a different or new direction. I have had to constantly remind myself that this is a long, slow process, a walk toward understanding one another. These are difficult and conflicting emotions to hold at once, but I also find a sense of respite in how empowering and beautiful it is to exist in the gray between these varied experiences.

I had to channel a lot of patience while my parents slowly got on board. Though they never explicitly told me to end my relationship with Sam, they did tell me that they wished I had chosen a Sikh guy. At one point, I told them that I would do whatever they wanted but that, eventually, when they were no longer here, I would be left with the choices they had made for me, which could leave me incredibly unhappy. I honestly think that drove home the point for my parents, and thankfully, they did come around. My mom enjoyed Sam's questions about learning how to cook Indian and Japanese food, and my dad started to look forward to watching sports and drinking beers with him when we'd visit.

As difficult as it was, I know that not all children of immigrants have had the luxuries that I had. I also know that it would have been a completely different story had I brought home someone who was Black or of the same gender. In a lot of immigrant households, colorism, casteism, anti-Blackness, and homophobia are still rampant. And I know that I have been allotted privilege in how I am perceived out in the world because I am with a white man. When Sam and I took a trip to Yellowstone early in our relationship, we stopped in a small town in Montana that was covered with Trump flags and posters. At a grocery-store checkout, the man behind the counter was being short with me and rude, but his entire demeanor changed when Sam walked up and stood next to me. It's not lost on me that this would have been an entirely different scenario had Sam had darker skin, worn a turban, or been of another ethnicity or race.

AFTER SAM PROPOSED to me in Barcelona in March 2018, everything seemed to get more complicated with my parents. Nothing had prepared us for how tough planning an intercultural wedding was going to be. There are very specific things a groom or a groom's family is expected to do in a Sikh wedding, and it was hard at first for my parents to compromise on certain traditions to make room for Sam's comfort and our American expectations of what a wedding should feel like. They struggled to grasp that our wedding was for us, not just for our community. My mom, like most desi mothers, took over the wedding planning and wanted everything to be exactly as *she* envisioned, going so far as to say that the wedding wasn't about me. I found myself mediating between the different cultural expectations of what a wedding is and who is planning it, but Sam and his family were open to just being along for the ride.

Thankfully, my sister stepped in when I needed her to help manage some of the stress with my mom. Eventually, we were able to create a wedding weekend that upheld the important Sikh traditions but had added twists to make it intercultural (e.g., a Sikh ceremony followed by a brewery reception where Sam played the drums in his band and I wore white).

I would be lying if I said that it was *everything* I wanted. It wasn't. The South Asian photographer/videographer chosen by my mom focused primarily on my family and parents, and we didn't even get a say in our wedding video song. I had hoped to do a "first look" or a pre-ceremony vow reading so that Sam and I could have a private moment of connection with each other on our wedding day. Traditionally, Sikh weddings are very solemn occasions: there is no smiling, the bride and groom never face each other, and the bride's family simultaneously grieves and celebrates the giving away of the daughter. It's a beautiful tradition, but it didn't feel like something that was for us. I was happy, and in love, and kept sneaking glances at Sam throughout, reveling in the privilege and gratitude I felt for being able to marry this wonderful man—something I know not all people, present and past, have been able to do.

Leading up to the wedding, I had massive anxiety over wondering whether my Sikh community was going to judge or reject Sam and my in-laws. I was also nervous about how overwhelmed Sam's family might be by the culture shock of this elaborately planned weekend. The truth is, I underestimated everyone. I got so caught up in what it means to marry outside my race and religion that I didn't give much credit to the love that was flowing around our relationship. My family and my family's friends were loving, patient, and kind, embracing my in-laws as new members of the community. And my in-laws were enthusiastic, flexible, and willing to learn, embracing my culture and traditions with open minds and hearts. I truly couldn't have asked for any more love or acceptance.

During my Sikh ceremony, my dad read the laavan from the Guru Granth Sahib, which meant that he sat in front of us through the entire traditional ceremony. I didn't make eye contact with him because I knew we were both processing a series of emotions, and it felt like a breach of his privacy. The wall of his stoicism crumbled a little bit.

After the fourth laav, or walk around the Guru Granth Sahib, Sam and I were officially husband and wife. As I looked up and

locked eyes with my dad, I immediately started bawling. In that moment, I felt so overwhelmed by his love for me, a love so much stronger than his own religious convictions or expectations or needs.
Despite my choosing a different path than the one he'd initially
wanted for me, my papa reached out through his worries and reser-
vations and met me where I was. I saw the weight of the sacrifices
and compromises he had made throughout his life to get me to where
I was—sitting next to the man I had chosen as my life partner—with
the support of the hundreds of people sitting behind us. His leaving
of his family over thirty years ago was the reason I was able to
choose Sam as my own.

AS WE WERE departing the gurdwara, my dad had told Sam to
take care of his most precious cargo. Thereafter, in true Indian dad
form, he started alluding to Sam's "ownership" of me. In my culture, I was considered my father's responsibility before marriage and
Sam's responsibility after. If I was doing something on my own, my
dad would usually ask where Sam was. If I wanted to buy something, he would usually say, "As long as Sam approves!" Shortly
after my wedding, I told my dad that I still wanted to plan another
father-daughter trip with him. For two years, we had gone on one
annually, and it was important to me that we uphold this new tradition. Of course, his first reaction was: "Will Sam be okay with that?"
I had to remind my dad that I did not need my husband's permission,
but yes, he would be.

I truly believe that as we grow, we often need to get to know ourselves again. The same goes for those close to us, too. These father-
daughter trips are a commitment to getting to know my immigrant
papa over and over again and hoping he will embrace me and my
growth in return.

Although my parents' acceptance of my relationship eventually took root, there was a person in our family tree, one who was unable to attend the wedding, whose support seemed paramount to me. My maternal grandmother, my last living grandparent at that time, was dying of cancer in Japan. Years earlier, when I had told her about Sam, she had been vehemently and explicitly unsupportive of my choice to be with a white man. But now that we were married, it was important to me that she meet him. We ended our honeymoon in Japan to see my extended family, and frankly, I didn't know what to expect. To my surprise, she showed compassion and openness to meeting him. I don't know if she was just resigned to the fact because she was nearing the end of her life, but I was grateful for it. I stuck by her side over the few days we were there, knowing this would probably be the last time I would see her. She wasn't talkative, but both Sam and I could feel her acceptance in the way she willingly shared her space and her silence with us. When it was time for us to leave, we never acknowledged it, but I knew that she knew we would never meet again. I cried when she put her hands upon my head and Sam's, giving us her blessing. She died several months later, and I will always cherish that moment.

Even though it's been several years since that day, I still don't know what to expect in my marriage with Sam. I know that this is a journey we will take together, but I also know that there will always be personal challenges I have to face alone. I am constantly reevaluating my identities and relearning what they mean to me. And Sam doesn't stand idly by while I navigate these crises alone: He looks up gurdwaras near our home. He takes bhangra lessons. In conversations with my nephews, he throws in Punjabi words where he can. He educates himself. The day we got engaged in Barcelona, we ventured to the local gurdwara to ask the gyani to do Ardaas—a Sikh prayer that is done before performing or after undertaking any significant task.

We won't ever be culturally conflict-free, but we have created shared expectations around our differences. The truth is, we aren't navigating this in only one direction; joining an all-white family from New England has included a learning curve for me, too. We set time aside to talk often. He's consistently checking himself. And when either of us feels frustrated by something the other's family does or says that feels countercultural, we never bury it. We always commit to hearing each other out and exploring ways to move forward. Navigating cultural issues is a delicate dance, but so far we have been able to engage in open and honest dialogue that will always be ongoing.

> My partner's race and religious beliefs don't affect my autonomy to explore my own. I am not betraying my family or culture by committing to a partnership that nurtures who I am, supports my experiences, and encourages my exploration in and out of the relationship.

According to the Pew Research Center, intermarriage is very common for second-generation immigrants. About 15 percent of children of immigrants in this country have chosen partners outside their races and/or ethnicities—almost double that of immigrants and their native-born counterparts (8 percent). Hispanic and Asian Americans, in particular, have the highest rates of intermarriage in the United States.

How do you navigate an interracial, intercultural relationship? This is one of the most common questions I get from people in the Brown Girl Therapy community—so much so that even Sam gets messages from strangers wanting to know how *he* navigated the experience in the beginning. The dilemma usually presents itself as some variation of "Help! I'm conflicted," or "I want my partner to integrate into my family," or "It's important that I remain close with my family." The conflict is real—trust me, I know. Family systems operate differently for everyone, and only you can decide what is worth doing or not doing; every action—*and* inaction—is a choice. But here are some tips for navigating this circumstance that I have shared with community members:

- If you haven't, talk to your partner to confirm that you're on the same page about your faith and culture and their importance—now and in the future. This is more important than anyone else's opinion. Most people say that they want to integrate their partner into their family, but it's also important to be *with* your partner on this journey. Don't expect them to deal with their feelings alone. Take responsibility for your role in bridging their relationship with your family. If you're serious about marriage, then you're choosing your partner as your family, too. By committing to your partner, your primary identity will shift from daughter/son/kid to partner. Both are important, but one naturally takes precedence. Are you ready to make this shift?

- You may want to be more explicit: "It's hard for me to know that you disapprove of X when you haven't even met them. I'm serious about our relationship, and it's really important to me that you meet them. Are you open to this?" You may even want to talk about your happiness with your partner, especially if your family hasn't met them: "I know you disapprove of X, but I'd like to tell you more about the qualities that I really appreciate in them." You may not get the answer or response you want, but you will get clarity on the situation.

- Loyalty to family comes up often in my work, and I urge you to explore these questions: How do guilt and loyalty serve your relationship with your family? What do they cost you?

- Be honest with yourself about your parents' disapproval. There's a difference between disapproval because your partner is harmful or bad and disapproval because your parents are simply disappointed. The former may require your willingness to listen to them and receive their feedback. The latter may reinforce a belief that you only deserve your family's love when you are doing things they support. Real love should never wear the guise of fear or control. Disappointing loved ones can be uncomfortable, but it doesn't necessarily mean that you are doing something wrong.

MARRYING SAM HAS made me want to reconnect even more strongly with my roots, my language, and my culture. I want to own the cultural knowledge and to embed it in my life and in our relationship. I think about our potential future kids and what it will mean for them to be half white, half Indian. Ultimately, there is no right or wrong way to be a child of immigrants. Am I better or worse because I married a white person? No. Is someone else better or worse because they married someone of the same religion and culture? No. Can intermarriage be a sign of assimilation? Yes. But assimilation isn't an all-or-nothing process. We must find what works for us to maintain relationships with our families and our cultures, embracing communities that allow us to feel less alone.

Identifying your core beliefs and tips for navigating guilt

- **It is important to remember that feelings are not necessarily fact.** You can feel like you're doing something wrong because someone else isn't happy with what you're doing. But it doesn't make what you're doing wrong. You can feel unworthy. You can feel like a failure. And these feelings can be so overpowering, but having them doesn't make them true. Nor should they stop you from doing the thing anyway. Question them and find evidence *against* them.
- **Identify any other emotions** that might be accompanying or buried under the guilt, such as resentment, disappointment, or anger.
- **Identify the values and standards** that are feeding the guilt by being crossed. Get clarity on whether these are yours or someone else's standards and values. And try to sit with what's important to you in that moment; this will help inform how you handle it.
- **Own your choices,** and remember that you are making decisions based on information and knowledge you have at the time. You can make amends, forgive yourself, and differ in how you want to handle situations.

- **Ask yourself:** *How can I lovingly detach from my parents' assumptions or beliefs? How can I challenge their assumptions and beliefs internally? What's true for me? What do I believe?*
  - Accept that guilt may always be an emotion you feel for being the first in your family to do or have access to something different. The goal may not be to eradicate it altogether but, rather, not to let it have a chokehold on you.
- **Reauthor the narrative that things are binary—good or bad, right or wrong, all or nothing.** Embrace the reality that two things can be true at the same time: you can make different choices than your family has made—choices that are inherently good for you—and you can feel guilty or sad that your parents don't approve or understand. This may be uncomfortable.
- **Parse unhelpful guilt from helpful guilt.** Is your guilt telling you that you need to change something about your behavior because it crosses a moral, personal, or cultural value that is important to *you*? Or is it simply rooted in obligation, people-pleasing, and perfectionism?
- **Change your self-talk** from "I should" to "I can" or "I deserve." This will help you detach from other people's values and step into your own.
- **Recognize when you are emotion monitoring, or being anticipative and hyperaware of how others are feeling.** Having empathy isn't bad, but it can swing into territory where you are absorbing others' feelings rather than acknowledging them as separate entities.
- **Remember:** You are doing your best in navigating new terrain and new family dynamics. Your courage to carry your parents' or family's momentum forward is a beautiful thing.

Chapter Ten

Getting Out of My Own Way

My dad and I were sitting at a wooden picnic table along the harbor in Halifax, Nova Scotia. It was May 2018, a year and a half after the excursion to Albuquerque and a couple of months after my Barcelona engagement. We were on our (real) second father-daughter trip.

The two of us had found our rhythm for spending time alone together. We both enjoy walking around aimlessly, my dad usually with his hands behind his back, often stopping to grab beers and french fries. We both prefer casual eateries over fancy restaurants. He relishes finding a crispy fish sandwich or fish and chips, and I relish hitting up a local bookstore. We like to spend our first day together going where the wind takes us and getting a sense of the place.

My dad loves a quaint port town, and we had just spent the day exploring, visiting breweries, and planning our itinerary for the following days—we would maximize the use of our rental car and venture to Lunenburg, a UNESCO World Heritage site, and Peggy's Cove. Wearing a lavender pagri and navy bomber jacket, my dad gazed over the half-drunk beers in front of us and into the distance. The atmosphere around us was buzzing with gleeful energy. Massive container ships were lined up in port, and other tourists strolled along the boardwalk that housed beer gardens, creameries, and waterfront restaurants. But my dad looked solemn. I've always been intimidated by this dignified look. He never feels compelled to fill the empty space the way my mom does, and he's more reflective than I've ever given him credit for. It took me decades to stop mistaking his quiet contemplation for a lack of care and to realize that intimacy with my dad lives in a shared silence. I've started to understand why there's so much he doesn't share. For most of his life, he has had to figure things out by himself, and he was simply taught to communicate differently than me. I hoped to continue to penetrate those walls and allow him to appreciate that he doesn't, in fact, need to live life in isolation or disconnection for fear of not being able to protect his loved ones.

He was blissfully unaware of my angst. I was bouncing my knees up and down and sitting on the edge of my seat, feeling ready to bolt at any moment. My anxiety was rapidly increasing, reminiscent of the many conversations I had had with my dad growing up. *I can't believe I have to address another big letdown with him.* I took a tiny sip of beer and gave myself a quick pep talk: *You have to do this. For months, you've held off being honest because you told yourself that you would say this face-to-face. You're an adult, for God's sake.* This would have to be it. I knew I would never fully summon the courage, but I needed to do it now so that we could have a couple of days to process and digest the thing together.

"I have something to tell you," I blurted out before I could change my mind.

After a deep breath, I continued: "And I'm scared to say it. I don't want you to be upset, but I want to be honest with you."

My dad put down his half-empty beer glass, popped a piece of calamari into his mouth, and straightened his back. "Okay," he said, locking eyes with me. *Here we go.*

"I'm just now finishing my bachelor's degree and will have it by the end of this year." His mouth went slightly agape, and I continued before he could say anything. "I'm not asking for anything from you. I paid for it myself, and I know that you probably assumed I had gotten my degree already, because I never corrected you when you'd mention it. But I just needed to get here on my own time."

One of the many, many things we'd fought about when I first moved to New York five years prior was his expectation for me to prioritize finishing my bachelor's as soon as I got settled in. I, of course, did not. I chose life experience over traditional education, but it was not something that we ever openly discussed again. In the beginning, he'd asked a few times whether I was doing it, and I'd waved him off with a vague reply—*I will* or *I'm looking into it.* Maybe he and my mom had no reason to question if I was telling the truth, or maybe he got tired of having the same conversation over and over again. Either way, I suspected that my parents were appeased on some level by the prestige and success I achieved at *HuffPost.*

As children of immigrants—or as anyone who struggles with the achievement behavior I have previously mentioned—we tend to believe that we are motivated by achievement because of the expectations placed on us. But the longer I do this work, the more I think we may actually be more motivated by a fear of failure and subsequent (external or internal) punishment. When milestones are reached or achievements are collected, so many of us remain unsatisfied. We mistake any praise we get for love, constantly needing to chase it down, searching for it in every corner.

We become highly motivated by specific traditional markers of success, which are less trophies than they are layers of armor that we hope will safeguard us from feeling belittled, invalidated, or unappreciated. We don't learn that there is pride and honor in trying—or trying again. In knowing when to stop. In slowing down. In making a hard choice to quit something that isn't right or healthy for us. In learning from a mistake.

After my proclamation in Halifax, the longest two minutes followed. I had wanted nothing more than Papa to be proud of me for these things: stepping away when it became too hard to go on, trusting myself to figure out a different way, and eventually choosing to take a chance on myself, even if my achievements weren't attained in the order or way he expected. It had taken a few years of living in New York and confronting not only my internalized narratives about success and worthiness but also my own fears—the imaginary demons that I believed were the reason why I was so "behind" in life. I had embraced being alone, single, and independent. I had proved that I'm not, in fact, scared of hard work. I had become insatiably curious and driven by a desire to learn. I had gotten to know myself as a professional outside the expectations of my family or community. And I had finally decided that it was time for me to go back to school and finish what I had started over a decade prior. I had challenged the culturally accepted notion that there is one right way to pursue an education and one right timeline for it. I had rewritten narratives that I had previously taken as absolute truths. I had only come to this decision after time away from an academic environment and after living at home to build up my self-efficacy, self-concept, and strength. I'd had to get there on my own.

By this point, my dad and I had been on a roller coaster together, and I felt like we were lurching to the top of a stomach-churning hill. It's a drop that many children of immigrants encounter when they finally face their parents in all of their vulnerable, different, and honest glory. As the sun set over the harbor, my dad finally replied:

"I had a feeling you never got the degree. Every time I asked where the degree was, you always changed the subject." I still wonder if he never pushed it because he wanted to stay in denial. Denial, in some ways, is a form of procrastination—a comfortable way to avoid reality. And in my experience, immigrant families are very skilled at it.

"You did it by yourself? You paid for it and everything?" he asked more intentionally, as if we were walking across a minefield together.

"Yes. Everything is taken care of. I just needed you to know the truth."

His expression lightened. "I'm proud of you for prioritizing this and for doing this on your own."

Our relationship had changed significantly in the five years since I had moved to New York City. But when I look back, I think this may have been the watershed moment when he started to accept who I was becoming, even if he couldn't always understand me.

A YEAR PRIOR to that evening in Halifax with my dad, I had told Sam that I didn't have my bachelor's degree. I said it was my biggest secret. He didn't seem concerned about why I didn't have the degree. He just asked: "Would you want to do it?"

It made me understand that the important thing wasn't what happened *then* but what I wanted *now*—a more nuanced and positive example of how the cultural differences between Sam and me presented themselves in our relationship. He didn't see failure or respond with fear the way my family had. This was refreshing to me. So much of the way I had framed my life was shaped by a sense of urgency to make up for lost time. I worked twice and thrice as hard to make friends as an adult, build a professional life and career, and chase a sense of competency through *other* achievements. I was constantly trying to pretend that I was exactly where my peers were. It had never occurred to me that being on a different path was not only okay but also a strength and something I could feel proud of myself for navigating.

So in 2017, half a decade after dropping out, I applied to a local online school with a continuing education program for professionals. Over the course of that first year, I didn't tell more than three or four people what I was doing. The shame was still raw. Though I was choosing to try again—a quality I never hesitate to applaud in others—I still felt like a disgrace. I didn't even tell most of my best friends because I was convinced they would realize that they had always known something was off about me. That I wasn't quite on their level.

At this point, I hadn't told my father, but I wanted someone in my family to know so that I wasn't carrying yet another secret alone. After getting accepted into the program, I decided to tell my brother and sister. The three of us were slowly moving away from the big-sibling-and-little-sibling dynamic, venturing into a more equal friendship fueled by mutual honesty, respect, and curiosity. They were both married with kids, my sister living in London and my brother in North Carolina, and I was a more independent version of myself than I had ever been. We had needed to let our lives grow in different directions before we could choose to bring one another along for the journey.

Self-Sabotaging Behavior

Through therapy and self-examination, I learned that there must come a point when we *really* have to hold ourselves accountable for our role in our own struggles and be honest with ourselves about where we want to go from there. Pursuing my bachelor's degree was a first step. It wasn't easy to commit. I was terrified: I had thus far sheltered myself from the possibility of more academic failure by simply avoiding it. But if I stayed in this cycle of paralysis and avoidance, I would be sabotaging myself and holding myself hostage to my previous circumstances. A common struggle I see in my work with children of immigrants is the internalization of limiting beliefs as truth. These are the same ones that become barriers to boundary setting or learning differentiation, and they ultimately keep us from our potential.

We don't believe we are good enough or deserve happiness or success, so we—knowingly and unknowingly—hold ourselves back. I was constantly asking myself: *What school would possibly take a chance on me after I failed and failed and failed again?* Many clients unconsciously self-sabotage because of an expectation to have complete certainty in their choices. To them, wavering in that certainty in and of itself indicates failure, so they refuse to acknowledge it, holding steadfast to the safest choice without examining it. I see clients who stay in jobs they hate, avoid learning new skills, and resist exploring new possibilities or taking even lower-stake risks. By self-sabotaging, we feed a dominant narrative, affirming and reinforcing it.

In *The Big Leap*, psychologist Gay Hendricks introduces the concept of the "Upper Limit Problem," which has been defined as "an internal threshold for the maximum degree of success and happiness you'll allow yourself to experience." According to Hendricks, this can be ingrained by false beliefs that you internalized at a young age and continue to carry. For example, maybe you believe, fundamentally, that you are undeserving because of what your immigrant parents or ancestors went through. If you start to achieve happiness, pleasure, rest, or peace, you may struggle with cognitive dissonance and discomfort around conflicting beliefs and experiences. You may start to hold yourself back from your pursuits.

Other Common Reasons
Why You May Self-Sabotage

- You were told that you should be or do one thing, so now you may try to make your life fit into that box, even if it doesn't feel right.
- You grew up in a household where you had to learn to be comfortable with instability, so as an adult you set your own upper-limit potential—or your own comfort level for success—and it inhibits your growth but provides a sense of security.
- You were told to do things well or not at all. So at the first sign of a hiccup, mistake, or roadblock, you give up altogether, feeling like you're a failure.
- You did not feel supported or heard (or deserving of being heard) when you were a child, so now you may struggle to communicate effectively, speak up for yourself, or clarify your needs.
- Your parents may have modeled control as a form of love. So as an adult, instead of being able to enjoy the process, the work, or the relationship, you find yourself focused on needing to know what happens next or deciding how things should go.
- You were taught to always put others first, so now you may struggle with how to prioritize yourself and your pursuits. The promises you make to others may supersede the promises you make to yourself, suggesting that your growth is less important.
- You were repeatedly told to be grateful for what you have and where you are. This may manifest itself in procrastination or avoidance of something new, different, or hard because you

fear how things may change to allow for your growth and happiness.

- You were taught that rejection is a failure and a flaw, so your self-concept has been intertwined with your levels of success. Now, when you do experience rejection, you internalize it and have a hard time bouncing back.
- You've been told to be humble, and thus you may subconsciously or consciously minimize your success so as not to show up someone else.

Perfectionism and Procrastination

Despite all the ways I had learned to embrace my own humanity through friendships and extracurricular activities, doing so in my career had always felt inconceivable. I've talked before about how we tend to learn and adopt perfectionism, and how it can exacerbate our tendencies toward impression management, where we seek to craft an external vision of ourselves in hopes of shaping how others perceive us. But it can also be waged internally and become an insidious form of self-sabotage.

In a Brown Girl Therapy poll, 93 percent of 5,477 children of immigrants reported that they also struggle with perfectionism. The concern around meeting unrealistic standards of exceptionalism can be paralyzing, and as such, you may struggle with taking risks, avoid things you aren't sure you're good at, or, worst of all, start to believe that you are lazy or incapable. And so when you are tasked with something, you want to do it amazingly well. You want to be the best. You want to *impress*. And you fear that anything less will feel like failure, or you fear consequences for not doing it well. Ultimately, you get sucked into a perfectionism-procrastination cycle.

I have witnessed this cycle of self-oriented perfectionism that so many of us children of immigrants learned in households or cultures that prioritize social perception. For example, I talked to one second-generation Nigerian immigrant who really wanted to go back to school for a completely different career than the one she had been working in for almost a decade. But for years she procrastinated when it came to researching programs or talking to anyone in the field. When I asked her why this seemingly low-risk task felt so difficult, she admitted she was scared that the people she talked to would tell her she wasn't good enough, *and* she was convinced that her parents would worry about why she was leaving a good job. So she wanted to please her parents and was paralyzed by self-oriented perfectionism and a fear of judgment—both of which caused her to sabotage her own happiness. On top of it all, she started to feel worse about herself for procrastinating over something that she genuinely wanted to explore. Even research suggests that perceived self-efficacy, or our belief that we can or cannot do the hard thing we are attempting, and self-sabotage are strongly related to procrastination. I, too, struggled with this perfectionism-procrastination cycle. After moving to New York City, I believed that I couldn't make even a single mistake, because I had already made them all. I was operating as if we had all been allotted only a certain number of mistakes in our lives, and I had gone through mine too early in life.

It's only now, years later and after studying mental health, that I understand the importance of asking certain questions: Who is benefiting from our perfectionism and self-doubts? From our silence? From our refusal to confront the tough questions? Often, the answer is people in power, or those who don't have our best interests at heart. It may be those who do love us but are unaware of our personal strengths or passions. You know, judge a fish by its ability to climb a tree and all that. I didn't realize that by constantly trying to be perfect, or to measure my value by others' metrics of success, I had tied my self-esteem to what would win me approval. From the get-go, this would always set me up for disappointment and potential failure. I had to start creating my own personal metrics for success and happiness.

Confronting our own core and/or self-limiting beliefs is a strategy for recognizing and reauthoring our dominant narratives. This forces us to be honest about how we are contributing to our stuckness. Systemic barriers aside, there often comes a point when many of us must take ownership of what happens next. In my case, I wanted a bachelor's degree so that I could pursue a career in psychotherapy. I had a clear goal, and to get there, that degree was the first and necessary step. Nothing else mattered anymore.

So I took online classes while continuing to work at *HuffPost*. I didn't tell people at work I was taking classes or putting things in motion for me to figure out my next steps (which would probably mean leaving the company), and because most of my friends didn't know, I carried on with my life outside work as though nothing were different. I often woke up really early or stayed up late doing homework assignments and studying for class in my room. I continued to be chased by a sense of urgency and fear, so I jammed all my classes together without any breaks. It never felt like enough, and I was constantly overwhelmed. I ended up taking twelve classes in one year. Looking back, though, I can recognize that this was the start of a new narrative—one in which I picked up the pen and started writing chapters for myself instead of living in a book written by my parents or someone else.

I needed to trust in the life experience I had gathered. I needed to believe that I wasn't the same person I had been when I started undergrad over a decade prior. I needed to have confidence that I could handle whatever happened, and if I couldn't, I needed to trust that I would find the support or tools to help me—the same way I had in the past. After all, confidence is not, and does not require, perfection; it requires self-knowing, in contrast to the tendency to prioritize other-knowing. In order to build confidence, you must learn to trust yourself, and in order to do that, you must be willing to get to know yourself—strengths, limitations, and all. This feels countercultural to many because it involves making space and time for your own needs, values, feelings, and ideas when you have likely been conditioned to put others first.

Confidence is a skill. Here are five tips and reflections for building confidence:

- Confidence is not about believing that things won't be difficult; rather, it is about knowing that difficulty is an inescapable part of pursuing anything worthwhile. Trust your judgment, even when things go wrong. Trust your capability, even when you make mistakes. And trust your qualities and worthiness, even when you experience rejection or failure.
- Practice reframing these thoughts as you notice them:
  - Replace *I should have known better* with *I am learning, and I trust that I will be better for overcoming this.*
  - Replace *I should always have the answer* with *I believe in myself to figure it out.*
  - Replace *I can't do this* with *I want to try this, and I can handle whatever happens.*
  - Replace *Maybe someone else will be better than me at this* with *Am I just scared to try, or do I truly need to seek out support?*

- Confidence doesn't look the same for everyone, especially according to different cultural values. For instance, being more soft-spoken doesn't necessarily mean you're not a confident person. Consider all of the cultural, social, and gender-based values you have learned and how they define confidence. Are these similar or different?

- Reflect on a time when you made a mistake or when something didn't go according to plan. How did you handle it? What did you learn from it? Remind yourself that you can get through things even when they are difficult.

- For an immediate confidence boost, listen to a song that makes you feel confident; exercise, move your body, or dance it out; or look yourself in the mirror and say an affirmation.

The Scarcity Mindset

When success is expected, you don't honor or celebrate it. Even more, because success is expected, it can be hard to admit that something was difficult or that you're proud of yourself for persisting. Though I never celebrated completing my associate's degree, I felt the pull to celebrate pursuing my bachelor's after so many hiccups. Telling my dad in Halifax was the first step. Eight months later, in the beginning of 2019, after finishing my program in December 2018, I told my best friends at my bachelorette party. It was the first time I admitted to my disappointments and talked about them in a way that didn't end in my breaking down. Though I recognize now that earning my bachelor's degree twelve years after I started isn't shameful, I was just then starting to take the bricks of shame out of the heavy backpack I had been lugging around for so long.

I was about to enter an entirely new chapter in my life, with little idea of where it was going to take me. For many children of immigrants, uncertainty is dreadful. It can feel like a sign of failure because it has potential for instability or insecurity. Often, this is rooted in the ways we have been conditioned to try to plan for *everything*. In my work, many second-generation Americans have expressed that they felt the need to create contingency plans, and then contingency plans for their contingency plans. They only felt safe knowing what was next and how to handle things going awry. Many community members have shared with me that creating contingency plans actually helps alleviate the anxiety they learned from their parents. One woman said that failure was never an option, so having a backup to still be able to succeed at *something* was better than nothing. Another member said he applied to thirty-two graduate programs, with the goal of making sure he got into one so that his parents would be proud. (He got into all of them, and it was a waste of money, according to him.) I've observed the direct connection between this tendency and catastrophizing—or assuming worst-case scenarios—in my work with clients. At its heart, contingency planning allows us to prepare for uncomfortable or unknown situations. This is not necessarily bad, but it can reinforce core beliefs about ourselves that may not be true. For example, if we feel like we should anticipate every scenario, and don't, we may feel like *we* did something wrong, reinforcing our perfectionist tendencies.

The need for this level of security or preparedness is also often a passed-down trait resulting from our immigrant parents' scarcity mindsets, or beliefs that there is never *enough* of something (time, resources, opportunities, safety, money, and so on). When on the precipice of uncertainty, we ultimately have two choices: we can either let fear stop us from trying and seeing what happens, or we can open our arms to opportunities we could never imagine.

In his book *Stumbling on Happiness*, Daniel Gilbert talks about how we utilize existing images and memories in order to consider the future. In this way, I hear about how many children of immigrants, and people in general, grapple with what their futures will look like. Many of us don't have role models for women in their twenties and thirties living independently; the stories we've been told about being single, having full-time careers, divorce, or other "negative" experiences revolve around being ostracized and unhappy. My past memories of school had created an idea of a future in which graduate school was bound to be terribly hard and sure to consign me to failure. I was so concerned about what was going to go wrong that I struggled to consider what could go right.

Some people naturally subscribe to the scarcity mindset, even if economic insecurity has never been a hardship in their lives. Stephen Covey, who coined the term in his book *The 7 Habits of Highly Effective People*, describes the scarcity mindset as seeing "life as having only so much, as though there were only one pie out there. And if someone were to get a big piece of the pie, it would mean less for everybody else." Many of us have become stuck with these scarcity beliefs, which impact how we speak to ourselves and how we show up at work and in relationships. The scarcity mindset can affect decision-making, decrease confidence, increase levels of stress, and exacerbate mental health struggles.

It's important to note that the scarcity mindset is real, and if you are struggling with economic or resource insecurity, then the behaviors and learned beliefs that stem from this mentality may be a result of living in survival mode. But surviving and being stuck in survival mode when you don't need to be are two different things.

The scarcity mindset can show up in so many specific and seemingly small ways that many children of immigrants don't even realize where it's coming from. It can look like:

- Resentment or fear when others are being acknowledged, as you think this takes away from your chance to be seen or heard.
- Hoarding things that you don't need right now, or no longer need, because you want to be prepared—just in case.
- Jealousy of others who are pursuing similar goals, because you worry that there's not enough room for all of you.
- A now-or-never mentality (e.g., feeling like you have to take any opportunity that arises right away because the chance won't come again).
- Charging less or accepting lower payments for your work or expertise because you believe that something is better than nothing.
- Maintaining whatever security you have, even if you aren't happy (e.g., staying in an unhealthy relationship because you think that it's better than being alone, that you can't find better, and/or that you don't have time to wait for something else).
- Resistance to change and/or stepping outside your comfort zone.
- Having a mindset of competitiveness rather than collaboration.
- Hyperfixation on what's not going right and what you don't have rather than on what's going right and what you do and can have.
- Chasing instant gratification or being stingy with your time, money, and energy if you won't see an immediate return on investment.
- Perfectionism and the need for control because you fear that one wrong move will take everything away.

- Assuming negative intentions in others (e.g., distrusting others with your ideas for fear they will steal them).
- Having a tendency toward negative self-talk or pessimistic thinking.
- Constant anxiety and risk avoidance for fear of losing what you do have.
- Subscribing to the idea that things are permanent and that when you make choices and take actions, or when things don't work out for you, you can never change them or repeat them in the future.
- Overcommitting or overscheduling yourself.

It doesn't help that I was raised in a household and community where it was normalized to be compared with peers to the point that everything felt like a zero-sum game. For me and so many other children of immigrants, there is a baseline belief that we have benefited at the *expense* of our loved ones or community.

Comparison culture and scarcity culture are rooted in capitalism and white-supremacist ideology (as I elaborate on in chapter eight). Many of our immigrant parents want to demonstrate their success to their families back home or simply alleviate their own guilt. This can be suffocating for children of immigrants, especially because it is not typically our personal happiness or sense of fulfillment being compared to others'; instead, it's often grades, degrees, salaries, and other material things. The thing is, comparing ourselves with other people is how we make and keep ourselves small. This may be entrenched in the fear our immigrant parents have for our well-being, or their fear of being outliers in the group/community. But we are allowed to live big lives and pursue big dreams.

Out of 5,328 children of immigrants who responded to one of my Instagram polls, 69 percent said that their parents pitted them against their siblings or peers. Another 75 percent of 5,349 children of immigrants said that they still struggle today, as adults, with feeling like they are in competition with their peers. Although not with intended malice, my own immigrant parents will frequently talk about something someone else is doing that I'm not doing. *So-and-so just had a baby. So-and-so got into the Ivy League. So-and-so just bought their parents a washing machine. So-and-so visits their parents once a month.*

Of course, this is where information asymmetry comes in—when we compare ourselves with others, we are often seeing very intentional and filtered personas. We have more information about our own shortcomings and struggles than we do about those of others, causing us to compare ourselves with information that skews more positively toward others and more negatively toward ourselves. I would find out years later that many of those college friends of mine with whom I'd first felt the balm of real acceptance—the same people from whom I'd hid the truth—had also struggled in college, and many of them struggled, too, with an internalized narrative of "not being enough."

IN HIS BOOK *Maps of Narrative Practice*, Michael White, the founder of Narrative Therapy, explains that instead of focusing on our needs, motives, drives, or personality traits, it may be more important to understand the "socially constructed conclusions" about these things. This concept has helped me understand my own constructed narrative about my life trajectory: because it was deemed socially and culturally irresponsible and wrong—in my family—to drop out of college, I constructed an identity around being a failure and not enough, and from that moment on, everything found a way to breathe more life into this version of me. Only by recognizing *where* the narrative was rooted could I then practice agency around my ownership—or rejection—of it. Most important, I was able to start celebrating myself and my determination to reach a goal—perhaps later than I wanted to but when I was supposed to. I was unlearning mindsets that were setting me up for failure and disappointment—the scarcity mindset, the approval mindset, the perfection mindset, the fixed mindset, and the victim mindset.

A part of this process was also making the conscious choice to stop seeing Dr. T. At the end of 2018, our sessions turned into a space for me to talk about my applications to graduate school and my desire to become a therapist. I even asked her questions about her own educational background and discussed my own research into which path to choose and which schools felt like good fits. Our time together had changed my life in many ways, but I also realized that we may have reached our ceiling as far as doing work together.

Therapists often joke that it's our job to work ourselves out of a job. We want clients to practice implementing their own skills and solutions and to be able to live independently and healthily outside their relationship with us. Sure, we all will face varied struggles in life, but the goal is to build a tool kit that will enable us to handle whatever comes our way. I felt like I finally had this. Not to mention that my sister and parents had separately commented on how different I was, using phrases like "less scary to talk to" and "more calm." Though they often hinted that this was because Sam made me a better person, I knew that just being in a relationship with him was a product of my emotional work to become a healthier person and let down my walls with those who made me feel safe. I was a different version of myself than I had been when Dr. T and I had started working together four years earlier, and it showed in the ways I was starting to conceptualize my life narrative and all the smaller stories that made it so.

I was about to turn thirty, and I had decided to start over with a new career in mental health. I was finally beginning to accept that life doesn't need to go in a certain order, and for most it never does! In thirty years, I'd had the opportunity to explore different career paths, take risks, marry a partner of my choice, go to therapy, and self-actualize. In their first thirty years, my parents had three children, learned and relearned societal customs and norms, proved themselves within different systems, and built a life from scratch—twice over. All of us had taken detours from our "expected" paths, and looking back, I was not only glad to note that similarity but also grateful to have taken the route I did.

Combating self-sabotaging behaviors and mindsets

Tips for Navigating Procrastination and Perfectionism

- Perfectionism can be a time suck. If you have been working on the same task or project for longer than you anticipated, ask yourself:
    - Am I using my time wisely?
    - By continuing to work on this, am I maximizing my impact?
    - What part of this actually needs to be perfect? Can I settle for "good enough" in other parts of this?
- Next time you feel yourself procrastinating, explore if you are clear on these three questions:
    - Do I know *how* to do it?
    - Do I need help figuring out *where* to start?
    - Do I have clarity on *why* I am doing this?
- Remember that there is a difference between procrastinating and taking a break or resting. Procrastination is often a deliberate avoidance or delay of the task at hand and usually

leads to negative effects, whereas resting or taking a break reflects an intentional choice to step away and recharge.

- You may procrastinate, or avoid the task/challenge at hand, because you don't want to face the difficult emotions—like anxiety, self-doubt, and even apathy—that will surface. When you recognize that you are procrastinating, identify the negative feelings that come up for you.
  - When you think about doing the task, how do you feel?
  - Is there a reason why you are avoiding this?
  - How can you manage this feeling rather than avoid it?

Unlearning the Scarcity Mindset

Reflections on Your Scarcity Mindset

- If/when you are presented with an opportunity and feel pressure to accept it, ask yourself: This is a good opportunity, but is it a good opportunity *for me*? Be honest with yourself about where the pressure is coming from and what you may be afraid of.
- Who makes you feel insecure, scarcity-minded, or competitive? Reflect on why you feel this way around that person or those people.
- Who makes you feel secure, abundant, and confident in what you can do and what you have? Reflect on why you feel this way around that person or those people.
- Sometimes, battling a scarcity mindset is less about having or being "more" and more about having or being "enough." Freewrite about what you have "enough" of and can be grateful for. What does "good enough" mean to you?

Moving Toward an Abundance Mindset

- Practice celebrating others. Instead of thinking, *She's smarter than me*, or instantly feeling jealous, pause and recognize that person's strength: *She worked so hard. I'm so happy she did well!* This might feel uncomfortable at first, but it will help you separate others' actions and achievements from your own. It will also help you recognize strengths, values, and characteristics (beyond achievements) in others that are worth celebrating, allowing you to see these things in yourself, too.

- Be mindful of whom you surround yourself with. If you are constantly around negative people, you may feel more inclined toward negativity, too! Realizing who makes you feel worse, or more negative, is a sign that you may need to set boundaries. (This can be daunting; see page 206 for more tips on setting boundaries.)

- Be honest with yourself about what you can control and what you are realistically up against within our greater systems of white supremacy, patriarchy, and capitalism. Then, find allies, mentors, and others with whom you can share problem-solving efforts and who will help you find agency in whatever ways you can.

- Challenge your binary thinking. Scarcity thrives on fear and on the black-and-white belief that certain things are right/good and other things are wrong/bad. Challenge the notion that your path, your success, your life, and your love must look a certain way in order to be worthy.

Reframing Scarcity

"Change scares me and can take away what I already have." →	"Change is uncomfortable, but with uncertainty comes opportunity for better or more than I know right now."
"I need to keep this thing, item, or relationship in my life even if it's not serving me—just in case." →	"I've outgrown this, and that's okay. Now it's time to make room for something else that serves me better."
"What if something goes wrong?" →	"What if something goes right?"
"I feel jealous of them for achieving the things I want." →	"That's not my timeline, and that's okay. It doesn't mean I can't achieve those things, too."
"That person/ group is getting attention, so no one cares what's going on with me." →	"The fact that other people are getting attention doesn't negate my own experiences."

"If I don't take this opportunity now, I may never get the chance to do it again."	→	"I'm allowed to say no to a good opportunity if the timing doesn't feel right. I can try again later."
"I need to figure it out right now."	→	"I will figure it out."
"What if this ends up being the wrong choice?"	→	"I'm allowed to change my mind later if I want to."

Chapter Eleven

Exploring My Bicultural
Identity Development

n November of 2018, a few months after my father-daughter trip to Halifax and a month shy of completing my bachelor's program, my mom and I were in India to go wedding shopping. The surrounding months were punctuated by arguments related to the wedding, and I had been thinking a lot about my identity, therapy, and mental health. I was navigating a series of professional and bicultural identity crises: How Indian do I have to be to be considered Indian enough? How does my bicultural identity impact my friendships? How do I continue to talk to my immigrant parents about mental health? How do I navigate the not-enoughness I feel in predominantly white spaces? Looking back, I can see that my work in media, my decision to pursue a career in mental health, and my own therapy journey had all been leading me to this moment.

So on our flight back, I registered the Instagram handle @Brown GirlTherapy. Once we landed back in the States, I did a callout on my personal Instagram account asking to hear from "South Asian women who have been to therapy or have wanted to go." Through my Instagram Stories, I asked follow-up questions about whether culture affected their relationships with therapy and what they wished their therapists would understand about their lived experiences as South Asian women. I didn't save any of the responses, but I remember being shocked by the number of messages I received from such a simple and unstructured callout. I witnessed a collective expression of frustration: angst over being misunderstood by clinicians and feeling like they were betraying their immigrant parents by even considering talking to professionals about their struggles. I had thought it was just me. So many folks in the community—those who message me, show up to community events, or speak up in corporate workshops—often say the same thing: *I thought it was just me.*

I was emboldened to further dissect these common feelings and how they were impacting my peers. It wasn't something that happened immediately—I continued wedding planning, got married in April 2019, was accepted to graduate school in D.C., and then went on my honeymoon. But the thoughts planted by the impromptu Instagram callout had been marinating in the back of my mind for months, and I felt called to explore what other South Asian women had shared with me. Finally, after my honeymoon, I decided to revisit the idea and the Instagram page, and I had only a couple of months left in New York, where there was a relatively large South Asian community. The urgency suddenly felt palpable.

As I started building Brown Girl Therapy, I decided to conduct a bit of market research to see what was already out there; I didn't want to join an oversaturated arena, but I did want to find a way to marry my twin passions of narrative storytelling and mental health advocacy. I had seen several online communities and social media pages dedicated to the Asian American community, a community with which I technically identify on a macro level, but I had never truly seen myself represented, since many of these communities targeted East or Southeast Asians. I had also discovered many on-line communities centering South Asian pop culture and social commentary but not mental health specifically. As such, I figured that I would focus on telling my story as a way to talk more broadly about mental health and see what happened. On Father's Day, I wrote a post about my immigrant papa and all he has done and lived through—things that aren't represented in the traditional marketing and noise around that holiday. The post reached thousands of people. I leaned into this pull, though I couldn't yet articulate *where* it was taking me. When I accumulated a few hundred followers, I decided to facilitate some meetups in New York City. I put out a call to anyone who wanted to join, shared my location, and waited. I sat on a sheet I had laid out near the Central Park carousel, with water bottles, pretzels, hummus, and a handful of pencils and notebooks. *Maybe people will want to take notes.* It was a sunny Saturday afternoon, and I was fidgeting, standing up to make sure people could see me if they were looking, then sitting with my head down, convinced that no one was going to come. It felt like a first date; it's safe to say that I had no idea what I was doing.

To my surprise, it turned out better than I could have imagined. Six women of South Asian descent showed up, including a pair of sisters from New Jersey and a Bangladeshi woman from Queens. I'd allotted an hour and a half for the meetup, which stretched into several hours of discussing mental health, grief, our relationships with our parents, colorism, chronic illness, careers, and dating. I was blown away by how willing each woman was to share, even though we were strangers to one another. Encouraged, I hosted a second meetup a month later in Washington Square Park; this time there were about fifteen women, all different from the first meetup. Again, we chatted for hours. As everyone was talking, I looked around in awe. Not only did I leave these meetups feeling seen and rejuvenated, but I also heard that others felt the same way. The ways that so many of these women, myself included, shared and showed their emotions in public with a group of strangers made me revel in the experience. All of us had been, to varying degrees, bereft of the tools or space needed to express ourselves and move through our emotions. In those parks, we were giving each other the space to be unrestrained—and to greedily and safely reach out to one another in newfound connection. Every one of us brought to the forefront a part of ourselves that we likely never felt safe exposing.

Being a child of immigrants is an identifier that I didn't use until I started Brown Girl Therapy. Of course, I always knew that my parents were immigrants, but I never made the connection between their experiences and my childhood struggles and learned behaviors/mindsets. It wasn't just through in-person meetups that I felt a sense of relatability. The stories I was sharing on Instagram had, to me, felt abnormal and unrelatable—until I realized that there were innumerable people out there living with the same internalized narratives and experiencing their struggles in silence and isolation, just like me. We all craved the sense of belonging and acceptance that we lacked in our daily lives. At the end of a recent corporate workshop, one attendee asked me how I learned to verbalize and give language to so many of these experiences. The truth is, I don't know. I do think that my sensitive nature has been my superpower. I spent years carefully observing how others perceived me and how my elders were feeling in any given situation, and I think that this, coupled with the significant amount of time I spent on my own trying to process my thoughts and feelings through reading, watching TV, or journaling, allowed me to develop an insight into family dynamics, cultural values, and the specific ways I straddled being either-or—even when I was too young to fully understand. What's more, my desperation for community and my mental health struggles shaped the way I viewed others, developed empathy, and started to understand myself as a product of multiple systems that were bigger than just me. These shared experiences in our communities are often so precise and so embedded in the fabric of our daily lives and identities that unless you put them under a cultural microscope, you often don't even know what you're looking at.

Though many of my followers are South Asian women, and though I initially formed the community to focus on this specific population, I came to realize that Brown Girl Therapy and its mission and themes extend well beyond this community. I heard from a Mexican American person who never thought that another human would relate to their experiences. A Vietnamese woman told me that one of my interviews gave her the tools she needed to have a breakthrough conversation with her mom, despite a significant language barrier. An older second-generation Nigerian parent mentioned that my posts, and the associated comments she reads, have allowed her to be more aware and intentional with her own kids. A biracial Egyptian woman reported that the community helped her find other biracial second gens to support one another's acute identity struggles. A Syrian man discussed how the community enabled him to connect his gender and birth order to his current behavior at work. Even children of white European immigrants have noted shock over how similar their parents are to other immigrant parents, despite the racial and cultural differences. After hearing from a diverse group of people, I decided to poll the community and found that over one hundred countries were represented within it. When the results came back, I was stupefied. How could so many of us, despite our different intersectional identities, have such similar shared experiences?

Bicultural Identity Development

It was through building Brown Girl Therapy—and hearing stories from others—while starting a career in mental health and navigating my own bicultural identity as a newlywed that I recognized how cyclical our identity development is as children of immigrants. We don't go through consecutive stages in order or on a certain timeline; instead, I theorize, we grow through many different bicultural identity crises. These are, of course, impacted by our acculturation experiences and those of our parents—geographical locations, access to cultural or religious communities, enforced traditions, retention of heritage languages, and so on. Research suggests that identity development tends to happen during the adolescent years, as we move through the fear of embarrassment, the need for approval, the need to belong, and the experience and resolution of normative conflicts. This is why many of us have some version of the "stinky lunchbox" story or can recollect the painful pause before our names were stumbled over during roll call in grade school. It's the same reason why I spent my early high school years trying to *fit in* by attempting to alter my skin and eye color.

As we get older, however, we start making adult choices—what career to pursue, whom to marry, where to live, whether to have kids or not and how to raise them if we do—and we start to grapple with our parents' mortality. We are flung back into the throes of questioning what is important to us and how we should carry on. For many of us, this may happen later than eighteen (age of adulthood be damned) because of familial and cultural expectations that we stay close—physically or emotionally, for better or for worse—to family. The age at which we reckon with the values and norms we've always lived by differs for us all.

Different researchers have created many different identity development models, trying to incorporate and pinpoint the distinctive experiences of racial and ethnic minorities. Among some of the prominent, William E. Cross created the Nigrescence model on Black racial identity development in 1971. Jean Kim created an Asian American identity development model in 1981. Jean Phinney created a three-stage model of ethnic identity formation in 1989. W. S. Carlos Poston created a biracial identity development model in 1990. Aureliano S. Ruiz developed the Latino ethnic identity model in 1990. And Derald Wing Sue and Stanley Sue created a racial and cultural identity development model in 1990 that was updated from the Minority Development model created in 1979 by Donald R. Atkinson, George Morten, and Derald Wing Sue. Kevin L. Nadal even hypothesized a Pilipino American identity development model in 2004. They all propose similar ideas and challenge the traditional or universal models of therapy; and they are all almost two decades old.

Sue and Sue's racial and cultural identity development model has five stages: conformity, dissonance, resistance and immersion, introspection, and integrative awareness. In the conformity stage, folks are more likely to adopt and prefer the dominant, or white, cultural values. They may even develop negative beliefs about their own cultures or races. In the dissonance stage, folks often question those messages and internalized beliefs, moving away from binary thinking that posits one as good and the other as bad. In the resistance and immersion stage, people feel angry and distrustful over the fact that things are not as they had been told when it comes to their racial or cultural identities. They may start to embrace positive attitudes toward their own cultures or races, appreciating diversity and devaluing dominant attitudes and norms. In the introspection stage, folks will question their experiences and start to explore their senses of loyalty and belonging. Finally, in the integrative awareness stage, they will at last feel more secure and confident in their racial and cultural identities, moving toward multiculturalism in all aspects of their lives and working toward fighting collective oppression. There's obviously truth to this racial identity model, and yet like all identity models, there's a particular focus on racial and ethnic development and cultural identity tends to be neglected.

In devising an alternative, I have built off these models and my professional work to theorize a bicultural/multicultural identity model with five stages. These are nonlinear and nonsequential; you may be at different depths in different stages depending on your relationship with your multiple cultural identities.

- **Conformity:** In this stage, you are motivated to develop performative behaviors in order to feel a semblance of belonging and acceptance within one or both of your cultural systems. This may not be a conscious choice (especially when you're younger), as there may be minimal awareness of how you feel about your bi/multicultural identity.
- **Isolation or Dissonance:** In this stage, you feel culturally conflicted. You may feel a sense of displacement from one, if not both/all, of your cultural communities. This can be particularly hard, as isolation and disconnection may increase the likelihood that you will struggle with mental health issues.
- **Awareness and Interrogation:** In this stage, you start to explore what it means to identify with a cultural group. You may start to question whether your values align with those of your culture(s). You start to unpack the experiences and feelings you have in relation to your different cultures, and what it means to identify with a dominant or marginalized identity. This stage is often correlated to exposure and learning.

- **Appreciation:** In this stage, you actively return to, or strengthen, your heritage cultural identity. By recognizing the benefits, strengths, and resilience of your heritage culture(s) and communities, you begin to unlearn narratives that the dominant society and culture imposed on you.

- **Negotiation and Fusion:** In this stage, you actively and critically assess how to integrate—or blend—your different cultures so that they complement each other and/or serve you in living truthfully. This can be particularly difficult when cultural values are not aligned with one another, and you might have to unlearn and question decades of conditioning and norms. You may practice new ways of being. You start to search for communities that share in your identity, and you start to feel more positively about your culture(s) and your sense of belonging within it/them. In this stage you become confident in what is important to you and what versions of your cultural identity you choose to uphold. This is usually accompanied by a sense of self-acceptance.

Reflections

- Which stage do you think you're in now? Why?
- What stages of identity development have you been in over the course of your life? What experiences or situations impacted this?
- What stage do you *want* to be in, and how do you think you can get there?
- What does a strong bi/multicultural identity mean or look like to you?

Along with our parents and bi/multicultural peers and loved ones, we are constantly negotiating our cultures, values, customs, and traditions. We make choices every day that lead us to embrace one culture over another, and prompt us to reconcile with any potential impact and recourse from those choices. *Who* we are in relationship with matters. *What* we consume matters. *Where* we exist, work, live, and love matters. A person is embedded in their systems, and thus their cultural identity development and relationship with their culture(s) are influenced by these external structures. To really understand and unpack your bi/multicultural identity, you have to start with the hunger you likely had as a kid to belong (in either or both of your cultures). In my work with children of immigrants, I have questions about their bi/multicultural identity development that I like to explore with them, and I invite you to explore these questions, too, with the forthcoming guided reflections on page 361.

Searching for "Home"

I'll never forget the first time I realized that people saw my turban-wearing brother and dad differently. I was thirteen, and it was after 9/11. My family was in New York City visiting my brother, who lived there at the time, and we were just walking down the street when a man with an Australian accent yelled, "Hey, bin Laden, go home!" His friend mimed playing a flute while shaking his head from side to side. No one said anything as they laughed and walked past us. We just pretended it didn't happen, but later that day, I overheard my mom nonchalantly mention to my dad that maybe they should consider moving back to India. That day, I learned two things: being brown makes me a "bad" kind of different, and America was not considered to be a permanent home for my family.

In the years after that incident with my family, the need to define "home" fell dormant, but after Trump was elected, moving out of the country was once again a prominent topic of conversation—not just for us but also for other immigrant families we knew. In late 2016, I was rooted in my independence. I had a stable career, and New York had been my home for three years. I was walking home from a writing class near Bryant Park when a white man in a suit hit on me. After I ignored him, he spat at me to "go home to where you came from" because no one wanted my "f*cking disease." Home. To where I came from. I was reminded, yet again, that I did not belong. What was home?

Even though they have been settled in the U.S. for nearly thirty-five years, my parents still talk about home as a faraway place. They, like many immigrants, carry nostalgia for places and times that may not even exist anymore due to cultural evolution, war, conflict, and natural change. Aunts, uncles, cousins, and extended family members span across the globe, from India, to Japan, to the U.K., to Canada, with touchstone nuclear-family homes in different cities—places to convene before we say our goodbyes and go our separate ways again.

Even my older siblings cycled through "homes"—spending years abroad, fleeing America altogether, or moving from state to state every few years. My sister and her husband finally bought a home in the U.K., and my brother, who is in his midforties, only recently did so in the United States. Putting roots down in a country that still doesn't really feel like home, even though it has been for decades. A lot of children of immigrants come from families that are dispersed *all* over the world, having fled countries willingly *and* unwillingly—and sometimes multiple times over, products of war, political regimes, and colonization. Through my work, I have heard many children of immigrants report an inability to pinpoint what and where "home" is—sometimes because the original place no longer exists—and they often gravitate temporarily to various cities and towns, wondering if one of them will stick.

On a recent family trip to India, I was reminded, again, of how fragmented my multicultural identity is. The smells and sounds and the ways my name and other words were pronounced elicited a deep and comforting familiarity, yet I stumbled to communicate with extended family members and locals. I was in a place where my skin color (in various shades) was the dominant one, but I was treated like a foreigner anyway. Seeing family members I had met only a few times in my life created formal and disconnected experiences. We're *from* somewhere, but we may never *live* there—never earn the privilege to call it home. Even more, for some, "home" evokes a sense of safety, but when systems and places are not always safe for us, we may turn to the space between our relationships where we can be received, and seen, in all our multiculturalism. The more I connect to my roots, the more important it is for me to be surrounded by people who either share in my intersectional identity and cultural identity or are curious about it in a way that allows me to bring my *whole* self to the relationship. So many of us continue to navigate, and will forever be navigating, where and what home means for us, while never feeling allowed to claim any one place as our own.

Building Bicultural Confidence

Biculturalism is often defined as a level of proficiency and comfort in the differing cultures (heritage and host) that encompass a person. Yet I hear from many immigrants, children of immigrants, and bi/multiracial folks regarding how *uncomfortable* they can feel in their cultural identities. In a Brown Girl Therapy Instagram poll, I asked how people felt about their bicultural or multicultural identities, and the responses were eye-opening. Of about 1,000 respondents, 23 percent said they solely feel pride toward their cultural identities; however, 26 percent said they feel either shame or confusion, and more than 50 percent said they feel *all three* of the above. When I explored further and asked about the main struggles they experienced in relation to their bicultural identities, hundreds said some version of "not fitting in" or "not knowing who I am." Many of us feel like we have to culturally code-switch and become different people in order to fit in to our different environments. And this is valid! This is also how *systems* are set up to make us feel—whether it's the systems founded in white supremacy and patriarchy or the systems inherited and inherently accepted as the norm in our families.

Our social and cultural identities can allow us to be part of a group, cultivating a sense of belonging by making us feel bound to something bigger than ourselves. That group membership can also be a source of community. However, many people I have worked with or heard from who are straddling two or more differing cultures are often also straddling the line between pride and shame. If our heritage culture is inherently group-oriented or collectivist, we may be more likely to experience levels of shame for not embracing the culture as wholly as our parents, families, and communities have embraced it. This may feel like a betrayal. In fact, our self-esteem can be shaped by how well we fulfill the values of our culture (say, how in line we are with our heritage cultural norms at home and how in line we are with our host culture at work). Research even suggests that in personal relationships, maintaining our heritage cultures is related to positive psychological well-being, whereas in our public life (school, work, etc.), adapting to the host culture is related to positive psychological well-being. Where does that leave us?

. . .

MY MULTICULTURAL IDENTITY had once felt fragile and un-
cool, only to morph into something I learned to make room for and
love. But the tension is still palpable. When I talk to family abroad,
across Canada, India, the U.K., and Japan, I find feelings of confu-
sion and betrayal surfacing. Not because I feel misunderstood or
othered by my own family, as I did growing up, but because I spent
a majority of my childhood as the American one (in my immediate
and extended family), which became a dominant part of my narrative. I am American, and I learned to embrace it. As I've gotten older,
I've come to realize that while I am grateful for the privileges, resources, and opportunities I have been allotted growing up and living in the U.S., I am *also* constantly confronting what it means to be
an American and navigating the (cultural and political) values tied
to that part of my identity. Further, I genuinely love being Indian—
it's special to me. But as I have come back to my roots, so has a
Western capitalist society commodified my culture (things like tur-
meric masks, making and drinking afternoon chai, hair oiling, etc.),
making me feel trapped between overprotection of what is ours and
guilt for what I hadn't claimed before.

When we feel ashamed of who we are or where we come from,
we contract. We begin to feel self-doubt and lose confidence, and we
learn to take up less space in situations or interactions with folks
who make us feel inadequate. However, when we feel pride in who
we are and where we come from, we expand. We can embrace the
confidence and take up space. They both have a cumulative effect
and can often be initiated by a single experience. For example, I have
always been too ashamed to speak Punjabi or practice it with my
family because whenever I would try as a teenager, I would often get
made fun of for poor pronunciation or my Americanized accent.

This is something that, decades later, I am still working through as I attempt to develop stronger language skills in my mother tongue. Conversely, during my recent monthlong trip to India, I learned that my great-grandfather was a freedom fighter, and I learned more stories about Sikhs during the Mughal Empire, leading me to feel more knowledgeable and competent, and thus more confident, in my cultural and religious identity. I felt a newfound pride in my family ancestry and my heritage.

Through having conversations in the community, it became clear to me that so many feel unsure about how to claim ownership over their differing identities. It's important to follow *your* curiosity about your culture rather than lean into what is expected of or forced on you. This may look like learning how to cook cultural foods, listening to cultural music, writing to, and building your own relationships with, relatives abroad, or going through old photos with parents and asking about the people in them. I hear from folks who didn't have their cultures passed down to them through family. And the truth is, if you want to embrace your culture, you have to seek it out for yourself.

There really is no *right* way to claim your identity. Instead of suggesting that there's a way to "successfully" achieve biculturalism, because you'll hold yourself to standards that you may never attain, I instead encourage building confidence in claiming your cultural identity. But what does this actually look like? It may require synthesizing your multiple cultures into a new and unique combination that is true to you. While many researchers explore multiple different processes that may lead to true biculturalism, I am most pulled toward the concepts of hybridizing biculturalism and alternating biculturalism. Second-generation immigrants are more likely to engage in hybridizing biculturalism, whereas first-generation immigrants are more likely to engage in alternating biculturalism. Hybridizing biculturalism consists of coming up with new and creative ways to integrate both cultures—such as by eating a home-cooked meal that is traditional to your heritage culture but has a Western twist, or by speaking a mix of two languages with friends who also speak both. It essentially creates a bridge between two cultural streams. Alternating biculturalism consists of shifting behaviors depending on the current cultural context—such as only speaking English at school but only speaking a heritage language at home, or only wearing traditional clothes to cultural community events but only wearing Western clothes elsewhere.

Those Sikh camps I attended every summer growing up shaped my multicultural identity and my ability to hybridize my cultures. There, I had peers and friends from across the United States. We woke up together at 6:00 a.m. to pray, then spent our days taking Punjabi language and kirtan classes, with breaks for lunch and recess-like activities. We'd take field trips to go bowling, watch fireworks, and even visit Hersheypark. As kids do, we'd also defy our camp counselors and stay up past nightly Rehraas Sahib in our bunks, giggling and telling each other stories. We were expected to perform religious hymns, and we also had annual talent shows in which we merged our Punjabi and American interests; one year I did a choreographed dance with some of my friends to Gloria Gaynor's "I Will Survive," followed by a bhangra performance with others.

For children of immigrants, and frankly BIPOC generally, the common Western advice to "be authentic and be yourself" doesn't feel right; rather, it may feel healthier and more appropriate to consider our cultural identities as something that we can blend, choose, or move between. This gives us individual agency to determine when it feels psychologically or emotionally safe or appropriate to deploy certain cultural values, behaviors, or norms depending on whom we are with and what environment we are in. Our ability to be authentic is informed by context, self-preservation, and a sense of safety. This also serves as a reminder that just because we thrive in one cultural environment doesn't necessarily mean we are rejecting a different part of our cultural identity.

IN 1996, STUART HALL, a Jamaican-born British sociologist known for his theories on cultural identity and multiculturalism, wrote an essay called "Cultural Identity and Diaspora." In it, he says: "Cultural identity is a matter of 'becoming' as well as of 'being.' It belongs to the future as much as to the past. It is not something which already exists, transcending place, time, history and culture. Cultural identities come from somewhere, have histories. But, like everything which is historical, they undergo constant transformation. Far from being eternally fixed in some essentialized past, they are subject to the continuous 'play' of history, culture and power." I return to this time and time again because it's a reminder of all the ways that our cultural identities can be forever in flux.

A phenomenon I observe in my work with children of immigrants is a desperation to have it all figured out. But as Hall suggests, our cultural identities are not only fluid but also products of access, power and oppression, privilege and marginalization, and history. I believe that part of building bicultural confidence is resisting categorization—and thus checklists for fitting into categories—altogether. Cultural fluency is less about knowing it all and more about familiarizing ourselves and being willing to learn. This includes exposing ourselves to our cultures in ways that feel digestible to *us*. Culture can be absorbed in different ways. Even more, through this approach to cultural exposure, we increase our own sense of agency to learn, explore, and decide *how* we identify with something and *what* we identify with. Research suggests that children of immigrants can partake in what is known as remote enculturation, or remote learning of one's heritage culture. In this context, we can take adult language or cooking classes, experience short-term exposure to our cultures through travel, maintain relationships with those abroad through the use of communication technology, or enjoy cultural media from afar. It's not passive, and we can't rely on how we were raised. We have to decide how we want to actively participate in our own bicultural identities.

When I ask people to tell me their favorite things about being bicultural—a question I ask in almost all of my workshops and community events—I am empowered by the responses. Some of the answers are obvious, like the food, music, and sense of community, and others are less so: *I am adaptable and empathetic. I am able to exist in multiple spaces. I can see different perspectives. I am open to trying new things because my existence in itself is new.* Our bicultural identities are a strength, a superpower.

We may not be able to change our cultural identities, but we can change our relationship to them. Instead of seeing the constant negotiation of your cultures as something burdensome or overwhelming, I encourage you to consider it a remarkable benefit and privilege. When you feel *stuck* between your differing cultures, try to remind yourself that you do have agency. You have the ability to move *through* different cultural systems. You have choice. Often, we feel trapped because we don't feel comfortable or confident allowing ourselves to expand in the way that our bi/multicultural identities encourage us to. A big part of building bicultural or multicultural confidence is rejecting an either-or mindset. This liberates us from having to try so hard to fit into any one box.

Reminder: It's never too late to reconnect with, or be curious about, your heritage culture. Recognize that the choice to build a bridge between your cultures in whatever way feels good to you is a powerful and personal drive toward honesty. You already are culturally enough.

Mental Health, Identity, and Culture

None of the above were represented or discussed in my education to become a therapist. My experiences of being a minority in the media, I would find, had broad overlap with my experiences as a minority in the counseling field.

When I started my graduate program in the fall of 2019, I was naive. My first class was Ethics in Counseling. My professor was a very well-known and well-respected older white man in the profession, and I initially felt grateful to be learning from him. A few weeks in, we were talking about the concept of dual relationships between counselors and clients. Of course, there are obviously harmful and problematic dual relationships that should always be avoided—for instance, don't have sex with a client, and don't treat your family members or friends. But beyond the extremes, what happens if you are a minoritized counselor who specializes in working with your community—a community lacking in representation in the field? Are you really supposed to create such rigid boundaries between every single person you meet who shares your identity? *Can* you? It seemed to me like some of these guidelines assumed that everyone lives in a big city and that everyone is unidentifiable to everyone else.

I decided to privately confront this professor, not only about these questions but also about my role as a public writer and content creator. I wanted to know how to balance becoming a therapist who did not center myself in the work but still strove to serve my community in ways that it had not been previously served. This professor told me in no uncertain terms that I should immediately delete all of my public-facing work and shut down Brown Girl Therapy. He didn't think it was professional or ethical. I was devastated. Was I really supposed to choose to silence myself as a vocal advocate for, and member of, a marginalized community in the name of ethics? *Who* would lose from that choice? Thankfully, and despite the fact that approximately 70 percent of full-time counselor educator faculty members are white, I had access to professors of color who were younger and who believed in me and my work so effortlessly that they refused to let me doubt what I was doing and why I was doing it. Their support was a tremendous factor in my continued building of Brown Girl Therapy, but that experience raised for me the first of many issues and questions about what we are taught and, even more so, what we are not taught as training clinicians.

WORKING IN THE MEDIA, I had been told for years that the very voices I wanted to uplift might not be mainstream enough. After being told that I should delete Brown Girl Therapy, I prioritized it as an act of defiance. So many of us struggle in silence, and I ached to find ways to dismantle the disconnection I had gotten used to. So I returned to my previous weapon of choice when it came to self-expression and connection: writing what I needed so desperately to hear myself. After my honeymoon, I had been creating content occasionally, but I wanted to be more deliberate about making time for it. I was feeling galvanized by what I was learning in school, but I was also navigating frustration and sadness over how little the common person understood about mental health, especially as it intersects with cultural identity. I wanted to democratize mental health education and knew then that accessibility would be a pillar of my work.

Social media can be an incredible resource—online spaces have a unique ability to offer mental health education and awareness to underrepresented populations in cultures where mental health is still highly stigmatized, and to create communities where people can feel validated in their experiences. It also helps people put language to what they've experienced or felt. Social media is obviously not a replacement for therapy. There are issues, of course, that arise in these online spaces, such as the perpetuation of wrongful stereotypes, the siloing of communities, and the spread of misinformation. But social media can be an accessible gateway to mental health care, and it allows for people to autonomously engage at their own pace and where they are without judgment.

I've seen firsthand how social media communities can provide psychological safety for folks who are otherwise marginalized, oppressed, or discriminated against. This includes a fulfillment of needs and shared emotional connection. Given that the counseling and psychology workforce lacks diversity, these online communities are doing invaluable work in curating culturally affirming resources and breaking stereotypes regarding mental health in marginalized populations. Furthermore, for children of immigrants, social media can actually help them claim their senses of heritage identity while also allowing them to stay connected with family members from their parents' origin countries.

One of the core tenets of group therapy is challenging the notion of othering. By bringing people with similar and different backgrounds together, we can connect over similarities—to feel less alone in our experiences—while also honoring our differences and learn-ing from each other. I wanted to create a space where children of immigrants felt included and represented, so I started facilitating conversation clubs and workshops for my community, and through nearly one hundred nonclinical groups, I witnessed the power of be-longing. It's unbelievable how much one hour with ten or so other people who nod their heads when you share a story can change the way you see yourself fitting into this world.

Representation in Mental Health

Having a public persona and being a therapist, I find that I am con-stantly navigating two different professional cultures—much like I am doing in my personal life as an Indian American. As is the case in so many arenas, there is such a lack of representation in the men-tal health-care world that when one person makes it through, there's oftentimes an expectation of them to represent all of the diverse sto-ries of all the people in the community of which they are a part. It's difficult not to be treated as a monolith. I get messages all the time from other children of immigrants who want to see their specific struggles represented or hear them discussed. It's unrealistic. I often feel suffocated by expectations to represent us all and have all the answers. But I'm human. I'm trying to be someone who shows up honestly and vulnerably and hopefully inspires more children of im-migrants to share their valuable stories and ideas, too.

On the flip side, the beauty of the way our community comes to-gether has been a source of empowerment for me. One of my first speaking engagements in 2020 came about because a psychologist who attended a few Brown Girl Therapy community events reached out to me, asking me to give a two-hour presentation to a group of clinicians on the clinical considerations of working with children of immigrants. A majority of the opportunities I have received since building Brown Girl Therapy have come solely from those within the community. I count among community members the reporters, writers, editors, and producers at media sites covering my work; the editor who brought me on as an advice columnist at *The Washington Post*; the multiple literary agents who initially reached out to work with me; and even one of my book editors. The ways we can make noise and take up space when we work together is beautiful, and it threatens the norm.

During the early years of building this community while I was in graduate school, I realized that my motivations were shifting. I was once motivated by achievement and affiliation, desperately wanting to feel accepted by my parents and to belong among my peers. In the aftermath of my depression, I was motivated by a need for change, which pushed me to move, go to therapy, and learn new skills. But in grad school, I began to find myself intrinsically motivated by a purpose bigger than myself. That's not to say I didn't need to prove myself as capable and smart. My grades mattered to me throughout graduate school, and I still felt the need to rewrite old narratives. We can choose to start over as many times as we need, and often, we must find compassion for what we are living through and what we may not yet be able to identify. Mental health struggles don't look the same for everyone. Healing doesn't look the same for everyone.

In D.C., while I looked for a new therapist in a new city, I was pulled to find a therapist of color. I wanted to spend more time sharing in sessions rather than explaining. I wanted all of my identities— Indian, American, woman, daughter, sister, content creator, public-facing writer, new therapist, newlywed, and so on—to be held together, and I believed that I had a better shot at this with someone of color.

. . .

COUNSELING AND MENTAL health are not one-size-fits-all, yet according to 2019 data from the American Psychological Association, about 83 percent of the U.S. psychology workforce is white. This is barely an improvement from ten years ago, when 85 percent of the workforce was white. Hispanic Americans represented the second-largest group at 7 percent, while Asian Americans represented 4 percent and African Americans just 3 percent. This doesn't even account for the lack of representation when it comes to disability, gender, sexuality, or religion. And it's not just the psychology workforce; in 2019, the Bureau of Labor Statistics found that close to 70 percent of U.S. social workers and 88 percent of mental health counselors were white.

I recognize how much privilege I have had to get to where I am today. When I was in graduate school—at a predominantly white institution, in a predominantly white field—it was not lost on me how many barriers there are to even just becoming a licensed therapist. Not only are the schools expensive, but the degree often entails years of unpaid work and internships. And once you do graduate, if you want to be on a licensure track, you again become overworked and underpaid for *at least* two years in order to get the hours you need under supervision, which some people have to pay to get, to qualify for state licensure. Phew. This is not possible for *so* many people of color who are already struggling because of systemic issues in the country.

The mental health profession was created by white people, and it was normed for white people. Asian Americans are three times less likely than their white counterparts to seek mental health care (and are the least likely of all ethnic groups to do so). Only one in three Black adults who need mental health care receives it, and only approximately 34 percent of Hispanic/Latine adults with mental illness receive treatment each year, compared with the U.S. average of 45 percent.

Mental health cannot be understood in isolation from identity and culture. There are several important ways that culture intersects with how we experience, perceive, and seek support for our mental health. Stigma and fear around mental health care often stem from a feeling of something "not being for us" and from a notion of it being harmful rather than helpful. In communities of color, discussions about mental health or therapy are often steeped in misunderstanding because of a lack of knowledge or access; most issues surrounding mental health care get grouped into a pile labeled "white people stuff." Solidarity within our communities can create trust and bridge generational and cultural gaps. Research has also shown a low retention rate for people of color who access care. This could be because of practical inaccessibility, but it could also be because of microaggressions in the room. Regardless of the reason, when someone has a bad experience with something they were hesitant to pursue in the first place, the field isn't just losing one client. Most likely, it is losing an entire community of people who distrust the system.

Even more, the expression of mental health symptoms can differ across cultures. Some may describe struggles as physical/somatic rather than mental/emotional. As I've previously mentioned, compared with Europeans and Americans, Asians are more likely to feel mental health struggles or mental illness in their bodies, or somatically, so medical doctors may be sought first. Also, Western definitions of mental health issues, such as depression and anxiety, don't necessarily translate across languages and cultures. For example, someone in the Latine community might describe symptoms of depression as "nervios" (nerves, in literal translation), which could be misconstrued as anxiety by a professional. Research suggests that shame and social anxiety are associated, but the *Diagnostic and Statistical Manual of Mental Disorders* criterion for social anxiety is a social situation "in which the individual is exposed to possible scrutiny by others." However, in an Eastern and collectivist context, a person may describe their social anxiety as a fear of embarrassing someone else or exposing them to scrutiny.

Members of marginalized groups may reject or distrust services due to historical and intergenerational trauma and racism experienced at the hands of professionals. Not to mention that bias and racism still creep in. For example, Black men (regardless of background) are more likely to receive a misdiagnosis of schizophrenia when expressing symptoms related to mood disorders or PTSD. And even if there isn't a diagnosis issue at stake, I have heard horror stories about, and have observed myself, how quickly a clinician may label a client as "resistant" before exploring *why* the resistance exists and *where* it comes from—especially on a cross-cultural level.

Social and cultural narratives that create barriers to mental health care are innumerable. These might revolve around the model minority myth or culturally defined masculinity (as well as many other stereotypes). People who subscribe to such narratives may struggle with asking for help or with being honest in therapy because of internalized beliefs that it will make them seem weak, less capable, or unworthy. Barriers may also arise simply because they were taught to show respect to those in positions of power and authority, and it may take time to dismantle that dynamic in the therapy room with them. Therapy as we know it *is* a Western construct, and yet many cultures have been practicing different sorts of healing and therapy for centuries, even as these practices may not be well integrated into the mainstream.

. . .

SEVERAL MONTHS BEFORE my last session with Dr. T in 2018, my parents came to visit me in New York. My dad had a work conference in the city, and they were staying at a hotel near the Rockefeller Center Christmas tree. My mom was excited to roam Midtown; she wanted to see the festive lights and storefront displays along Fifth Avenue and pop over to Bryant Park's Winter Village for last-minute shopping. Before arriving, they had made it clear that they expected me to maximize our time together and to stay with them in their one-room, two-bed hotel room. It didn't matter that I had an apartment not too far away. It didn't matter that I was in my late twenties. It didn't matter—and wasn't even conceivable to them—that I didn't want to. As an unmarried daughter, I was expected to do as they asked—they were visiting from so far away, after all.

I decided to set a boundary, one in which I still spent the whole weekend with them but refused to stay in their hotel with them. I was telling Dr. T about the psychological discomfort I felt over not staying with them, and she instinctively made a face. Who's to say what she was thinking, but she did suggest, without any curiosity about how this expectation was impacting me or what I thought of it, that I was an adult and therefore shouldn't have to stay with them. At that moment, I remember feeling judged, though I didn't actually say anything. In my case, this didn't negate the significant work we did together, but for others, it might.

When the mental health-care system does not look, sound, or think like you, it can be easy to feel like you do not deserve quality care unless you can fit yourself into the box of what Western mental health care is "supposed" to look like. This prevents so many people from wanting to seek help. Toxic parents? Cut them out. Struggling at work? Advocate for your needs. Navigating microaggressions? Are you sure there isn't something you can do differently?

My experience with Dr. T suggests that a client can either join in, pointing out everything wrong with their culture and using it as a scapegoat for mental health issues, completely turning their back on where they come from, or they can defend everything about their culture, even when some of its expectations and values are contributing to their struggle. This further perpetuates the idea that children of immigrants must maintain all-or-nothing mindsets when it comes to their families and cultures. We already grapple with feeling like we have to abandon the spaces we occupy. We already swallow our fears and frictions, pretending like they don't exist. We already engage with enablers and sympathizers in our workplaces and daily lives. Therapy should be a refuge where we can remove our armor, explore being who we've never dared to be, and sort through our issues—not have them exacerbated.

These feelings of cultural frustration were brewing in me long before I even realized, and I didn't have the language then that I do now to explain cultural humility or to stress how Eurocentric and colonial Western models of therapy are. I didn't know that, to some degree, Dr. T was pathologizing collectivism, whether she realized it or not. All I knew was that something wasn't sitting right with me. It stayed in the pit of my stomach, causing discomfort, but I would often just wait for it to pass. I never had the courage to explore it because I was convinced that it wasn't valid and that it was something only I struggled with. Now, years later, I hurt for others who may be experiencing this very thing, perhaps repeatedly, without realizing that it's *not* them.

Mental Health Care Moving Forward

Being culturally sensitive is not always about sharing an identity or a language. And sometimes being culturally sensitive is not about the details of what is being said but rather, it may be more about the internal process for a client to even admit certain things. It's about creating space that gives clients permission to speak their truths. That said, I've had multiple clients or parents of adolescent clients talk solely in Hindi or Punjabi during sessions to discuss concerns or reference family members or religious/cultural traditions. One of my adolescent clients was allowed to seek therapy for the first time because their parents were comfortable with my family's Punjab origins. "You get it. You get us," their parent said to me the first time I spoke with them. This is significant for many of us who have felt like we have to constantly hide parts of ourselves.

Cultural sensitivity offers a sense of safety to people who may not otherwise come to the table. Anecdotally, I have gotten a number of requests from folks who were referred to me by my current clients. Because I was vetted by people they trusted, they gained more trust in the unknown of the therapy process.

I grapple to this day with what my place is in the broken mental health system that still perpetuates heteronormativity. I have found myself frustrated by being put into a box and expected to speak to the experiences of those in my community, but I also feel impassioned to address the lack of representation in the field altogether. In developing myself as a therapist, I believe that I will always face the challenges of what is expected or encouraged in the field from an individualistic perspective and what feels more culturally responsible and sensitive when it comes to the cultures in which my clients (and I) exist. I cannot show up as a blank slate when I am a product of all the values, norms, and expectations that I have navigated in my life. Sometimes, this means that I will have to broach the topic of boundaries or shared community spaces and remind clients that, yes, maybe I will "get it," but I will still follow up with questions and curiosity to make sure I'm not making assumptions, either.

I believe it is imperative that the system diversify itself to provide accessible resources to marginalized communities. We need to challenge what therapy "must" look like, as well as the tools and evaluations we turn to in our work. I never want to pathologize cultural norms, but I simultaneously recognize that what is "normal" may not be healthy for—and may actually be harmful to—someone who experiences it. Symptomology looks different and is understood differently across cultures. We must recognize that grief, religion, spirituality, collectivism, anxiety, and depression are subjective experiences based on cultural roots and not universally applicable objective criteria. After all, social and cultural norms are not to be equated with therapeutic goals.

Near the end of graduate school, I was able to put all of these things together for myself. Intentionally seeking out a therapist of color was a step toward integrating my understanding that therapeutic goals were not, and do not have to be, fundamentally at odds with growing into my bicultural identity.

Reflecting on and understanding your bicultural identity development

Negotiating Family and Cultures

- What cultural traditions and norms were embedded in your childhood?
- How does your current relationship with your ethnic culture(s) and host culture compare or contrast with that of your siblings, parents, cousins, or other family members?
- Where did your family have the most resistance to the host culture? What were your parents scared of for you when you were growing up? Alternatively, how much did your family embrace the host culture and its values?
- How was internalized racism modeled to you or reinforced? How did you internalize racism growing up?
- How do you find yourself negotiating your different cultures when you are with your family?
- How did language retention or loss of language impact your

relationship with your family members and your heritage culture(s)?

Peers

- Who were your friends growing up? How did they compare with you in terms of identity and culture?
- Did where you grew up affect the people to whom you had access? In what ways?
- Did your peers make you feel proud or ashamed of your ethnic culture(s) growing up? How so?
- Who are your friends now? How do they (or do they not) nurture certain cultural identities in you?

Systems of Socialization

- Did you go to a school or work in an environment that had a lot of bicultural kids or kids that looked like you? How may this have impacted you?
- Did you regularly attend camps, religious events, or cultural community gatherings that fostered your ethnic identity? Did you have access to these spaces?
- Were your holidays or languages represented in your schools, universities, and/or workplaces?
- At work, do you feel encouraged to show up as your whole self on your team? Why or why not?
- How is your bicultural identity strengthened or weakened by the systems in which you currently live, love, and work?
- How comfortable are you blending your different cultures in different spaces you occupy? Be specific.

Reflections on Your Bicultural Conflict

Reality: You may have been expected to exhibit and maintain values and norms that you don't wholly embody but that are part of the country you live in.	Reflection: How have I internalized pressure from my peers or my socialized environment? In what ways do the expectations align (or misalign) with my own goals?
Reality: Feeling torn between identities creates a disconnect from each culture and community.	Reflection: How am I involved in each community or culture? How do I strengthen one or the other in a way that feels true to who I am?
Reality: It's natural and normal to crave identity approval and respect.	Reflection: How has my lack of an integrated bicultural identity fostered performative behavior that isn't true to who I am?
Reality: In order to feel secure in your identity and build a strong bicultural one, you may have to reevaluate what is/isn't working for you.	Reflection: How do I want to further develop my biculturalism? What can I learn or consume? Whom can I surround myself with? Who doesn't nurture my identities?

Building Bicultural Confidence

- Whose cultural definitions and expectations are you living by? From whom are you seeking validation? Exploring this may allow you to separate your worthiness and your cultural identity from the expectations and definitions they uphold.
- Think about the childhood label that your family gave you. Maybe you were the "obedient" one or the "sensitive" one. How did this affect your relationship with your cultural identity and/or your experience of cultural impostor syndrome?
- At what point will you know that you are "culturally enough"?
- Often, people who feel like they aren't enough are unable to articulate tangible goals that will make them feel otherwise. The truth is, you may be setting unrealistic expectations for yourself, deepening your feelings of self-doubt and unworthiness. The goalposts may always be moving, but you are already enough.
- The previous question brings another one to light: Do you feel culturally invalidated by certain people or environments? If so, you may need to reevaluate your relationships with these people or your presence in these spaces.
- How do certain cultural values and norms serve you or cost you? Even more, what's at stake for others who uphold certain expectations and values?
- Reflect on experiences and sources of shame in your heritage or host culture.
- Reflect on experiences and sources of pride in your heritage or host culture.
- Think of up to five ways you can intentionally build cultural confidence and knowledge.

Chapter Twelve

Uncovering My Family History

n building Brown Girl Therapy, I have learned that the internal conflicts and isolation many children of immigrants live with are the result of not being taught certain things about where we come from. It doesn't seem all that important whether this knowledge is deliberately withheld from us with the intention of protecting us, or whether it is simply left unshared because of an underlying assumption that we already possess it. I hear stories from children of immigrants who are shamed for not already knowing family details that they haven't been told, or who feel like they have to pry morsels of information from their family members, one crumb at a time. I crave these little pieces of my own family story: the favorite foods, the random forgotten memories that reappear with a song or a mention of a closed-down restaurant, and the inside jokes between siblings who have since become emotionally distant. In my work as a therapist, it's often the small, seemingly unimportant or unrelated things that lead to a deeper excavation of something significant.

In a graduate class on family counseling, we were asked to do a family genogram, tracking three generations of our family tree, along with ages, genders, education, and any other patterns or identifiers we wanted to explore. I knew that I would want to track immigration patterns, but first I needed the most basic information about my family. I wrote down my grandparents' names (the three I remembered) and then called my parents. I didn't know how old they were when they died, how many siblings they had, what their birth orders were, or where their siblings, if they were even still alive, resided. I couldn't tell you how old my aunts and uncles were, beyond who was older and who was younger. I couldn't even tell you their full names, because every one of my blood-related uncles has a nickname totally unrelated to his birth name. Shame crept in for having to ask these most basic questions, though this is actually a very common struggle for many of us.

I remember being at the hospital in Kobe when my dadaji was dying. I was six years old. Beyond that, I have only one other memory of this grandfather: he would give me yen so that I could go to Lawson with my cousins to buy okaki and ramune. *How, again, did he die?* Unless I'm at a doctor's office filling out a complete medical history, I've always found some of these questions to be irrelevant, and for many people, they are. But for children of immigrants, the incessant wondering over whether we are enough can stem from a lack of knowledge about where—and who—we come from.

A genogram is useful in mapping out the family system to provide a visual of patterns, and it allows for the recording of hereditary identifiers—medical, mental health—as well as emotional connections and relationship dynamics. It is a family systems intervention used to gain insight into patterns across generations. I tend to use genograms with many of my first- and second-generation immigrant clients who feel stuck when it comes to understanding their own bicultural identities or where their dominant narratives come from. Genograms present values and patterns that may be unseeable at first, but much like optical illusions, they can, with time and patience, reveal a different perspective. In order to understand who you are, it isn't necessary to understand where you come from, but it can often help. Having minimal access to their family stories and family experiences can leave children of immigrants feeling unmoored and disconnected from their heritage, which compounds the constant self-mistrust and delusion I've previously discussed. What has been repeated yet overlooked? What is passed down and by whom? What is modeled? Who broke a cycle or made a different choice? How did that impact their family relationships and life?

A part of writing this book was about my wanting to see the inner worlds of my loved ones, alive and gone: to perform a kind of autopsy on their brains and get a glimpse into which parts were impacted and which parts were atrophied due to their own life experiences. I ache to be able to know what thoughts and feelings are going on in the internal worlds of my parents and siblings—we are such an interconnected and enmeshed system, yet there are doors locked, hallways closed off, and entire levels removed.

When we are told only parts of our loved ones' stories, we fill in the gaps with our own preconceptions or misconceived notions. Sometimes, in a desperate search for clues and connections, we try to ascribe meaning to things where there may really be none. My dad recently told me that he and my mom decided to move to the U.S. because his job in London was over and he didn't want to go back to India for fear of not being able to do the work he wanted there and for fear of disappointing his own father. It had absolutely nothing to do with "giving his kids a better life," as I had always presumed. I was flabbergasted! I've created an entire identity—and narrative—around my immigrant parents' desire to give me a better life and more opportunities. Yes, they did put their kids first and provide more opportunities and resources. But this was a perfect illustration of how we allow assumptions to get in the way of true intimacy, reinforcing impression management even in our own homes.

It was a two-way street: because my parents did not share their pre-migration story with me, I was never able to make the connection between my dad's actions and my own and to understand our shared inability to handle disappointment or rejection. Instead of addressing it, we ran away—he to an entirely new country and me to a new state.

In trying to make sense of my own story, I have fallen in love with other people's stories. It's why I loved editing other people's personal essays, and it's why I practice narrative therapy as a therapist. We rely on stories to ground us in where we come from and the people we love. But what happens when the people who raise you, or have high expectations of you, or expect to be a priority don't share their stories with you? I have always been an open book, and maybe that's because so many of my loved ones hold their cards so close to their chest. In trying to reconcile with my own memory and childhood trauma, through writing this book, I have discovered the importance of collective memory, or family stories, no matter how limited.

Intergenerational Narratives

In many immigrant families, there aren't always heirlooms or artifacts to pass down from one generation to the next. The legacies of families and communities live in generational narratives or oral stories that are sometimes communicated in fragments, handed to children of immigrants like pieces of a puzzle needing to be put together. My own personal and familial history has many missing pieces scattered across different continents and oceans. The ties that once connected me to those who made me have stretched and weakened, and I am constantly losing my grip.

Research suggests that intergenerational narratives help us create meaning and build positive self-concepts, and they help us construct our own identities through the lens of history. They can serve as "a means of achieving a sense of generativity, in ways that may also contribute to family identity and individual well-being," and they are as beneficial to children as they are to immigrant parents/grandparents who share these stories. In wanting to learn from and connect with our elders—promoting intergenerational relationships—we may also shift away from authoritarian filial piety to reciprocal filial piety, wanting to break the cycle not only for ourselves but also for *them*. Intergenerational narratives can expand our knowledge about our families' strength and resilience. They teach us about our elders. They help us understand what our communities have endured. They relay our truths. For many of us, storytelling is a cultural practice, and even more, it is an indispensably integral part of connecting with our ancestors, a way to combat the multiple layers of colonization and white supremacy that erode our existence. It allows for us to choose connection over disconnection and bridge generational divides. Intergenerational narratives can pass down lessons, traditions, and ways of being, as well as encourage examination of the origin of things that "have always been this way," demystifying why and when and how these things came to be within our families and communities at large. Our intergenerational narratives can also empower us through intergenerational resilience—reminding us of not only the inherited fears and traumas we carry but also the inherited dreams and perseverance.

At my wedding, my dad's speech centered around my bravery. He told all four-hundred-something attendees at the traditional Indian reception that I was someone who did things even when I was scared. He called me fearless. He admitted to not always being able to understand why I did things, but he was proud of me for doing them anyway. He confessed to feeling out of his depth when I told him that I was going to travel alone abroad, and pursue a creative career, and voluntarily swim fifty feet underwater while learning to scuba dive, and jump off swinging beams even though I was terrified. I kept him on his toes; he couldn't figure out why I would choose fear and uncertainty when those were the very things he had spent his life trying to protect me from. He didn't grasp that all growth is uncomfortable and that if I avoided what I was afraid of, I would become stagnant. For all the ways my dad has resisted change throughout my life, that day he proved to me that his own adaptability and resilience were so like mine. They had enabled him to live in a new country far, far away from his own family, without anyone showing him the way. Just by being born and raised in a different country than those before us, we children of immigrants are automatically tasked with the internal or external burden of our parents' sacrifices, but we also carry the strength of their resilience, adaptability, resourcefulness, and resolve.

Our family members may be the gatekeepers, but there can be so many things that keep us from even getting to the gate. I had always assumed it was a language barrier that stopped me from being able to know things about my grandmothers while they were alive, but in reality it was a generational difference in communication. When I visited Japan one summer, I joined my grandmother for her daily walk, slowly down the steep street in the Minotani district. When we got to the public park and sat on a bench, I dove in.

"It's been twenty-five years since Nanaji died. Do you miss him?" I inquired.

"What's the point of missing him?" she replied curtly.

I pushed. "It must have been so difficult to live through the Kobe earthquake."

"It was a long time ago."

She seemed irritated that I was bringing up the past. On the one hand, I felt guilty for asking questions that might surface feelings and thoughts she had long ago processed or suppressed altogether for the sake of her own sanity and survival. On the other hand, this mindset of "not harping on the past" was such a common one among children of immigrants. The impact of stoicism reverberates through multigenerational relationships, so deeply burying past experiences that they become inaccessible. Even more, to cope, many of our elders look only to what they can control—today and tomorrow.

As I knew them, both of my grandmothers were always looking forward, not back, and I imagine now that this had been their coping skill. I wanted to hear about my nanima's past. She wanted to know what was in my future.

In several workshops I've hosted and interviews I've conducted, I've heard more or less the same from peers and community members. I've gotten many questions about how to approach impasses. I've found that two paths in tandem work for me: The first is to do what research I can on my own. I give myself history lessons on the places where my family members have lived during the times they lived there. I read books and articles about wars and genocides and natural disasters. Without being able to ask them, I'll never know if these roads lead me to their realities, but I do know they add color to the black-and-white photographs of their lives that I hold so closely. Through this research, I try to understand family dynamics, gender dynamics, inherited dreams and fears, and, ultimately, the trauma that still lives in my own DNA. The second path is finding different ways to approach the same topic.

I used to tiptoe around family conversations because I didn't want to potentially retrigger my own parents or learn about a history I wouldn't be able to avoid. However, as I've gotten older, I've felt desperate for any scraps I can get. While I was always mindful of how to best initiate these conversations without causing my loved ones pain, becoming a therapist has taught me how to broach difficult conversations. I will no longer shy away from the discomfort, nor will I miss an opportunity to use immediacy and dive deeper into a passing comment or judgment. Sometimes it's not the heavy conversations but the smaller details that open up where—and who—we come from. *Does that remind you of your childhood? Do you remember what you were preoccupied with? Did your parents know you started to drink alcohol? Do you see things differently? Where did you get this recipe? Who taught you that?*

The thing about intergenerational narratives is that they can not only spotlight strength and resilience but also teach us who to distrust. They can cast a glare on prejudices and biases and pinpoint imperfections and mistakes made. We don't get to pick and choose what we will find when we open the family suitcase. I've worked with clients who were estranged and kept away from certain family members because of their parents' own personal conflicts with those family members. I've worked with other folks who demonstrated a general distrust of entire religious or cultural populations because of historical wars and learned beliefs from their elders. Interrogating why we have certain views and feelings can allow us to question if we should be upholding them at all.

Intergenerational Trauma

Due to the COVID-19 pandemic and scheduling issues, my third father-daughter trip with my papa didn't take place until the fall of 2021. Instead of traveling by plane, he decided to drive up and visit me in Washington, D.C. He had dinner with me and Sam, and the next day we drove alone to Harpers Ferry—a little over an hour northwest of the city. We ate lunch and roamed around. I didn't have a list of questions prepared or a piece of news I needed to disburden myself of, so we talked about work and enjoyed the sights in comfortable silence.

We learned about civil rights activism at the Storer College and Niagara Movement exhibits. We stopped in a historic candy shop showcasing popular retro candy and sundry teas. It was a short trip, about half a day, and on the drive back, I asked him point-blank about trauma. He was a bit vague and dismissive at first, but I pressed a little harder than I ever had. My dad isn't someone who stays on the phone longer than three minutes (if that), let alone a talker, so I knew I had to broach this subject in person. I had come to realize that my parents had so thoroughly internalized this "forward-thinking" mindset, just like *their* parents before them, that they struggled to even consider what they had experienced or lived through.

"What is trauma?" my dad asked in response to my bringing it up.

"Well, how would *you* define it?" I volleyed back, putting on my therapist hat.

"I don't think I have ever been through trauma," he said matter-of-factly.

"What about your family?"

"No," he responded quickly.

I wasn't going to let up. "Okay. What about your immigration experience?"

"No."

"Is that because it worked out?"

"I don't know."

I took a pause. *Maybe there's nothing here*, I thought. I'd been taught in graduate school that a good therapist possesses the ability to ask the same question in a variety of ways so they can elicit the answer without being pushy. So many community members had told me that asking their parents direct questions didn't tend to produce the answers they were seeking. As such, I had learned to start slowly, with something only tangentially related, in order to ease into the conversation. My enthusiasm for this particular conversation, which had led to my being so direct, was creating a barrier where I didn't want one. So I turned to what I was learning about Indian history during the time when my dad lived in Punjab.

"The Indo-Pakistani War was in 1965; how old were you when that happened?" I asked.

"I must have been twelve." He softened.

"Wow. I can't imagine living through that," I said, nudgingly.

"For about two weeks, we had to black out our windows with panels every day, and we would often hide in the trenches we dug up in the backyard when we would hear the sirens alerting us of the enemy planes, in case we got bombed." I don't know what shocked me more: that he said this so nonchalantly, or that he had lived through this and never would have given it a second thought if I hadn't asked.

"And you wouldn't consider that to be trauma?" I gently pushed.

"No. It wasn't long. And we ended up being fine, and I forgot about that until just now."

I'm happy that my dad seems to feel like this experience didn't affect him, but I also recognize that "trauma" may be a foreign concept to someone who grew up in India when he did, as a boy, with parents who had zero understanding of mental health. When I asked community members how their parents view "trauma," there were many outliers, but the majority shared a similar experience, with parents who focused on powering through and remaining unaffected.

I also asked community members to tell me about conversations in which a family member divulged something that seemed traumatic but brushed it off or referenced it matter-of-factly. Some community members mentioned incest, substance abuse, domestic violence, and other harmful family dynamics that were never addressed or, worse, swept under the rug, with no repercussions for the perpetrators or care for the victims. Other community members described how their parents had lived through or fled from invasions of their "home" countries or natural disasters, such as floods that carried off belongings and sometimes other family members. Some shared heart-wrenching and detailed stories of genocide, poverty, and survival. These stories highlighted the different ways in which our brains—and our relatives' brains—interpret experiences. As we age, they become things that we harp on, process, or leave sitting ignored in the basements of our brains.

I continued the conversation with my dad, and then my mom, over the following weeks. I learned about how certain family members who lived in Delhi were impacted by the 1984 Sikh genocide. A few women in my extended family were given poison pills to carry in case they got caught. They could take them to avoid rape and murder in the streets, the fate of many Sikh women who were captured during that time. I learned that my maternal grandmother and grandfather watched my great-grandfather get stabbed in the neck and killed. I was sure I had misheard my mom when she told me this. As soon as I started to open my mouth, she went on: "They ended up taking care of my uncle who was there, too, because he never recovered from that moment."

I also learned that both of my grandmothers got married at a very young age—each at sixteen—around the time of the 1947 Partition of India, because marriage was perceived as one of the securest ways to ensure their physical safety. My parents told me stories about how their families, fearing post-partition religious persecution, had fled across the border into India, leaving behind their homes, livelihoods, and everything else they knew. In fact, in an effort to reconnect with *their* own family narratives, my parents took a life-changing trip to Pakistan just a couple of years ago; they wanted to see where their family members had lived and planted roots before the partition.

A few months prior to the trip, my mom sent me a text to ask if two pictures looked like the same place (a before and after of a building), which happened to be my maternal grandfather's bank. When they arrived, they only had old family photographs and name-based reputations to go by. They had to ask around in Rawalpindi to find the streets and buildings that our ancestors had occupied. They saw the school that my nani, my maternal grandmother, attended, and they were able to find an aunt's and grandparents' houses, which still exist today. My heart filled up, because I know firsthand how disconnecting it can feel to not have "proof" of where—or whom—you come from and to desperately ache for more.

I asked my mom about my maternal grandfather's death only a few months before the Kobe earthquake of 1995, causing my grandmother to lose her partner of about fifty years and the home and belongings she shared with him all at once. "Yeah, but she never looked back," my mom explained. "She didn't even go back for what was left of her things. She's always been one to focus on moving forward." I just can't understand this. On the one hand, I want to respect and appreciate the resilience my family has built, but on the other hand, I want to scream with rage that we are just going to pretend like this is all normal!

Research suggests that when one family member experiences intense trauma, there is a transgenerational impact on mental health, scarcity mindset, attachment styles, and parenting styles. I also can't help but wonder how much these experiences changed my family's epigenetics and how much they still live in my literal DNA and body today. I find myself with many more questions than answers and no way to really, truly know what lives on in me and in the way I show up in my own daily life.

There is still so much I don't know. I am curious about the untreated mental illness and medical issues within my family. There was speculation about one of my grandmothers, whom some family members called "paranoid," and there was (unsurprisingly) speculation about the uncle who saw his dad get stabbed in front of him. Given what I know now, I believe that he likely lived with untreated PTSD after that incident.

The multiple migration patterns in the family histories of many children of immigrants make it that much more difficult to trace the stories of their families. I have a friend who identifies as Indo-Caribbean, and we often reflect on how many layers of trauma and grief are embedded in her family history. She's never been to India, nor does she know where her family is from, exactly. She isn't South Asian, but she is often mistaken as such because of her name, skin color, and religion. Her family is from Guyana, and she can trace her ancestry to those who were taken from India as indentured laborers in the 1800s. Complicate this with the fact that all of her living family members reside in North America. Such complex diasporic histories can exacerbate the sense of unknowing we feel toward our own people, making us even less aware of what we may still hold within our bodies and minds.

Intergenerational trauma is not just the big, onetime experiences that our families have lived through; it's also the oppression experienced on a day-to-day basis—through patriarchal family systems, harmful immigration experiences, workplace discrimination, microaggressions, relational trauma, infidelity, secret divorce, and other types of abuse.

Each generation might experience something collectively, but each person experiences this thing and more in unique and individualized ways. I have to wonder how my great-grandparents' and grandparents' experiences of war, oppression, and abuse may have impacted my own parents and their siblings. Or how my parents' immigration experiences, discrimination, and marital issues have impacted my own mental health struggles, attachment issues, and learned behaviors.

As a mental health professional, I understand that pain and unprocessed trauma can be passed down in one way or another, usually in the form of dysfunctional behaviors and norms or dysregulated emotions. I also understand that difficulty discussing trauma, or denying that it exists, may itself be a sign of trauma. For example, someone who experienced war, genocide, or poverty may utilize mind-numbing substances, internalize shame, or develop anxiety or depression because of it. When this person has kids, they will likely project these learned behaviors and narratives through their parenting style. As a result, their child may experience trauma and its effects. These may not be insidious, but the trauma will continue to be passed on until someone decides to confront and heal from it.

> When we talk about responses to trauma and the coping skills we have acquired through traumatic experiences, it's important to also remember that they are not all bad. Let me be clear: my experiences of trauma harmed me. I wish I hadn't had to live through them, *and* I acknowledge that I have certain strengths as a result of my trauma. I am courageous, resilient, persistent, observant, dedicated, resourceful, empathetic, and so much more. This is not to say that we should be grateful for the hardships—or abuse—we experience but, rather, that all learned coping skills were adaptive—mechanisms we relied on for a sense of safety—at one point or another in our lives, and some can actually continue to benefit us . . . until maybe they don't. Once again, nothing is black or white, and self-awareness is key to recognizing these behaviors and patterns.

Disenfranchised Grief

As a child of immigrants, I often find that I am grieving information I don't have and relationships I've never known. As the youngest in my immediate family and on my dad's side of the family, I have the fewest lucid memories of my time with my grandparents. When my nanima, my maternal grandmother and final grandparent, passed away in 2019, I was devastated in the same way I had been when my paternal grandmother passed on three years earlier. My nanima, who lived in Japan, was the grandparent I felt closest to. When I lost her, I felt like the last root in my family tree had been pulled out. There's a void where she was—and all of us branches are here because of her—but I can't feel or see her anymore.

Our families have had to navigate different immigration experiences, often with no time or resources to look back. These migratory patterns have meant a loss of support, security, social status and capital, family roles, and cultural competency. While immigrating to a new country may be a choice for some, as it was for my family, for other first-generation immigrants, there may be compounding layers to the experience, such as living without documentation, fleeing war or violence as a refugee, and dealing with transracial adoption. It is also not unusual for women, especially in South Asia, to enter arranged marriages and then be expected to move to where their husbands live. All the women in my maternal family either immigrated to the countries where their husbands already lived or immigrated with their husbands (my uncles and cousins) right after marriage. My own sister-in-law, for example, moved to the United States from Dubai to be with my brother and her new family—my family—when they got married over a decade ago. She still struggles to reconcile with the fact that her own parents no longer consider her *their* daughter now that she is married.

These issues and travails are not socially or culturally acknowledged in the West, leading to disenfranchisement. Disenfranchised grief is defined as grief "that persons experience when they incur a loss that is not or cannot be openly acknowledged, publicly mourned, or socially supported." Disenfranchised grief frequently negates the likelihood of closure. When our grief is not recognized, where does it go?

For first-generation immigrants, disenfranchised grief may be complicated by everyday reminders of their loss of social support, security, status, and cultural norms, making it difficult for them to completely embrace their new homes and cultures, prolonging their own grief and potentially causing other mental health struggles. This intergenerational grief can be passed down, creating dysfunction, anxiety, and other aftereffects that impact a second-generation immigrant's mental health, especially because the grief was never originally mourned or processed in previous generations. As such, children of immigrants are often navigating their own grief while their parents do the same.

Another phenomenon that I see in the child-of-immigrant community is anticipatory grief. Through building my own genogram, I was fascinated to learn that both of my grandmothers were widows for exactly twenty-five years and that both of their husbands died at age sixty-nine. It's a coincidence I don't like to think about, because as I write this, my dad is three months away from turning seventy and just had his own medical scare that continues to exacerbate his, and my, feelings about mortality, legacy, and family. This anticipatory grief can also create a sense of urgency within us to try to force the relationship we ache for, to find peace, to heal, to access the stories and experiences that others within our families carry. For

those living in multigenerational households, access may be more realistic, compared with those who have a physical or language barrier
in place.

Ultimately, the multiple layers of grief culminate in a form of cultural bereavement, a concept initially developed and studied in the
'90s as a way to approach working with refugees and understanding
their distress. It was known to be associated with a loss of home,
identity, cultural values, and social structures and networks. I've
heard the saying that therapists become therapists to heal themselves
and to do "mesearch," or research on something important or relevant to their own experiences. As my curiosity about my family intensified in graduate school, I took every opportunity I got to turn
research and final papers into topics about the child-of-immigrant
experience. I covered all the ground I could, from researching cultural perspectives in career counseling to learning about cultural bereavement in grief counseling. It was in this grief counseling class
that I decided to write my final paper on grief in the second-
generation immigrant population, but since there wasn't much specific research available, my professor told me to theorize it using
other research—making connections where they hadn't yet been
made for this community. Through this paper, I was able to connect
the disenfranchised grief that children of immigrants feel with the
cultural bereavement that is constant in our day-to-day lives.

For us children of immigrants, grief can also present as cultural
impostor syndrome, wherein we no longer feel a sense of grounding
or belonging in either our host cultures or our heritage cultures.
These feelings vary across second-generation immigrant experiences
and can be impacted by access to community, language, traditions,
and extended family members; parentification; and family history.
Cultural bereavement is further complicated by transnational grieving, or grieving from a distance, and it can be unacknowledged by

Western counterparts who don't share in the experience. As such, it can be harder to let the grief out, speak openly about it, or even process it.

Every time I post on Instagram about this topic, I get the most engagement from people in the community, which tells me that I must be far from alone in this experience. And it's given me the opportunity to sit with and process my own grief in new ways. I always just assumed that everyone else knew how to navigate and manage this type of grief, but it seems that many, many of us are in the same boat.

As a therapist, I had a client who lost a grandparent while we were working together, and she stumbled into the depths of multi-layered grief—because she was biracial, she was losing not just a grandparent but also a connection to her ancestry and ethnic culture. Some stories about her grandparents and their experiences were only openly discussed *after* his passing, which complicated her relationship with her family history even further. I felt honored to be able to do therapeutic work with her and make space for these multiple layers of grief. After all, grief doesn't look the same for everyone, and even in the *DSM*, it is usually explored only in relation to an actual death. There are different cultural expressions of, and rituals pertaining to, grief that are not taught or even completely understood by Western-trained clinicians; this may lead to unnecessary pathologizing and unhelpful or harmful care.

Healing our grief, our intergenerational trauma, and constructing strong bicultural identities looks different for each of us. This can take many forms: It may be actively looking for something, or it may be resting and choosing to slow down. For some of us, it's about finding answers. And for others of us, it's merely about being heard, having the space to tell our stories in full. To connect with them or feel agency over them—whether they're family histories or things that happened to us personally. This can look like therapy, reconnection to family and roots, or choosing a different path altogether.

Our grief will reappear throughout our lives, even shape-shifting, as we deepen our understanding, pursue our own growth, or reach different milestones. Grief requires reprocessing. It will remain dormant for years only to tackle us to the ground when we least expect it.

Reconnecting with My History

I made many assumptions about my family members, grouping them all together in their experiences and endeavors. My genogram unveiled many truths, allowing me to collect more pieces of my identity puzzle. My family has lived, and still does live, all over the world, and I knew that this was something I would want to highlight within my own genogram. It was during this assignment that I learned about my family history in Iran. At sixteen, my grandmother was arranged to marry my grandfather, who decided to move them to Kobe, Japan, to start an auto import-export business. There, the next three generations have continued to live and have families—all Indian by descent. Conversely, my dad, who married and settled in Punjab, India, and never left the country. Or so I thought. I learned through this exercise that my paternal grandfather did a one-year pediatric anesthesia fellowship at Harvard in 1952, just before my dad was born, and that a few years later, when my dad was eight, they lived in Edinburgh for three years. Though the majority of my family members on both sides have stayed where they are in Japan and India, I do currently have cousins and siblings across Japan, India, England, Canada, and the United States.

When I trace the birth orders of those in the older generations, I see that both of my parents are the oldest siblings in their families, and they both left their families when they were barely adults. This consequently impacted their relationships with their younger siblings—relationships that have fused and separated at different points in time. Seeing a visual representation of the dynamics between my parents and their own siblings has shed some light on ours. I theorize that because *they* felt untethered to their families of origin, they tightly tethered themselves to me and my siblings. This has definitely contributed to the development of enmeshment and codependency in my immediate family.

Now, if I were to document my parents' or siblings' versions of our family, the genogram would likely look different. The factual content would be the same, but the crucial markers of relational dynamics and personal characteristics attributed to relatives would differ and be based on our own unique experiences and memories. My brother and sister are the oldest grandchildren on either side, and our parents are the oldest children in their families, which is almost in direct opposition to my experience. They have the most family memories and are able to make their own judgments, whereas I am beholden to other people's perspectives and versions of incidents and relationships.

I often witness a parent highlighting the parts of a family narrative that can confirm the story they either have to tell themselves to move on or want to tell themselves to be right. At one point or another, my mom and all my maternal uncles have mentioned or joked about how terrifying my grandfather was, but the more time that passes and the more they age—and reflect on parts of their own lives and relationships—the less objectivity I get when it comes to who my grandparents were as people. Like in a game of telephone, the truth of our family history depends on who you ask. So many members of the community have shared their shock over only lately discovering basic information—for example, how many siblings their parents or grandparents actually had, as a few were estranged or had died, and no one talked about it. My own mom recently took to our family's WhatsApp group to circulate a picture of my grandmother with a younger boy. We all asked who the boy was; apparently, he was a great-uncle of mine who died as a young kid. None of us kids knew. Other community members reported making discoveries about things that were never discussed: mental illness, secret past divorces and estrangements, incest involving still-present family members, child abuse, and substance abuse. Some had learned that family members they had always thought were related by blood actually weren't. In the last year, I found out that my great-grandfather was adopted. Like me, many people are only learning as adults that their ancestors were freedom fighters.

The genogram and the hard conversations with my parents have allowed me to see them not as my mom and dad but as humans, products of their own environments and circumstances. This does not absolve them of the pain they have caused me, but it enables me to better understand where they come from and how they came to be who I know them as today. We are all interconnected, and in a family system where much may go unspoken, a genogram is a powerful way to identify hidden themes and struggles, as well as to reveal untold knowledge and historical events that have impacted our family members through generations, thus impacting us today.

I uncovered not only family and intergenerational narratives but also dynamics in which I actively played a role. For example, in reflecting on my own family dynamics, I have discovered that I may be less forgiving of my mom than of my dad. At the end of the day, there's never been a question of whether she loved me in the way I sometimes doubted that my dad did, but I have often found myself holding her to a different set of standards—dare I say, the same standards that have been placed on *me* under conventional cultural and patriarchal systems. My mom is not a quiet woman, but she is often relegated to the sidelines, much like other immigrant women and much like she has been in this book. That's something I'm trying to be more mindful of moving forward.

My mom and I are very similar. We not only look the same but also communicate in the same very direct way, sometimes to the point that we forget to filter our words. We both have struggled with giving other people the space and support to shine and grow without us, sometimes centering ourselves in situations and relationships where we don't completely belong. We both have an inclination toward making things personal and taking things personally. We both fear being forgotten or overlooked by those we love. I have abandoned some of these ways with the help of therapy, but when we are alone together, we often both demand to be heard and struggle to listen to the other.

I continue to interrogate my observations of my family. (The therapist in me can't help it! It's a free case study!) And I continue to use my observations as a way to broach more difficult conversations. Each one serves as a building block for a bridge—from me to them, from my past to my present, from my ancestral experiences to my cultural identity. These interrogations also allow me to face the reality of which narratives are at play and which ones are being overlooked. These explorations are ongoing, and I have had to make peace with the fact that while my curiosity and good intentions can take me to unknown places with my loved ones, there's only so much I can ever truly know or understand.

Regardless of how determined I am to learn more about my

family, there will always be a limit to how far back I can go, given the facts that people have died and tangible trails don't necessarily exist. And that's okay—it just leaves us where we began this story: we don't need to gather every last detail for our narratives to be valid.

How to cope

with cultural bereavement

and disenfranchised grief

One grief theory that resonates with me is the continuing bonds theory. Instead of detaching from our grief, we should find ways to strengthen and continue our bonds with our families and cultures as we move forward.* A lot of this work is about rediscovering meaning. Here are tips for coping with cultural bereavement and disenfranchised grief:

- Consider relearning your family language(s), but remember that this is not a prerequisite for claiming ownership of your ethnic culture!
- Research the historical context of your grandparents' and ancestors' experiences.
- Home in on intergenerational narratives that can help you create meaning.

---

*If you have access to your immigrant parents, grandparents, or extended family members, check out a list of questions and activities designed to bridge the familial gap on my website, www.sahajkaurkohli.com.

- Reconnect to your ancestral wisdom. Consider what your grandparents or great-grandparents did to heal or take care of themselves.

- Reacquaint yourself with foods and recipes that have been passed down in your family or that have significant meaning to your family members or culture.

- Intentionally choose religious and cultural traditions, and values, to uphold.

- Continuously reassess whom you choose to surround yourself with and how you can strengthen relationships with people who encourage evolvement of your bi/multicultural identity.

- Find community with other folks who may be sharing in your experiences and feelings. You are definitely not alone!

- Remember that closure is defined by having a sense of resolution or conclusion, but in reality, grief is ongoing. You don't move on from it; you learn to build a life around it.

- Normalize bereavement's ambiguity to honor your grief truthfully. Reject either-or thinking.

- Consider taking a pilgrimage of your own to an accessible country or site that is significant in your culture or religion. Experiencing self-chosen places like this in new ways, as an adult, can have a significant impact on how you connect to your roots.

- Embrace the duality. My version is: I am Indian, *and* I am American. I am grateful for the privileges I have had growing up in America, *and* I am devastated by lost time and access to my extended family members. What's yours?

- Have self-compassion. Try not to ruminate on what could or should have been, and instead consider how you can broach this discomfort with curiosity.

- Embrace optimism in the face of tragedy. This involves not only finding meaning and purpose but also rooting deeper into your values. Life involves suffering and pain *and* hope and meaning. Think about the ways in which your family has historically shown strength and resilience. Consider what you *can* control and the influence you do have over your own life.

- Transnational grieving can complicate the experience of loss and is rarely addressed in Western contexts. If you were not able to say goodbye to someone who lived afar or whom you had limited access to, how can you honor their passing or the loss of connection with your own ritual or ceremony at home?

EXERCISE

Write a letter to loved ones or ancestors who are no longer alive. What would you want to ask them? What would you want to say to them? If applicable, remember that you are a child/grandchild/ great-grandchild of survivors of colonialism. Reflect on this on a microscale and a macroscale.

Epilogue

We are used to thinking of growth or emergence as a singular upward trajectory, further emphasized by Western ideas of mental health, but remember, we're often living in an upward spiral. We are progressing, but it's not linear. We are growing, but it is not without times of retreat. We are learning, but it is not without making mistakes. We embrace change, but it may not be without hesitation or resistance. We are climbing, but we may have to consistently decide if we are willing to backtrack to meet our loved ones and community where they are. We are making the most of the circumstances we are living in when we can, but we don't always have to be trying to. And sometimes we have days where we fall apart, but when we're ready, we can put ourselves back together with the pieces that serve us. It's important to remember that we will often have to heal from the same thing more than once, and that's okay!

In the capitalist Western models of wellness, we are often sold quick fixes. (And they're usually on sale, so get them now!) But the reality is that living well—with ourselves and with others—looks different for everyone. There is no single path, and there is no right answer. Life is not a test we are trying to ace.

A TRUTH WE rarely talk about: self-reflection and self-actualization are inherently painful processes. Many children of immigrants have access to resources their parents didn't have, and prioritizing healing and growth is great and all . . . but I can't responsibly promote these without also acknowledging and admitting to what it *really* feels like—and how incredibly painful and hard it can be—to emotionally outgrow your parents and family. You love them, but you can't heal them. You love them, but you understand things that they don't have language for. You love them, but you're left having to rationalize their behaviors while simultaneously working through how those may be affecting you. As children of immigrants, we constantly grapple with what gets lost in layers of cultural translation—this isn't the case in all family dynamics, of course—and as such, many of us learn over and over and over again how to practice extreme empathy and understanding for others' shortcomings.

None of this is to suggest that our version of healing and growth will make us *better* than our immigrant parents, but it does open pathways to us that may still be inaccessible to them. This is a privilege and a burden, as are a lot of the experiences of children of immigrants. And when we make internal shifts, the external world responds, whether we like it or not. Many children of immigrants ask how to pursue healing when those around them don't. We cannot make our parents access the help they may need. We cannot make people face the problems we've learned to identify as unhealthy or toxic. We can only focus on what is important to us and how we can navigate, and claim, the agency we do have within the systems, relationships, and spaces we live in. The truth remains that the amount of emotional labor required to compensate for the lack of emotional maturity among parents or family members is exhausting. Even simple questions may be debilitating and triggering. But accepting what we cannot change does not mean we forgive; it means we release ourselves from the pressure to do the impossible.

It's terrifying to change something that has "always been this way," and what's more, it can be lonely, and even boring, when we outgrow and unlearn living in dysfunction or chaos. Tolerating discomfort requires identifying impulses that may be rooted in negative and unhealthy experiences. It will often be painful for family and community members, but that doesn't mean it's bad or wrong. If you are resistant to making a change in a relationship, reflect on what you're scared of. Sometimes we self-sabotage our own relationships because we can't handle them changing.

For so long, I talked myself out of trusting what I really experienced in order to preserve good memories and override negative ones. This allowed me to maintain the same relationship dynamics with people I really love. I was scared of what change would do to the relationships, and I wasn't ready to find out. Many children of immigrants ask me: What's the point of trying to change if *they're* not going to change? The truth is, we can't change others, but we can change how *we* engage with or respond to them. One of the hardest things about being a therapist is challenging clients. I want to offer validation and make room for them to unlearn the narratives that are hurting, not helping, them, but they also have to interrogate their stories and be honest about their roles in upholding them. Many of my clients have avoided or feared making any changes because they have come to accept that being in relationships with some of their loved ones requires accepting dysfunction. One client refused to call her single mom out on her emotional behavior because she knew that if she did, her mom would stop talking to her. She wasn't ready to accept that consequence. These are choices that keep us stuck, but they are choices nonetheless. Even inaction is a choice. It makes sense that it can take some time to move forward with such a choice. After all, when one person in a family system changes, the entire system changes with them.

In changing the way I engage with family, I have been able to change our relationship. I prioritize finding moments of intimacy with my mom—who only wants to be appreciated for her acts of service—and hearing her big belly laugh, or finding times to coax out the jokester in my dad, and I realize that my narrative is changing. Laughing and reaching common ground with the people whom I felt so misunderstood by has healed me. I have been able to witness the ways in which reparenting myself has allowed me to reparent my parents.

Recently and very randomly, Papa—the man of few words who *always* thinks he knows best—apologized for how he treated me as a child. He's been honest about knowing that he could have been a better father and husband and acknowledging that he didn't have a framework for how to parent other than how he was parented himself. Hearing what I've been wanting him to admit for my whole life should have made me feel overpowering relief and validation, but instead I felt uncomfortable and instinctually wanted to wave it away. *It's okay! No big deal! No worries!* It's not my job—or yours—to protect family members from the truth. Easier said than done, I know.

I am also painfully aware that not all of us will get the apology or acknowledgment we desire. It may feel like negotiating our cultures and our values is driving a wedge between us and our loved ones. Unfortunately, for some of us, it is. When I asked the Brown Girl Therapy community about estrangement, many folks said that they have had to figure out what low contact looks like, while others expressed that no contact was the only way. In cases like the latter, where a relationship with relatives simply is not possible, reparenting ourselves becomes key. Forgiveness is not required to begin our own healing journeys. If we don't try to connect with and care for our inner children, we will continue to live in shame, rigidity, criticism, and self-doubt.

Change is hard, but it's not impossible. When we are stuck in a hole, we often look up and become discouraged when we see how deep we are. We wait and hope that someone will find us and rescue us. But all we really need to do is focus on the first rung of the ladder right in front of us. If we can make it to the first rung, we can tackle the second one when we get there and are ready.

Through my own healing and expansion of knowledge and language on wellness, I hope to bring my parents, family, and community on this journey alongside me. In considering personal growth and pursuing healing in a collectivist culture, an essential truth is this: our healing extends beyond us.

As children of immigrants, we have been given by our parents the opportunity to make different choices. A lot of the growth work we do often involves writing new narratives and breaking generational cycles. Personal healing is collective healing. Our parents and our ancestors are resilient, and now we get to challenge the systems that required them to be so. We heal ourselves by healing those before us and those after us. On my thirty-second birthday, as my family members (forcibly) went around to share one thing they like about me, my mom told me that my determination to make change and advocate for mental health care honestly gives her strength. This is single-handedly one of the ultimate metrics of success in the work I do.

Though progress may not always look the way we want it to, this doesn't mean that we aren't starting a ripple effect of healing across generations by pursuing our own healing. Trauma may change our brain chemistry and our relationships, but so does healing. There are always opportunities for new interpretations of our pasts, and for new commitments to change our futures. Remember: You are writing your family history right *now*. What cycle do you want to be responsible for?

Acknowledgments

This book is a product of so many before me. I don't think I can possibly list all the people without forgetting many others, so I will just say a blanket and heartfelt thank you to the writers, scholars, advocates, community leaders, and freedom fighters who paved the way for this book to exist.

To the Brown Girl Therapy community, I don't have enough words to emphasize how honored I am to have your support. The endless messages, comments, emails, and love I have received from you kept me going when this book felt like an impossible task. I am so grateful to each of you who have brought me into your lives and workplaces; to those of you who have shared or continue to share your stories with me; and to all of you who have entrusted me to be a voice for our experiences. This book is a culmination of all our voices. I hope I made you proud. Almost every professional opportunity, speaking engagement, and media interview I have received since starting Brown Girl Therapy in 2019 has been at the hands of someone in this community. I specifically want to name Neema Patel, who is no longer with us, but who made my dream of being an advice columnist come true. Your friendship, however brief, will stay with me forever. Many others also leveraged their own access and privilege to amplify my voice and my work. I promise to continue to pay it forward.

A huge thank you to my editors Emily Wunderlich, Nidhi Pugalia, and the entire team at Penguin Life and Viking: Your constant belief in this book made all the difference in this world. Thank you for being unflappable in all those moments when I would text you frantically, convinced I was going to press ctrl + A and delete it all. Thank you for asking more of me when I didn't think there was anything left. You were always right—there was more; I was just afraid. You nudged me toward the fringes of—and then way past—the perimeter of my comfort zone, but you held my hand through it all. The years in which I wrote this book have been some of the most personally testing for me. I appreciate your patience as I sometimes missed and pushed deadlines. I have been able to truly give myself to this book only because you gave me grace when I needed to take care of myself or my loved ones first. I don't take that for granted. You're wonderful, incisive, and compassionate editors; and you have become dear friends.

Susana Alvarez, Celeste Fine, Elizabeth Pratt, and the Park & Fine Literary team: Thank you for your unwavering belief in this book. I am so lucky you saw what I wanted and needed to do, reminding me of this over the years when I would doubt myself. Thank you for being on my team every step of the way.

To my early readers, Dom Harrington, Ali Cherry, Bagmi Das, Thu-Hong Nguyen, Mazen Istanbouli, and Chandani Kohli, your smart and gentle notes on my pages were everything. Thank you, thank you, thank you.

Dr. Mina Attia, Dr. Almeta McCannon, Dr. Maya Georgieva, Dr. Bagmi Das, Dr. Harvey Peters, Dr. Delishia Pittman, and all my supervisors, teachers, and advisers, your mentorship has meant so much to me. You never turned me away when I was exasperated or anxious or unsure of how to continue on this path of mine. Thanks for believing in me and encouraging me not to give up. Your voice and representation in the mental health field matters.

To my fellow therapist friends, my coconspirators in challenging the system we work within, I am so inspired by each of you. The road is long, but it's much easier to navigate with you by my side.

To my past and present therapists and psychiatrists, you changed my life.

To my clients, I am humbled to be on this journey with you every week.

To my friends, you know who you are. Thank you for wholly and unquestionably accepting every version of me. You hold me tight, but you also give me room to expand and contract and evolve—again and again and again. The phone calls, texts, quality time, patience, encouragement, memes, dancing, crying, and many memories—they grounded me. You ground me. I hope we find each other in every lifetime.

Ajay and Chan, I am so fortunate to have known you both the longest. You've cheered me on when I have felt small, and you've humbled me when my head gets too big. You've known me through it all. I love being your annoying little sister. Thank you for always being generous and tenderhearted. I can't wait for the world to realize you're both much cooler than I am.

To my little ones, Zoravar, Azad, Izzat, Raunaq, and Nanki—thank you for being such a source of joy in my life. This book is really for each of you. I hope you never feel alone in your journeys and I hope you know Sahaj Bhua/Masi will always have a soft place for you to land if and when you ever need it. You are all so wildly curious and brave, and your mere existence has allowed me to heal parts of my own inner child. I am so grateful to your parents for bringing you into my life. I cherish each of you, always and forever.

Papa and Mom, I love you so much. Thank you for being willing to go *there* with me. Neither of you backed down from this challenge even as it changed our relationship, and even as it required you to explore and self-examine in ways you may not have necessarily wanted to. Thank you for not hesitating to give me your blessing to write what I needed to write, and for trusting me to share our stories with the world. Our relationships have changed in innumerable ways, and they could have gone in vastly different directions. At the end of the day, your love for me overpowered your need for control and comfort. I, and my stories, would not exist without either of you.

Finally, and always, my most supportive reader, confidant, cheerleader, adventure buddy, and love—Sam. I love you. Thanks for feeding me, nurturing me, and supporting me on this journey. Thanks for reading every iteration of this book, and for letting me watch you read them to observe your facial reactions. Your unwavering love gave me agency to face my own demons and to write this book. I am a different person than when I started this endeavor, and you've undeniably loved me through it all. From day one, and without hesitation, you took my dreams in as your very own. I am so very lucky to be loved by you.

Notes

INTRODUCTION

4   **"ongoing process of adaptation":** Tsui-Sui Annie Kao and Betsy Huang, "Bicultural Straddling Among Immigrant Adolescents: A Concept Analysis," *Journal of Holistic Nursing* 33, no. 3 (September 2015): 269–81.

10   **A study utilizing data:** Amanda Mancenido, Emily C. Williams, and Anjum Hajat, "Examining Psychological Distress across Intersections of Immigrant Generational Status, Race, Poverty, and Gender," *Community Mental Health Journal* 56, no. 7 (October 2020): 1269–74.

10   **one in four children:** "Children in U.S. Immigrant Families," Migration Policy Institute, January 16, 2019, https://www.migrationpolicy.org/programs/data-hub/charts/children-immigrant-families.

14   **the 2020 *World Migration Report*:** Marie McAuliffe and Binod Khadria, eds., *World Migration Report 2020* (Geneva: International Organization for Migration, 2019), https://publications.iom.int/system/files/pdf/wmr_2020.pdf, page 73.

14   **number-one destination for immigrants:** Anusha Natarajan, Mohamad Moslimani, and Mark Hugo Lopez, "Key Facts About Recent Trends in Global Migration," Pew Research Center, December 16, 2022, https://www.pewresearch.org/short-reads/2022/12/16/key-facts-about-recent-trends-in-global-migration/.

14   **Hispanic immigrants living:** Mark Hugo Lopez and Mohamad Moslimani, *Latinos See U.S. as Better than Place of Family's Ancestry for Opportunity, Raising Kids, Health Care Access* (Washington, D.C.: Pew Research Center, 2022), https://www.pewresearch.org/race-ethnicity/2022/01/20/latinos-see-u-s-as-better-than-place-of-familys-ancestry-for-opportunity-raising-kids-health-care-access.

14   **one in five Black people:** Christine Tamir and Monica Anderson, *One-in-Ten Black People Living in the U.S. Are Immigrants* (Washington, D.C.: Pew Research Center, 2022), https://www.pewresearch.org/race-ethnicity/2022/01/20/one-in-ten-black-people-living-in-the-u-s-are-immigrants/.

14   **Asian Americans made up:** Abby Budiman and Neil G. Ruiz, "Key Facts About Asian Americans, a Diverse and Growing Population," Pew Research Center,

April 29, 2021, https://www.pewresearch.org/short-reads/2021/04/29/key-facts -about-asian-americans/.

15 **intersectionality of your identity:** Kimberle Crenshaw, "Demarginalizing the Intersection of Race and Sex: A Black Feminist Critique of Antidiscrimination Doctrine, Feminist Theory and Antiracist Politics," *University of Chicago Legal Forum* 1989, no. 1 (1989): 139–67, http://chicagounbound.uchicago.edu/uclf/vol 1989/iss1/8.

CHAPTER ONE: OUR STORIES MATTER, TOO

21 **sum of all the stories:** Michael White, *Maps of Narrative Practice* (New York: W. W. Norton & Co., 2007).

22 **Narrative identity is defined:** Dan P. McAdams and Kate C. McLean, "Narrative Identity," *Current Directions in Psychological Science* 22, no. 3 (2013): 233–38, https://doi.org/10.1177/0963721413475622.

37 **"Trauma in a person":** *Talk Easy with Sam Fragoso* (podcast), "How Do We Heal? (with Resmaa Menakem)," November 15, 2020, https://talkeasypod.com/resmaa -menakem/.

39 **emotional and affectional neglect:** Kimberly Holland, "Childhood Emotional Neglect: How It Can Impact You Now and Later," Healthline, updated October 21, 2021, https://www.healthline.com/health/mental-health/childhood-emotional -neglect.

40 **As Dr. Jonice Webb:** Jonice Webb and Christine Musello, *Running on Empty: Overcome Your Childhood Emotional Neglect* (New York: Morgan James Publishing, 2012), p. 65.

47 **This is known as parentification:** Mary West, "What to Know About Parentification," *Medical News Today*, April 29, 2022, https://www.medicalnewstoday.com /articles/parentification.

47 **Research even suggests that parentification:** Radhika Rana and Ashapurna Das, "Parentification: A Review Paper," *International Journal of Indian Psychology 9*, no. 1 (2021): 44–50, https://www.researchgate.net/publication/351101281_Paren tification_A_Review_Paper.

CHAPTER TWO: WHEN THINGS DON'T GO ACCORDING TO PLAN

61 **form of impression management:** Esraa Al-Shatti and Marc Ohana, "Impression Management and Career Related Outcomes: A Systematic Literature Review," *Frontiers in Psychology* 12 (July 2021): art. 701694, https://doi.org/10.3389/fpsyg .2021.701694.

62 **We all engage in:** Hila Riemer and Sharon Shavitt, "Impression Management in Survey Responding: Easier for Collectivists or Individualists?," *Journal of Consumer Psychology* 21, no. 2 (April 2011): 157–68, https://doi.org/10.1016/j.jcps.2010 .10.001.

62 **researchers in China found:** Wangshuai Wang et al., "The Cost of Impression Management to Life Satisfaction: Sense of Control and Loneliness as Mediators," *Psychology Research and Behavior Management* 13 (2020): 407–17, https://doi .org/10.2147/prbm.s238344.

63 **praise may actually:** Eddie Brummelman et al., "On Feeding Those Hungry for Praise: Person Praise Backfires in Children with Low Self-Esteem," *Journal of Experimental Psychology: General* 143, no. 1 (2014): 9–14, https://doi.org/10.1037 /a0031917.

66 **One in three freshman college:** Randy P. Auerbach et al., "WHO World Mental Health Surveys International College Student Project: Prevalence and Distribution of Mental Disorders," *Journal of Abnormal Psychology* 127, no. 7 (October 2018): 623–38, https://doi.org/10.1037/abn0000362.

66 **among students of color:** Tamar Kodish et al., "Enhancing Racial/Ethnic Equity in College Student Mental Health through Innovative Screening and Treatment," *Administration and Policy in Mental Health and Mental Health Services Research* 49, no. 2 (March 2022): 267–82, https://doi.org/10.1007/s10488-021-01163-1.

66 **less than their white peers:** Sarah Ketchen Lipson et al., "Mental Health Disparities Among College Students of Color," *Journal of Adolescent Health* 63, no. 3 (September 2018): 348–56, https://doi.org/10.1016/j.jadohealth.2018.04.014.

70 **According to the Pew Research Center, despite:** D'Vera Cohn and Wendy Wang, "Portrait of Asian Americans," in *The Rise of Asian Americans*, ed. Paul Taylor (Washington, D.C.: Pew Research Center, 2012), https://www.pewresearch.org/social-trends/2012/06/19/chapter-1-portrait-of-asian-americans.

70 **many Asian American children:** Neil G. Ruiz, Sunny Shao, and Sono Shah, "What It Means to Be Asian in America," Pew Research Center, August 2, 2022, https://www.pewresearch.org/race-ethnicity/2022/08/02/what-it-means-to-be-asian-in-america/.

CHAPTER THREE: BUT WHAT
WILL PEOPLE SAY?

81 **Dr. Donald Winnicott:** Val Richards and Gillian Wilce, eds., *The Person Who Is Me: Contemporary Perspectives on the True and False Self* (London: Karnac Books, 1996).

84 **every sixty-eight seconds:** "Scope of the Problem: Statistics," RAINN, accessed July 17, 2023, https://www.rainn.org/statistics/scope-problem.

84 **And according to the CDC:** "Fast Facts: Preventing Sexual Violence," Centers for Disease Control and Prevention, last modified June 22, 2022, https://www.cdc.gov/violenceprevention/sexualviolence/fastfact.html.

85 **cultures that prioritize family honor:** Gurvinder Kalra and Dinesh Bhugra, "Sexual Violence against Women: Understanding Cross-Cultural Intersections," *Indian Journal of Psychiatry* 55, no. 3 (2013): 244, https://doi.org/10.4103/0019-5545.117139.

93 **different types of trauma responses:** Crystal Raypole, "The Beginner's Guide to Trauma Responses," Healthline, August 26, 2021, https://www.healthline.com/health/mental-health/fight-flight-freeze-fawn#takeaway.

94 **notes that people:** Pete Walker, *Complex PTSD: From Surviving to Thriving* (Lafayette, Calif.: Azure Coyote, 2013).

95 **inclined toward problem-solving:** Marisa J. Perera and Edward C. Chang, eds., *Biopsychosocial Approaches to Understanding Health in South Asian Americans* (New York: Springer, 2018).

96 **That's why research suggests:** "Medication or Therapy for Depression? Or Both?," Harvard Health Publishing, May 26, 2020, https://www.health.harvard.edu/staying-healthy/medication-or-therapy-for-depression-or-both.

99 **support from medical doctors:** "Latinx/Hispanic Communities and Mental Health," Mental Health America, accessed July 17, 2023, https://mhanational.org/issues/latinxhispanic-communities-and-mental-health.

99 **somaticized as physical symptoms:** Kelly Guanhua Yang et al., "Disparities in Mental Health Care Utilization and Perceived Need Among Asian Americans: 2012–2016,"

Psychiatric Services 71, no. 1 (2020): 21–27, https://doi.org/10.1176/appi.ps.2019 00126.

99 **"the ability to notice":** Annie Keough, "Making Room for Self-Compassion," Wellzesta, April 11, 2022, https://articles.wellzesta.com/making-room-for-self -compassion.

CHAPTER FOUR: WHAT'S FAITH GOT TO DO WITH IT?

109 **model of acculturation:** Seth J. Schwartz et al., "Rethinking the Concept of Acculturation: Implications for Theory and Research," *American Psychologist* 65, no. 4 (2010): 237–51, https://doi.org/10.1037/a0019330.

109 **Berry and other researchers:** Linda P. Juang and Moin Syed, "The Evolution of Acculturation and Development Models for Understanding Immigrant Children and Youth Adjustment," *Child Development Perspectives* 13, no. 4 (December 2019): 241–46, https://doi.org/10.1111/cdep.12346.

111 **known as the acculturation gap:** Eva H. Telzer, "Expanding the Acculturation Gap-Distress Model: An Integrative Review of Research," *Human Development* 53, no. 6 (February 2011): 313–40, https://doi.org/10.1159/000322476.

111 **A meta-analytic review of research:** P. Priscilla Lui, "Intergenerational Cultural Conflict, Mental Health, and Educational Outcomes Among Asian and Latino/a Americans: Qualitative and Meta-analytic Review," *Psychological Bulletin* 141, no. 2 (2015): 404–46, https://doi.org/10.1037/a0038449.

111 **joint or multigenerational households:** D'Vera Cohn et al., "The Demographics of Multigenerational Households," in *Financial Issues Top the List of Reasons U.S. Adults Live in Multigenerational Homes* (Washington, D.C.: Pew Research Center, 2022), 11–16, https://www.pewresearch.org/social-trends/2022/03/24/the -demographics-of-multigenerational-households/.

115 **known as the perpetual foreigner:** "Combatting the AAPI Perpetual Foreigner Stereotype," New American Economy Research Fund, May 20, 2021, https://research .newamericaneconomy.org/report/aapi-perpetual-foreigner-stereotype/.

115 **The statistics bear this out:** "Updated 2021 Hate Crimes Statistics," United States Department of Justice, updated March 28, 2023, https://www.justice.gov/crs /highlights/2021-hate-crime-statistics.

115 **An important contextual part:** John D. Cowden and Kelly Kreisler, "Development in Children of Immigrant Families," *Pediatric Clinics of North America* 63, no. 5 (October 2016): 775–93, https://doi.org/10.1016/j.pcl.2016.06.005.

124 **beneficial to our well-being:** Daniella Mahfoud et al., "The Co-moderating Effect of Social Support and Religiosity in the Association between Psychological Distress and Coping Strategies in a Sample of Lebanese Adults," *BMC Psychology* 11 (2023): art. 61, https://doi.org/10.1186/s40359-023-01102-9.

126 **major barrier for people:** U.S. Department of Health and Human Services, "Culture Counts: The Influence of Culture and Society on Mental Health," in *Mental Health: Culture, Race, and Ethnicity—A Supplement to Mental Health: A Report of the Surgeon General* (Rockville, Md.: U.S. Department of Health and Human Services, 2001), 23–42, https://www.ncbi.nlm.nih.gov/books/NBK44243 /pdf/Bookshelf_NBK44243.pdf.

127 **can be adaptive:** Allison P. Sederlund, Lawrence R. Burns, and William Rogers, "Multidimensional Models of Perfectionism and Procrastination: Seeking Determinants of Both," *International Journal of Environmental Research and Public Health* 17, no. 14 (July 2020): art. 5099, https://doi.org/10.3390/ijerph17145099.

129 **One study examined:** Thomas Curran and Andrew P. Hill, "Perfectionism Is Increasing over Time: A Meta-analysis of Birth Cohort Differences from 1989 to

2016," *Psychological Bulletin* 145, no. 4 (2019): 410–29, https://doi.org/10.1037/bul0000138.

129 **linked to depression:** Katerina Rnic et al., "Examining the Link between Multidimensional Perfectionism and Depression: A Longitudinal Study of the Intervening Effects of Social Disconnection," *Journal of Social and Clinical Psychology* 40, no. 4 (August 2021): 277–303, https://doi.org/10.1521/jscp.2021.40.4.277.

132 **In a 2018 study:** Léa Pessin and Bruno Arpino, "Navigating between Two Cultures: Immigrants' Gender Attitudes toward Working Women," *Demographic Research* 38 (March 2018): 967–1016, https://doi.org/10.4054/demres.2018.38.35.

133 **Religiosity and spirituality:** Mahfoud et al., "The Co-moderating Effect of Social Support and Religiosity," art. 61.

134 **from within their communities:** Amelia Seraphia Derr, "Mental Health Service Use Among Immigrants in the United States: A Systematic Review," *Psychiatric Services* 67, no. 3 (March 2016): 265–74, https://doi.org/10.1176/appi.ps.201500004.

134 **useful tool of support:** Randy Hebert et al., "Positive and Negative Religious Coping and Well-Being in Women with Breast Cancer," *Journal of Palliative Medicine* 12, no. 6 (June 2009): 537–45, https://doi.org/10.1089/jpm.2008.0250.

CHAPTER FIVE: FEELING MY WAY THROUGH

143 **differences in regulation strategies:** Vivian A. Dzokoto et al., "Emotion Norms, Display Rules, and Regulation in the Akan Society of Ghana: An Exploration Using Proverbs," *Frontiers in Psychology* 9 (October 2018): art. 1916, https://doi.org/10.3389/fpsyg.2018.01916.

144 **Suppressing your emotions:** Benjamin P. Chapman et al., "Emotion Suppression and Mortality Risk over a 12-Year Follow-Up," *Journal of Psychosomatic Research* 75, no. 4 (October 2013): 381–85, https://doi.org/10.1016/j.jpsychores.2013.07.014.

144 **One culturally bound illness:** Hyo-Weon Suh et al., "How Suppressed Anger Can Become an Illness: A Qualitative Systematic Review of the Experiences and Perspectives of Hwabyung Patients in Korea," *Frontiers in Psychiatry* 12 (2021): art. 637029, https://doi.org/10.3389/fpsyt.2021.637029.

144 **rooted in certain Korean:** Jieun Lee, Amy Wachholtz, and Keum-Hyeong Choi, "A Review of the Korean Cultural Syndrome Hwa-Byung: Suggestions for Theory and Intervention," *Journal of Asia Pacific Counseling* 4, no. 1 (2014): 49–64, https://doi.org/10.18401/2014.4.1.4.

145 **greater adherence to certain values:** Mehwish Shahid et al., "Asian Americans' Mental Health Help-Seeking Attitudes: The Relative and Unique Roles of Cultural Values and Ethnic Identity," *Asian American Journal of Psychology* 12, no. 2 (2021): 138–46, https://doi.org/10.1037/aap0000230.

145 **people in non-Western cultures:** Joshua Stephen Eng, "Emotion Regulation and Culture: The Effects of Cultural Models of Self on Western and East Asian Differences in Suppression and Reappraisal" (PhD diss., UC Berkeley, 2012), https://escholarship.org/uc/item/3fg3k1p0.

145 **In her book *Between Us*:** Batja Mesquita, *Between Us: How Cultures Create Emotions* (New York: W. W. Norton & Co., 2022), p. 23.

146 **rate positive emotions:** Nicole Senft et al., "Who Emphasizes Positivity? An Exploration of Emotion Values in People of Latino, Asian, and European Heritage Living in the United States," *Emotion* 21, no. 4 (2021): 707–19, https://doi.org/10.1037/emo0000737.

146 **Maybe we experienced childhood trauma:** Hilary A. Marusak et al., "Childhood Trauma Exposure Disrupts the Automatic Regulation of Emotional Processing," *Neuropsychopharmacology* 40, no. 5 (March 2015): 1250–58, https://doi.org/10.1038/npp.2014.311.

147 **the prefrontal cortex:** Mariam Arain et al., "Maturation of the Adolescent Brain," *Neuropsychiatric Disease and Treatment* 9 (2013): 449–61, https://doi.org/10.2147/ndt.s39776.

148 **In her book *Adult Children*:** Lindsay C. Gibson, *Adult Children of Emotionally Immature Parents: How to Heal from Distant, Rejecting, or Self-Involved Parents* (Oakland, Calif.: New Harbinger Publications, 2015), p. 32.

149 **many defense mechanisms:** Carlos Blanco et al., "Approximating Defense Mechanisms in a National Study of Adults: Prevalence and Correlates with Functioning," *Translational Psychiatry* 13, no. 1 (2023): art. 21, https://doi.org/10.1038/s41398-022-02303-3.

151 **As Mesquita points out:** Mesquita, *Between Us.*

151 **a cultural mismatch:** Jozefien De Leersnyder, "Emotional Acculturation: A First Review," *Current Opinion in Psychology* 17 (October 2017): 67–73, https://doi.org/10.1016/j.copsyc.2017.06.007.

152 **by UCLA psychologists:** Jared B. Torre and Matthew D. Lieberman, "Putting Feelings into Words: Affect Labeling as Implicit Emotion Regulation," *Emotion Review* 10, no. 2 (2018): 116–24, https://doi.org/10.1177/1754073917742706.

155 **Developed by psychiatrist Donald:** Paul Yelsma, Norman M. Brown, and Jeff Elison, "Shame-Focused Coping Styles and Their Associations with Self-Esteem," *Psychological Reports* 90, no. 3 (2002): 1179–89, https://doi.org/10.2466/pr0.2002.90.3c.1179.

157 **One study found:** Jiyoung Park et al., "Social Status and Anger Expression: The Cultural Moderation Hypothesis," *Emotion* 13, no. 6 (2013): 1122–31, https://doi.org/10.1037/a0034273.

162 **contribute to learned helplessness:** Jayne Leonard, "What Is Learned Helplessness?," *Medical News Today*, updated May 23, 2023, https://www.medicalnewstoday.com/articles/325355.

163 **our personal self-esteem:** Hongfei Du, Ronnel B. King, and Peilian Chi, "Self-Esteem and Subjective Well-Being Revisited: The Roles of Personal, Relational, and Collective Self-Esteem," *Plos One* 12, no. 8 (2017): e0183958, https://doi.org/10.1371/journal.pone.0183958.

168 **One of the pillars:** Michael White, *Maps of Narrative Practice* (New York: W. W. Norton & Co., 2007), p. 82.

CHAPTER SIX: WHERE DO MY PARENTS END AND I BEGIN?

180 **prioritize filial piety:** Amy J. Lim, Clement Yong Hao Lau, and Chi-Ying Cheng, "Applying the Dual Filial Piety Model in the United States: A Comparison of Filial Piety between Asian Americans and Caucasian Americans," *Frontiers in Psychology* 12 (February 2022): art. 786609, https://doi.org/10.3389/fpsyg.2021.786609.

181 **One study researching this value:** Belinda Campos et al., "Familism and Psychological Health: The Intervening Role of Closeness and Social Support," *Cultural Diversity & Ethnic Minority Psychology* 20, no. 2 (2014): 191–201, https://doi.org/10.1037/a0034094.

181 **Filial piety emphasizes:** Kaidi Wu et al., "Perception of Sibling Relationships and Birth Order Among Asian American and European American Emerging Adults,"

Journal of Family Issues 39, no. 13 (2018): 3641–63, https://doi.org/10.1177/0192513x18783465.

181 **posit a vertical social hierarchy:** Wu et al., "Perception of Sibling Relationships," 3641–63.

182 **An enmeshed family is one:** Ingrid Bacon and Jeff Conway, "Co-dependency and Enmeshment—a Fusion of Concepts," *International Journal of Mental Health and Addiction* (April 2022), https://doi.org/10.1007/s11469-022-00810-4.

183 **In Western models of family:** Mary Moussa Rogers, "Understanding Family Dynamics in a Cross-Cultural Sample" (PhD diss., Mississippi State University, 2021), https://scholarsjunction.msstate.edu/td/5240/, p. 5.

185 **internalizers versus externalizers:** Lindsay C. Gibson, *Adult Children of Emotionally Immature Parents: How to Heal from Distant, Rejecting, or Self-Involved Parents* (Oakland, Calif.: New Harbinger Publications, 2015), p. 89.

187 **codependency is often a reaction:** Melody Beattie, *Codependent No More: How to Stop Controlling Others and Start Caring for Yourself* (Center City, Minn.: Hazelden, 1986).

191 **intergenerational cultural dissonance:** Yoonsun Choi, Michael He, and Tracy W. Harachi, "Intergenerational Cultural Dissonance, Parent–Child Conflict and Bonding, and Youth Problem Behaviors Among Vietnamese and Cambodian Immigrant Families," *Journal of Youth and Adolescence* 37, no. 1 (2008): 85–96, https://doi.org/10.1007/s10964-007-9217-z.

CHAPTER SEVEN: INVESTING IN COMMUNITY CARE AND SELF-CARE

216 **with our caregivers:** Hio Wa Mak, Gregory M. Fosco, and Mark E. Feinberg, "The Role of Family for Youth Friendships: Examining a Social Anxiety Mechanism," *Journal of Youth and Adolescence* 47, no. 2 (2018): 306–20, https://doi.org/10.1007/s10964-017-0738-9.

216 **their lack of friendships:** Peiqi Lu et al., "Friendship Importance Around the World: Links to Cultural Factors, Health, and Well-Being," *Frontiers in Psychology* 11 (January 2021): art. 570839, https://doi.org/10.3389/fpsyg.2020.570839.

229 **this kind of linguistic framing:** Caitlin M. Fausey and Lera Boroditsky, "Subtle Linguistic Cues Influence Perceived Blame and Financial Liability," *Psychonomic Bulletin & Review* 17, no. 5 (October 2010): 644–50, https://doi.org/10.3758/pbr.17.5.644.

CHAPTER EIGHT: WHEN YOU'RE THE ONLY ONE

246 **a groundbreaking article:** Tema Okun, "(Divorcing) White Supremacy Culture: Coming Home to Who We Really Are," White Supremacy Culture (website), updated August 2023, https://www.whitesupremacyculture.info/.

247 **workplaces try to be meritocracies:** Emilio J. Castilla and Stephen Benard, "The Paradox of Meritocracy in Organizations," *Administrative Science Quarterly* 55, no. 4 (2010): 543–676, https://doi.org/10.2189/asqu.2010.55.4.543.

247 **are the least likely:** Buck Gee and Denise Peck, "Asian Americans Are the Least Likely Group in the U.S. to Be Promoted to Management," *Harvard Business Review*, May 31, 2018, https://hbr.org/2018/05/asian-americans-are-the-least-likely-group-in-the-u-s-to-be-promoted-to-management.

247 **least represented group:** "Leadership Roles Remain Out of Reach for Many Women of Color," McKinsey & Company, October 7, 2021, https://www

.mckinsey.com/featured-insights/sustainable-inclusive-growth/chart-of-the-day/leadership-roles-remain-out-of-reach-for-many-women-of-color.

254 **frequently and intensely:** Afran Ahmed et al., "Why Is There a Higher Rate of Impostor Syndrome Among BIPOC?," *Across the Spectrum of Socioeconomics* 1, no. 2 (2020): 1–17, https://doi.org/10.5281/zenodo.4310477.

254 **reframed impostor syndrome:** Ruchika Tulshyan and Jodi-Ann Burey, "Stop Telling Women They Have Imposter Syndrome," *Harvard Business Review*, February 11, 2021, https://hbr.org/2021/02/stop-telling-women-they-have-imposter-syndrome.

254 **highly demanding family system:** George P. Chrousos, Alexios-Fotios A. Mentis, and Efthimios Dardiotis, "Focusing on the Neuro-Psycho-Biological and Evolutionary Underpinnings of the Imposter Syndrome," *Frontiers in Psychology* 11 (July 2020): art. 1553, https://doi.org/10.3389/fpsyg.2020.01553.

254 **Even parentification can lead:** Denise M. Castro, Rebecca A. Jones, and Hamid Mirsalimi, "Parentification and the Impostor Phenomenon: An Empirical Investigation," *American Journal of Family Therapy* 32, no. 3 (2004): 205–16, https://doi.org/10.1080/01926180490425676.

258 **we call high-context cultures:** "Context Is Everything: Communicating in High- and Low-Context Cultures," So You're an American? (U.S. Department of State web resource), accessed July 17, 2023, https://www.state.gov/courses/answering difficultquestions/html/app.htm.htm?p=module3_p3.htm.

260 **"self-image, status or career":** William A. Kahn, "Psychological Conditions of Personal Engagement and Disengagement at Work," *Academy of Management Journal* 33, no. 4 (1990): 692–724, https://www.jstor.org/stable/256287.

261 **HuffPost Union had reported:** HuffPost Union (@HuffPostUnion), "In the past 2 years, @HuffPost lost at least 28 staff of color—incl. 25 women of color," Twitter, September 15, 2020, 12:07 p.m., https://twitter.com/HuffPostUnion/status/1305 901092224393217.

268 **if you are feeling unsupported:** Christina Maslach and Michael P. Leiter, "Understanding the Burnout Experience: Recent Research and Its Implications for Psychiatry," *World Psychiatry* 15, no. 2 (June 2016), pp. 103–111, https://www.ncbi.nlm.nih.gov/pmc/articles/PMC4911781/.

CHAPTER NINE: LOVE OR LOYALTY

274 **with an attachment style:** Amir Levine and Rachel Heller, *Attached: The New Science of Adult Attachment and How It Can Help You Find—and Keep—Love* (New York: TarcherPerigee, 2010).

286 **I have observed how immigrant:** Laurie Meyers, "Asian-American Mental Health," *Monitor on Psychology* 37, no. 2 (February 2006): 44, https://www.apa.org/monitor/feb06/health.

290 **Persistent and unhelpful guilt:** Carlos Tilghman-Osborne, David A. Cole, and Julia W. Felton, "Definition and Measurement of Guilt: Implications for Clinical Research and Practice," *Clinical Psychology Review* 30, no. 5 (July 2010): 536–46, https://doi.org/10.1016/j.cpr.2010.03.007.

291 **may be more motivated:** Marlies de Groot et al., "Group-Based Shame, Guilt, and Regret across Cultures," *European Journal of Social Psychology* 51, no. 7 (2021): 1198–1212, https://doi.org/10.1002/ejsp.2808.

292 **pain and often anxiety:** Melody Beattie, *Codependent No More: How to Stop Controlling Others and Start Caring for Yourself* (Center City, Minn.: Hazelden, 1986), p. 232.

300 **Hispanic and Asian Americans:** Paul Taylor, "Chapter 1: Overview," in *Second-Generation Americans: A Portrait of the Adult Children of Immigrants* (Washing-

ton, D.C.: Pew Research Center, 2013), 7–18, https://www.pewresearch.org/social trends/2013/02/07/second-generation-americans/.

CHAPTER TEN: GETTING OUT OF MY OWN WAY

311 **psychologist Gay Hendricks:** Gay Hendricks, *The Big Leap: Conquer Your Hidden Fear and Take Life to the Next Level*, 3rd ed. (New York: HarperOne, 2010).

311 **"an internal threshold":** Darya Sinusoid, "The Big Leap: Book Overview & Key Takeaways," *Shortform*, June 2, 2022, https://www.shortform.com/blog/the-big -leap-book/.

314 **perceived self-efficacy:** Bo Yan and Xiaomin Zhang, "What Research Has Been Conducted on Procrastination? Evidence from a Systematical Bibliometric Analysis," *Frontiers in Psychology* 13 (February 2022): art. 809044, https://doi.org /10.3389/fpsyg.2022.809044.

319 **Daniel Gilbert talks about:** Daniel Gilbert, *Stumbling on Happiness* (New York: Vintage Books, 2007).

319 **who coined the term:** Stephen R. Covey, *The 7 Habits of Highly Effective People: Powerful Lessons in Personal Change*, rev. 30th ed. (New York: Simon & Schuster, 2020).

319 **scarcity mindset can affect:** Inge Huijsmans et al., "A Scarcity Mindset Alters Neural Processing Underlying Consumer Decision Making," *Proceedings of the National Academy of Sciences* 116, no. 24 (2019): 11699–704, https://doi.org /10.1073/pnas.1818572116.

319 **exacerbate mental health struggles:** "Scarcity Mindset: Causes and How to Overcome It," Cleveland Clinic, November 30, 2022, https://health.clevelandclinic .org/scarcity-mindset/.

322 **founder of Narrative Therapy:** Michael White, *Maps of Narrative Practice* (New York: W. W. Norton & Co., 2007), p. 107.

CHAPTER ELEVEN: EXPLORING MY BICULTURAL IDENTITY DEVELOPMENT

336 **during the adolescent years:** Jennifer H. Pfeifer and Elliot T. Berkman, "The Development of Self and Identity in Adolescence: Neural Evidence and Implications for a Value-Based Choice Perspective on Motivated Behavior," *Child Development Perspectives* 12, no. 3 (September 2018): 158–64, https://doi.org/10.1111 /cdep.12279.

337 **the Nigrescence model:** William E. Cross Jr., "The Psychology of Nigrescence: Revising the Cross Model," *Handbook of Multicultural Counseling*, J. G. Ponteretto et al., eds. (1995): 93–122, https://psycnet.apa.org/record/1995-98648-006.

337 **Jean Kim created:** Jean H. Kim, "Processes of Asian American Identity Development: A Study of Japanese American Women's Perceptions of Their Struggle to Achieve Positive Identities as Americans of Asian Ancestry" (PhD diss., University of Massachusetts Amherst, 1981), https://doi.org/10.7275/11192479.

337 **Jean Phinney created:** Jean S. Phinney, "Stages of Ethnic Identity Development in Minority Group Adolescents," *Journal of Early Adolescence* 9, no. 1–2 (1989): 34–49, https://doi.org/10.1177/0272431689091004.

337 **W. S. Carlos Poston created:** W. S. Carlos Poston, "The Biracial Identity Development Model: A Needed Addition," *Journal of Counseling & Development* 69, no. 2 (1990): 152–55, https://doi.org/10.1002/j.1556-6676.1990.tb01477.x.

337 **Latino ethnic identity model:** Cross, "The Psychology of Nigrescence."

337   **Derald Wing Sue and Stanley Sue:** D. W. Sue and D. Sue, *Counseling the Culturally Different: Theory and Practice*, 3rd ed. (New York: John Wiley & Sons, 1999), pp. 235–42.

337   **Pilipino American identity development:** Kevin L. Nadal, "Pilipino American Identity Development Model," *Journal of Multicultural Counseling and Development* 32, no. 1 (January 2004), https://www.researchgate.net/publication/26447 1415_Pilipino_American_Identity_Development_Model.

337   **Biculturalism is often defined:** Seth J. Schwartz and Jennifer B. Unger, "Biculturalism and Context: What Is Biculturalism, and When Is It Adaptive?," *Human Development* 53, no. 1 (March 2010): 26–32, https://doi.org/10.1159/0002 68137.

343   **self-esteem can be shaped:** CNRS (Délégation Paris Michel-Ange), "Culture Influences Young People's Self-Esteem: Fulfillment of Value Priorities of Other Individuals Important to Youth," ScienceDaily, February 24, 2014, https://www .sciencedaily.com/releases/2014/02/140224081027.htm.

343   **that in personal relationships:** Linda P. Juang and Moin Syed, "The Evolution of Acculturation and Development Models for Understanding Immigrant Children and Youth Adjustment," *Child Development Perspectives* 13, no. 4 (December 2019): 241–46, https://doi.org/10.1111/cdep.12346.

345   **It may require synthesizing:** Schwartz and Unger, "Biculturalism and Context."

345   **I am most pulled:** Alan Meca et al., "Biculturalism and Bicultural Identity Development: A Relational Model of Bicultural Systems," in *Youth in Superdiverse Societies: Growing Up with Globalization, Diversity, and Acculturation*, ed. Peter F. Titzmann and Philipp Jugert (London: Routledge, 2019), 41–57, https://doi .org//10.4324/9781351040266-5.

345   **in hybridizing biculturalism:** Colleen Ward et al., "Hybrid and Alternating Identity Styles as Strategies for Managing Multicultural Identities," *Journal of Cross-Cultural Psychology* 49, no. 9 (2018): 1402–39, https://doi.org/10.1177/002202 2118782641.

347   **Jamaican-born British sociologist:** S. Hall, "Cultural Identity and Diaspora," in *Identity: Community, Culture, Difference*, ed. J. Rutherford (London: Lawrence & Wishart, 1990), 222–37.

348   **known as remote enculturation:** Alexandria L. West et al., "More than the Sum of Its Parts: A Transformative Theory of Biculturalism," *Journal of Cross-Cultural Psychology* 48, no. 7 (2017): 963–90, https://doi.org/10.1177/0022022117709533.

350   **approximately 70 percent:** Council for Accreditation of Counseling and Related Educational Programs, *CACREP Vital Statistics 2020: Results from a National Survey of Accredited Programs*, www.cacrep.org/wp-content/uploads/2023/01 /Vital-Stats-Report-2020.pdf.

351   **Social media can be an incredible:** Mohammad Delwar Hossain and Aaron S. Veenstra, "Social Capital and Relationship Maintenance: Uses of Social Media Among the South Asian Diaspora in the U.S.," *Asian Journal of Communication* 27, no. 1 (2017): 1–17, https://doi.org/10.1080/01292986.2016.1240817.

354   **according to 2019 data:** Charlotte Huff, "Psychology's Diversity Problem," American Psychological Association, October 1, 2021, https://www.apa.org/monitor /2021/10/feature-diversity-problem.

354   **Bureau of Labor Statistics found:** "Employed Persons by Detailed Occupation, Sex, Race, and Hispanic or Latino Ethnicity," U.S. Bureau of Labor Statistics, last modified January 25, 2023, https://www.bls.gov/cps/cpsaat11.htm.

354   **Asian Americans are three times:** "Asian American / Pacific Islander Communities and Mental Health," Mental Health America, accessed July 17, 2023, https:// www.mhanational.org/issues/asian-american-pacific-islander-communities-and -mental-health.

354 **Only one in three:** "Black/African American," National Alliance on Mental Illness, accessed July 24, 2023, https://www.nami.org/Your-Journey/Identity-and-Cultural-Dimensions/Black-African-American.

355 **approximately 34 percent:** Louise Morales-Brown, "What to Know About Mental Health Conditions and the Latinx Community," *Medical News Today*, September 23, 2021, https://www.medicalnewstoday.com/articles/latino-mental-health.

355 **a low retention rate:** John E. Zeber et al., "The Impact of Race and Ethnicity on Rates of Return to Psychotherapy for Depression," *Depression and Anxiety* 34, no. 12 (December 2017): 1157–63, https://doi.org/10.1002/da.22696.

355 **compared with Europeans:** Kelly Guanhua Yang et al., "Disparities in Mental Health Care Utilization and Perceived Need Among Asian Americans: 2012–2016," *Psychiatric Services* 71, no. 1 (2020): 21–27, https://doi.org/10.1176/appi.ps.201900126.

355 **depression as "nervios":** Louise Morales-Brown, "What Role Does Hispanic Culture Play in Depression?," *Medical News Today*, August 31, 2021, https://www.medicalnewstoday.com/articles/depression-in-hispanic-culture.

356 **shame and social anxiety are associated:** Erik Hedman et al., "Shame and Guilt in Social Anxiety Disorder: Effects of Cognitive Behavior Therapy and Association with Social Anxiety and Depressive Symptoms," *Plos One* 8, no. 4 (April 2013): e61713, https://doi.org/10.1371/journal.pone.0061713.

356 **a misdiagnosis of schizophrenia:** Sonya C. Faber et al., "The Weaponization of Medicine: Early Psychosis in the Black Community and the Need for Racially Informed Mental Healthcare," *Frontiers in Psychiatry* 14 (February 2023), https://doi.org/10.3389/fpsyt.2023.1098292.

CHAPTER TWELVE: UNCOVERING
MY FAMILY HISTORY

366 **A genogram is useful:** "Introduction to the Genogram," GenoPro, accessed July 24, 2023, https://genopro.com/genogram/.

368 **help us create meaning:** Robyn Fivush, Jennifer G. Bohanek, and Widaad Zaman, "Personal and Intergenerational Narratives in Relation to Adolescents' Well-Being," *New Directions for Child and Adolescent Development* 2011, no. 131 (Spring 2011): 45–57, https://doi.org/10.1002/cd.288.

369 **"a means of achieving":** Natalie Merrill and Robyn Fivush, "Intergenerational Narratives and Identity across Development," *Developmental Review* 40 (June 2016): 72–92, https://doi.org/10.1016/j.dr.2016.03.001.

376 **a transgenerational impact:** Gina Ryder and Taneasha White, "How Intergenerational Trauma Impacts Families," PsychCentral, updated on April 15, 2022, https://psychcentral.com/lib/how-intergenerational-trauma-impacts-families#next-steps.

378 **I understand that pain:** Rachel Yehuda and Amy Lehrner, "Intergenerational Transmission of Trauma Effects: Putative Role of Epigenetic Mechanisms," *World Psychiatry* 17, no. 3 (October 2018): 243–57, https://doi.org/10.1002/wps.20568.

380 **"that persons experience":** Saba Mughal et al., "Grief Reaction," StatPearls, last updated May 22, 2022, https://www.ncbi.nlm.nih.gov/books/NBK507832/.

380 **the likelihood of closure:** Pauline Boss and Donna Carnes, "The Myth of Closure," *Family Process* 51, no. 4 (December 2012): 456–69, https://doi.org/10.1111/famp.12005.

381 **multiple layers of grief culminate:** Maurice Eisenbruch, "The Cultural Bereavement Interview: A New Clinical Research Approach for Refugees," *The Psychiatric Clinics of North America* 13, no. 4 (December 1990): 715–35.

Index